NICHOLAS WISEMAN

Courtesy of the National Gallery of Ireland

Nicholas Cardinal Wiseman

Nicholas Wiseman

by

BRIAN FOTHERGILL

FABER AND FABER LTD
24 Russell Square
London

First published in mcmlxiii
by Faber and Faber Limited
24 Russell Square, London, W.C.1
Printed in Great Britain by
Western Printing Services Ltd., Bristol

© *Arthur Brian Fothergill*
1963

To
Stephen and Kitt Jenkins

CONTENTS

9

First meeting with Dr. Walsh—Success of Wiseman's lectures in London—Newman's comments—A commemorative medal—The Dublin Review.

Last years in Rome—Ideas for a liberally educated Priesthood—First encounter with Manning—Gladstone in Rome—Early moves for the restoration of the Hierarchy—Impatience at the Bishops' delays—Their dissatisfaction with Wiseman—Prayers for the Conversion of England—Opposition of Dr. Baines.

Cardinal Acton—The number of Vicariates raised to eight—Wiseman consecrated bishop—Essay on the Donatist heresy—Impressions of his character as President of Oscott—Appearance and personality—His hopes for the Oxford Movement.

Tract XC—Pugin, de Lisle and the Tractarians—Differing views of Wiseman and de Lisle on the Anglican Church—Wiseman's cautious attitude—Letter to Newman on Tract XC—Newman retires to Littlemore—Wiseman criticized by the Old Catholics—Sibthorpe—Newman resigns his living—Wiseman visits Spain.

More conversions—W. G. Ward deprived of his degrees—Received into the Catholic Church—Impatience at Newman's delays—His last days as an Anglican—Visits Wiseman at Oscott—Problems raised by the conversions—Newman goes to Rome—Accepts Wiseman's suggestion of becoming an Oratorian—A strange episode in Rome.

Irish immigrants—The new religious Orders—Retreats—Architectural disputes—Renewed call for a Hierarchy—Pius IX—Wiseman puts the case for the Hierarchy at Rome—Pro-Vicar Apostolic in London—A diplomatic mission—Opening of St. George's, Southwark—Louis-Philippe in exile—Revolution in

FOREWORD

Cardinal Wiseman is one of the neglected figures of the Nineteenth Century; he has been overshadowed by his two great contemporaries, Newman and Manning, whose submission to the Roman Catholic Church owed so much to his influence. Any attempt to reassess his life must still rely to a great extent upon Wilfrid Ward's *Life and Times of Cardinal Wiseman*, first published in 1897. The present work has drawn largely upon these two volumes (referred to in the footnotes as 'Ward'), the archives of the Archdiocese of Westminster (upon which Ward's volumes are largely based), and the Talbot Correspondence in the archives of the Venerable English College, Rome. The author has also had access to the archives of the Roman Catholic Diocese of Southwark, a source which was not available to previous biographers of the Cardinal. He must express his deep gratitude to his Eminence Cardinal Godfrey, Archbishop of Westminster, to the Right Rev. Mgr. Cyril C. Cowderoy, Bishop of Southwark, and to the Right Rev. Mgr. Gerard W. Tickle, Rector of the Venerable English College, Rome, for kindly allowing him the use of these archives.

The author is also indebted to the Editor of the *Venerable Magazine*, Rome, for permission to quote from the Fano Papers, which consist of copies of letters and documents from the archives of Count Gabrielli-Wiseman; to Mr. Joseph H. Vaughan and the Rev. Father Alfonso de Zulueta for kindly showing him Wiseman papers in their possession, and to the Director of the National Gallery of Ireland for permission to reproduce Henry Doyle's water-colour portrait of the Cardinal. He is also grateful for help from Mrs. Minna Carney, and the Rev. Father Bernard Trevett who provided invaluable assistance in Rome.

I

For the Roman Catholic Church, probably no century since the time of the Reformation opened with such dismal prospects for the future as did the nineteenth. The spirit of rationalism and anti-clericalism, which had spread across Europe in the wake of the French Revolution, seemed everywhere to be triumphant. The eighteenth century, which had espoused Reason and proliferated scepticism, ended with the Church humiliated, its wealth plundered, and its Sovereign Pontiff led into captivity to die a prisoner of the Revolution at Valence. In the death of Pius VI many people saw the death of Catholicism; few imagined it capable of any general revival; none would have forecast that within the next sixty years France itself would be the scene of a religious revival centred on an ultramontane conception of the papal office; and that by 1870 the Holy See, shorn of its temporal power, would have re-established and defined its spiritual authority in a manner unbelievable to the men of 1800.

With the triumphal return of Pius VII to Rome after the fall of Napoleon a new era seemed at first to have begun; but the Pope was old and worn out with suffering, and in restoring the Papal States by brilliant diplomacy at the Congress of Vienna, Cardinal Consalvi was, in fact, merely saddling the Church with a problem which was to dissipate its energy in the late nineteenth century to the detriment of its spiritual life and universal mission. The policy of ensuing pontiffs did little to reconcile the Church to the new spirit of liberalism and in the pontificates of Leo XII and Gregory XVI the Holy See seemed to be inseparably identified with the cause of reaction. So, at least, it must have appeared to those who struggled in various

15

countries against the renascent absolutism that flourished under Metternich in Vienna, under Charles X in Paris, and in the minor principalities that still cluttered the peninsula of Italy. Even the waltz came under the ban of Leo XII[1] and a reactionary Archbishop of Paris felt it necessary to remind his congregation that their Saviour, as well as being the Son of God, was also very well connected on His mother's side, having an excellent claim to be the heir to the throne of Judea.[2] In such an atmosphere a religious revival must have seemed unlikely. But, inspired by such men as Lamennais, Montalembert and Lacordaire, the Church in France was to spring into new life; in Austria the anti-Roman ecclesiastical policy established by Joseph II was finally to give way before the new ultramontanism; and in England, where for the past hundred years the Catholic community had consisted of a dwindling band of quiet, devout, unobtrusive families with their dependants and followers, free from persecution but still fettered by penal laws, emancipation was to come in 1829, to be followed just over twenty years later by the restoration of the hierarchy and by a flow of converts from the Church of England destined to change the whole complexion of Catholic life. It is in this context that one name stands out above all others, the Roman-educated Englishman, friend of Montalembert and Lacordaire, whose great intellectual endowments combined with an imagination of a singular quality made him so unique an instrument in the restoration of Catholic life in England—the name of Nicholas Wiseman, the first man since Reginald Pole to come from Rome to England in the sacred purple of a Roman Cardinal.

The years 1840 to 1860 in particular, so far as the Catholic Church in England is concerned, are what might be called the Wiseman era; that is from the year when he was consecrated bishop until the period when declining health made it inevitable that his influence at the centre of things should decline while other men contended for the disputed succession. But while in England his influence predominated he was also recognized abroad as a churchman and scholar of European repute, a powerful figure in the Roman *Curia*, a man of wide culture and broad interests who combined with a deep

---

[1] In 1826
[2] P. Spencer: *Politics of Belief in Nineteenth-Century France*, p. 58.

spirituality an almost childlike delight in the dignity of his position as a Prince of the Church. This was the period when men of high intellect, brought up in the esoteric atmosphere of the ancient universities, were turning their thoughts towards the Catholic Church, and it was Wiseman, almost alone on the Catholic side, who was able to meet them on terms of absolute equality. His words, read at a time of crisis, were to have a decisive effect upon the mind of John Henry Newman when he stood at the spiritual crossroads; and it was to Wiseman that Manning looked when he made the fateful step that led him into the Church of Rome. Both Manning and Newman have tended to overshadow Wiseman, as he himself predicted. When writing to a friend in 1841 he declared that 'if the Oxford Divines entered the Church, we must be ready to fall into the shade and take up our position in the background',[1] and if this has, to a large extent, been the case, we must also remember that it was almost entirely due to Wiseman that Newman found a welcome in the Catholic Church despite the hostility felt by many of the old Catholics to his previous position as an Anglican; a position which they, as much as his Protestant co-religionists, considered to be insincere. It was Wiseman who laid the foundation, by his sympathetic understanding and eager co-operation, for all the great benefits that were to accrue to Catholicism from the conversions resulting from the Oxford Movement.

The future Cardinal was born in Spain on the 3rd[2] of August 1802 at half an hour past midnight at his parents' house in Seville, and baptized the day following in the Church of Santa Cruz by an Irish Capuchin, James Ryan, known in religion as Father Bonaventure de Irlanda. He was given the names of Nicholas Patrick Stephen. The child's grandfather, James Wiseman, of Waterford in Ireland, had settled in Seville at the end of the eighteenth century where he was in business as a merchant; the Cardinal's father, also called James, was the youngest son, and was also described as a merchant. Nicholas Wiseman was the son of James's second marriage to Xaviera Strange, whom he had married in 1800 while on a visit to

---

[1] E S Purcell: *Ambrose Phillipps de Lisle*, Vol. 1, p. 290.
[2] Not August 2 as in Ward. The authority for August 3 is based on the diary kept by Wiseman's father and on the record of Baptism (Appendix A).

London. James had previously been married to Mariana Dunphy, who had died in 1793 after presenting her husband with four daughters, one of whom had died in infancy. By his second marriage James Wiseman had two other children, James, born in February 1801 in London, and Francesca, afterwards Countess Gabrielli, born in August 1804. Barely five months after the birth of his youngest daughter James Wiseman died suddenly of an apoplectic fit. 'What made this event the more melancholy,' his widow wrote on a page of her husband's diary, 'was (that) the deceased was sitting at table with a party of friends celebrating the birthday of his eldest daughter who was present. . . . May his soul find mercy from his Creator who was pleased to cut him off in so sudden and un-expected a manner, and may the charity and humanity which he showed every person in distress find merit in the sight of the Almighty, who disposes of everything in this life for his honour and Glory.'[1] Shortly after her husband's death Xaviera Wiseman brought her family of small children back to Ireland, but the young Nicholas was not without memories of the land of his birth. 'Though only three years old when he left Spain,' writes Wilfrid Ward, 'Nicholas Wiseman used to recall in later life seeing the prize crews brought ashore at Cadiz after the battle of Trafalgar; and he criticized Mr. Stanfield's great picture "The Victory" as inaccurate, because his sailor at the port-hole had no pigtail. Wiseman's memory proved quite accurate, and Mr. Stanfield painted in the pigtail.'[2]

On returning to Ireland the Wiseman children attended a school at Waterford and it was here that Nicholas first learnt to speak English, having, until then, spoken only Spanish. His Irish school days, however, did not last long, and in March 1810, he was sent over to England to enrol at St. Cuthbert's College at Ushaw. This College had been founded near Durham in the latter years of the eighteenth century by the priests of the English college of the university of Douai when these fathers had been driven from their continental home at the time of the reign of terror in 1793. The traditions of the place went back to the days of Cardinal Allen, who had founded the college in 1568, and it was here that Wiseman first

[1] *Memorie sulla nascita del Card. Nicola Wiseman scritte da Suo Padre* (ex archives of Count Carlo Gabrielli-Wiseman from the transcription property of *Venerabile* magazine, Rome). The passage quoted is in the writing of Wiseman's mother.
[2] Ward, Vol. I, p. 4.

came into contact with the peculiar *ethos* of English Catholic life. It must be remembered that the Act of Catholic Emancipation was not to be passed for another nineteen years and that memories of penal times were still very much alive in an institution which had given many martyrs to the Faith. Catholics lived a secluded life, content to practise their religion in peace and quiet while they remembered that the fires of persecution might flare out again as they had done in the Gordon Riots only a generation before. William Bernard Ullathorne, three years junior to Wiseman and later to be a fellow bishop at the restoration of the hierarchy, writing of his own boyhood tells us that 'in those days it was not considered safe to wear a religious habit, even within the monastery', and while describing his early days as a Benedictine novice he continues: 'I had never before seen the Benediction of the Blessed Sacrament or heard the Litany sung, as it now came so sweetly to my ears and soul, and I had never before seen a cope.'[1]

Such was the contrast that the young Wiseman found at Ushaw after his earliest memories of life in Catholic Spain. It is no surprise to learn that he was not entirely happy as a student there. 'I was always considered stupid and dull by my companions,' he told his nephew many years later, 'and made hardly any friends, and never got any notice or favour from superiors. But I knew that I was reading a great deal more than others without saying a word about it, both in study time and out of it, and I made myself happy enough. I am sure I never said a witty or clever thing all the time I was at college, but I used to think a good deal.'[2] He did, however, make one friendship while at Ushaw, despite the considerable difference in age between himself and the man who was to remain his friend and counsellor while life lasted. This was John Lingard, the distinguished historian, then Vice-President of the college and later to be offered, but to decline, a Cardinal's hat. Wiseman was only eight when he entered Ushaw, but Lingard must quickly have noticed the latent ability in the quiet and retiring child, and gave him encouragement and kind attention. Wiseman was grateful for these 'specific acts of thoughtful and delicate kindness, which showed a tender heart' and remembered them many years afterwards, when

[1] W. B. Ullathorne: *From Cabin-Boy to Archbishop*, pp. 31 and 36.
[2] Ward, Vol. I, p. 7.

19

he wrote that 'though he went from college soon after, and I later left the country and saw him not again for fifteen years, yet there grew up an understanding first, and by degrees a correspondence and an intimacy between us, which continued to the close of his life'.[1]

The general impression we get of Wiseman during his years at Ushaw is of a reserved and studious boy, hard-working but not yet particularly outstanding among his fellow students. 'A somewhat gawky youth,' Ward described him, 'with limbs ill knit together, betokening the absence of all aptitude for athletics, sauntering about with a book under his arm, oftener alone than in company.' It was while at St. Cuthbert's that Wiseman finally determined to enter the priesthood. We can fairly assume that this idea was never very far from his mind. We know that his mother, shortly after his birth, laid him on the altar of the Cathedral of Seville, and dedicated him to the service of the Church. While such an act of maternal piety, which may seem excessive to a less demonstrative age, was in no sense binding as to the future choice of career for her son, it suggests with some degree of certainty that any indication of a priestly vocation would have been vigorously encouraged. It is said that Wiseman, while still a student at Ushaw, was forced to shelter from a thunder storm in a cottage, and that while for half an hour the storm raged, his mind, always susceptible to romantic impressions, was made up with respect to his future. It would seem that this was no sudden or dramatic change, as might have been the case had some other career been previously in mind, now abandoned for the better choice, but rather that which had long been in the back of his mind was now, to the accompaniment of thunder and lightning, acknowledged and accepted as his life's vocation.

Another incident of these years is important in consideration of what was to lie ahead. When he was about ten or twelve years old Wiseman was staying with his mother in Durham at a time when a parliamentary election was in progress. Their house was opposite to an inn where a boisterous crowd had gathered to hear an election address, and young Nicholas, attracted by the commotion outside, appeared at a window to watch the exciting scene. The house, however, was known to be a Catholic one, and when the boy was seen

---

[1] Quoted by Ward, Vol. I, p. 8.

looking-on the crowd began to shout and to use those expressions of anti-Catholic abuse which were then the commonplace of English anti-Papal demonstrations and which may still be heard by the curious at election time in Northern Ireland. We can assume that the crowd was not particularly nice in its choice of epithets, and Wiseman learnt for the first time something of the latent hatred still felt by the majority of his fellow countrymen for 'the bishop of Rome and all his detestable enormities'. Later on many years of residence abroad softened this impression until he was ready to believe that such feelings had quite died out in England. The reaction to his pastoral letter 'From out of the Flaminian Gate' was to show that he was sadly mistaken.

Mrs. Wiseman later settled near Paris, about the time Nicholas was leaving Ushaw for Rome, and we have a picture of him and of his school at that period in the memoirs of Barbara Charlton: 'In those days there was a considerable English colony in Versailles and we children had plenty of dances and picnics, and private theatricals. But my two sisters always preferred to anything else a visit to Mrs. Wiseman and her daughter, who afterwards became Comtesse Gabrielli. . . . I remember their son and brother, the future Cardinal, coming to Versailles, a thin, delicate-looking youth, who even then, when he must have come straight from Ushaw, was made much of by the Catholics as a young man of extraordinary ability and promise. Ushaw, though a rough school, was always celebrated, before and after the Vice-Presidency of Lingard, for turning out the best-informed Catholics. There was no espionage, no encouragement for boys to tell tales of one another, and so the spirit of the school was good. I never saw Wiseman from the day he dined with my parents at Versailles in 1826[1] until he was a Cardinal and dined with us . . . in Eaton Place twenty-five years later, on which occasion I got Gunter to make a cake in the shape of a Cardinal's hat that amused him highly. At that time he was hugely stout and coarse-looking, having a strong resemblance to his good and kind mother.'[2]

Nicholas Wiseman was a student at Ushaw from 1810 until 1818. When he left the college in the latter year he was no more than

---

[1] Wiseman was by then a member of the English College at Rome.
[2] *The Recollections of a Northumberland Lady, 1815–1866*, edited by L. E. O. Charlton, pp. 55–56.

sixteen. With the exception of one or two extended visits he was not to live in England again until he returned as a bishop in the year 1840 when he was thirty-eight years old. It is important to remember that the most formative years of his life were spent, and the greater part of his education was completed, in a foreign country and at the very centre of the Catholic world; in surroundings, and under circumstances, as far removed as could be from the conditions of England and of English Catholicism at the period of Catholic emancipation. Though he continued always stalwartly, almost self-consciously, insistent on his character as an Englishman and delighted in those robust qualities which this condition implied in the nineteenth century, it cannot be denied that his knowledge of England and of the peculiar idiosyncrasies of the British way of life, particularly in its predominantly Protestant aspect, became very much of a closed book to him; and the more closed the book was the more he seemed to consider himself well read in it. To men like Ullathorne and Errington, who understood so well the background of English Catholicism from which they were sprung, this aspect of Wiseman's was always to be a major difficulty and was to make work with him bewildering and co-operation often unsuccessful. It was also to make him appear to the old Catholics (as they came to be called) as the champion of foreign ideas and exotic, Italianate forms of religious devotion, when he became leader of the English hierarchy. He was to find himself more at home with enthusiastic converts like F. W. Faber, avid for everything that was Italian and Roman, and (as it seemed to the old Catholics) lacking in those qualities of reticence which the long traditions of penal times had made the distinguishing feature of the Church in England.

II

At the end of the year 1818 Nicholas Wiseman was sent, with five other students from Ushaw, to the recently reopened English College at Rome; and as this place was to be his home for the next twenty-two years, a word should be said about its history. The *Venerabile Collegio Inglese* had originally been a *hospitium* for English pilgrims to the tomb of the Apostle, and as such could trace its descent to Saxon times. After the breach with Rome the house first became a place of refuge for English Catholic priests until in 1578 it was converted into a college by Pope Gregory XIII, and so it remained until 1798 when the English College, in company with many other ancient institutions of Rome, was plundered by the French revolutionary armies. For the next twenty years it was to remain derelict and empty until, at the suggestion of Cardinal Consalvi, it was reopened by Pius VII with Consalvi as 'Cardinal Protector'. Thus, under the protection of the powerful Secretary of State, the college opened its doors once more to the little band of Englishmen who alighted there at the end of their long journey on the 18th of December 1818, not only strangers in a strange country, but having to start from the very beginning in the task of rehabilitating the old college whose empty halls must have given them a grim enough welcome. 'Wide and lofty corridors; a noble staircase leading to vast and airy halls succeeding one another;' so Wiseman later described his new home, 'a spacious garden, glowing with the lemon and orange, and presenting to one's first approach a perspective in fresco by Pozzi,—engraved by him in his celebrated work on perspective; a library, airy, large, and cheerful, whose shelves, however, exhibited a specimen of what antiquarians

23

call '*opus tumultuarium*' in the piled up disorganized volumes from folio to duodecimo, that crammed them; a refectory, wainscoted in polished walnut, and above that, St. George and the Dragon by the same artist, ready to drop on to the floor from the groined ceiling; still better, a chapel, unfurnished indeed, but illuminated from floor to roof with the Saints of England and with celestial glories, leading to the altar . . ., such were the first features of our future abode, as, alone and undirected, we wandered through the solemn building, and made it, after years of silence, re-echo to the sound of English voices, and give back the bounding tread of those who had returned to claim their own.'[1]

The journey to Rome itself had not been without its excitements, as Wiseman described in a long letter to his mother written the following April: 'Saturday the 18 of October was the most fatal day of our voyage. It was rough weather all the day and towards 10 at night the wind became more favourable, but the sea still remained very high. On a sudden we were alarmed with a cry: "All hands on deck!" We all ran up and found that a man had just fallen overboard. It was truly awful to hear the cries of the poor man in the water. Ropes and spars were thrown over to no purpose, and our captain with another sailor went out in a boat, with danger of their lives, but were too late. The man lost was a black and our best sailor. We tossed about the ocean for some days longer, till on the eve of All Saints we saw Lisbon rock after having been 22 days without seeing land.' Accidents were not confined to human beings; later, in the Mediterranean: 'A dog which we had on board went mad and after howling round the deck and refusing water, went to the stern and jumpt overboard.'[2] Eventually Rome was reached without further mishap to man or beast, and the students soon settled down to their new life. By April Wiseman was able to tell his mother that he could understand Italian easily and could '*gabble* with tolerable fluency'.

The ceremonies of the Church always had a fascination for Wiseman, and after the austerities of life in England he was able to delight in the full pageantry of the papacy. In the letter from which we have already quoted he gives an account of his first encounter with the splendid Liturgy as it was performed in the great Basilica

[1] Cardinal Wiseman: *Recollections of the Last Four Popes*, p. 7.
[2] English College Archives. *Venerabile* magazine, Vol. IV, No. 2, April 1929.

of St. Peter's. 'On Easter Sunday we went to St. Peter's and heard a grand mass celebrated in the presence of His Holiness by Cardinal Matteio and after the ceremony, secured a place to see the Pope give his benediction. He was carried on a sumptuous chair of crimson velvet and gold, and in a rich cope and his tiara with a triple crown, surrounded by Bishops and Cardinals, he appeared in the grand balcony over the front door. It was something above earthly to see an Emperor and Empress, a queen, dukes and princes of the highest blood kneeling before the sovereign vicar of Christ, with thousands of people of all nations. The bells tolled, the band played for a few minutes and all was silent. The Pope recited a short prayer, then rose slowly up, joined his hands and gave his benediction to the whole world. Instantly, the cannons fired, the bells rang, and the band played. All was silent again. He again rose, and in the same manner gave his blessing to the people assembled.'

The pontiff who Wiseman saw on this occasion was the aged Pius VII, the former prisoner of Napoleon, whose long and eventful reign was now drawing towards its close. Earlier, on Christmas eve 1818, he had received a small group of students from the English College, Wiseman among them, in audience at the Quirinal palace, receiving them standing up and shaking hands with each one of them in turn, remarking that he hoped they would do honour both to Rome and to their own country. It was Wiseman's first encounter with the person of the Vicar of Christ, all of whose successors he was to know personally and serve faithfully until the hour of his death. Forty years later he was to write of this first papal audience: 'The friendly and almost national grasp of the hand—(after due homage had been willingly paid)—between the Head of the Catholic Church, venerable by his very age, and a youth who had nothing even to promise; the first exhortation on entering a course of ecclesiastical study—its very inaugural discourse, from him who was believed to be the fountain of spiritual wisdom on earth;—these surely formed a double tie, not to be broken, but rather strengthened by every subsequent experience.'[1]

Dr. Robert Gradwell, the Rector of the College, had already been some time in Rome when this first batch of students arrived, so that they were soon able to get down to their studies and adapt

[1] Wiseman: *Recollections of the Last Four Popes*, p. 14.

themselves to the steady routine of an ecclesiastical seminary which, as Wilfrid Ward has described it in Wiseman's time, was rigorous enough: 'The students rose then, as now, at 5–30. Half an hour's meditation was followed by Mass and breakfast. Every day, except Thursday and Sunday, lectures were attended on philosophy, theology, canon law, Church history, Biblical exegesis, as the case might be: and the rest of the morning was devoted to study. The midday dinner was preceded by the daily "examination of conscience". After dinner came a visit to the Blessed Sacrament and, a little later, the *siesta*. A space in the afternoon was allotted to a walk through the city, either to some object of interest—a church or a museum—or to one of the Palazzos, or to Monte Pincio, where friends would meet the collegians and exchange greetings or converse. Nearly all the colleges—and among them the English— would take their walk *in camerata*—that is to say, the students walking two abreast, in double file. Outside the city or on Monte Pincio this order was relaxed for the time, and students might disperse, reassembling for their return home. The bell towards sunset for the *Ave Maria* would summon the *camerata* back to college, and the rest of the day was spent chiefly in study and prayer.'[1]

Wiseman settled down happily to this life of study, soon distinguishing himself as one of the most promising scholars of the College, developing early an interest in the Syriac and Arabic languages in the study of which he was later to gain a European reputation. He also fully enjoyed the life and atmosphere of the Eternal City, steeping himself in its history, studying its ancient monuments, and delighting in its artistic treasures. While still at Ushaw he had prepared himself for these agreeable pursuits having formed, with some other students, a society for the study of Roman antiquities. Wiseman was now able to visit all those famous shrines, churches, and palaces which had been the subject of his research in distant County Durham; gaze with delight and discrimination at the frescoed walls and painted ceilings with their brilliant array of colours, in which pagan and Christian mythology seemed to vie with each other on such terms of equality as might have alarmed the sombre Spaniards or scandalized the northern English Protestants among whom his early school days had been passed. Both art and

---

[1] Ward, Vol. I, p. 27.

music appealed strongly to his sensitive nature. He was a proficient musician and enjoyed assisting in the musical parts of the divine office.

As well as their house in Rome the English College owned a villa or country house in the village of Monte Porzio in the Alban Hills above Frascati, and here they would pass the hottest months of the year when the papal court moved to Castel Gandolfo and all who could escaped from the heat of Rome. Wiseman became deeply attached to this summer residence, especially later when he became himself Rector of the College, and it was often in his thoughts in the last years of his life when he was head of the Catholic hierarchy in England. He then looked back to those distant Italian summers as to a time of peaceful tranquillity, though in fact the Roman countryside was often, in the early nineteenth century, the very opposite of peaceful. In 1820, while Wiseman was still a young student, a monastery of Camaldolese anchorites, visible from the terrace of the English College's summer residence, was surprised by a company of *banditti* and the unfortunate monks taken into captivity, only to be rescued at the eleventh hour by the intervention of a detachment of soldiers who were dispatched to the bandits in place of the ransom they had demanded. The brigands were eventually forced to retreat, abandoning their venerable hostages unscathed, save for one who had been wounded in the leg. They were able to return to their monastery and resume their religious life unmolested, having taken the precaution (as Wiseman describes in his *Recollections*) of having the walls of their retreat 'built up to a formidable height, and slashed with rows of loop-holes, so as to be defensible by the fire-arms of secular servants.' Once more the English students could hear the bell calling the monks to their religious duties and were perhaps not surprised when their ears also caught 'the deep bay of enormous and fierce ban-dogs', whose angry, but under the circumstances, comforting bark 'echoed through the night, more unceasing than the bell'.

Three years after this exciting event Pius VII closed his long and eventful reign in his eighty-third year. The fatal illness of Napoleon's former prisoner began on the fourteenth anniversary of his arrest by General Radet. On that day the aged Pope had a fall in his apartments in the Quirinal Palace which resulted in a fractured femur. The Pope lingered for some weeks in gradually failing health,

27

and finally died on the 20th August 1823. As the Pontiff lay dying in his Roman palace the great Benedictine monastery and Basilica of St. Paul *fuori le Mura*, where the Pope had spent some years as a young monk, was almost totally destroyed by fire. The news of the devastation of this ancient monument of Christendom, which had stood since the fourth century on the traditional site of the apostle's tomb, was carefully concealed from the Pope, whose last hours were saved from this additional sorrow; but Wiseman was one of those who witnessed the great church go up in flames. 'Melancholy indeed was the scene,' he wrote. 'The tottering external walls were all that was permitted to be seen, even from a respectful distance; for it was impossible to know how long they would stand. A clear space was therefore kept round, in which the skilful and intrepid fire-brigade—an admirably organized body—were using all their appliances to prevent the flames breaking out from the smouldering ruins.'[1] While the ancient Basilica was burning masses were being offered in all the churches of Rome with the special prayers 'for the Pontiff at the point of death'. The next day Pius VII breathed his last and an epoch in the history of the church was over. The ancient ceremonies that surround the obsequies of a Vicar of Christ took their course. Clothed in pontifical vestments the body lay in state in a chapel of St. Peter's, where the faithful crowded to pay their homage and kiss for the last time the embroidered cross on the slipper of the dead Pope. 'This last act of reverence to the mortal remains of the immortal Pius,' Wiseman tells us, 'the writer well recollects performing.'

A short interval after the funeral the conclave assembled to elect a successor. Wiseman was among the throng that watched the princes of the church process into the Quirinal palace, where, on this occasion, the election was to take place. The last pontifical election had taken place in 1800, and during the revolutionary occupation of Rome had been held in the island monastery of S. Giorgio Maggiore in the Venetian Lagoon, so that few people in Rome on that day could claim to have witnessed such a spectacle before. Wiseman later described the scene as 'Cardinals never before seen by them, or not for many years, pass before them; eager eyes scan and measure them, and try to conjecture, from fancied

[1] *Recollections of the Last Four Popes*, p. 126.

28

omens in eye, or figure, or expression, who will shortly be the sovereign of their fair city, and, what is much more, the Head of the Catholic Church from the rising to the setting sun.'[1] In the event it was Cardinal Annibale della Genga, a man of the *ancien régime*, who had been consecrated bishop in 1793 at the hands of Henry, Cardinal of York, the last of the Stuarts, who now mounted the throne of St. Peter to begin a reign of over five disastrous years under the name of Leo XII.

For Wiseman, however, the details of papal administration were as yet of minor importance; he was now busily preparing for his public examination for the degree of Doctor of Divinity, which he was to take the next year, on 7th July 1824, when he was only twenty-one years old. It was not an enviable ordeal. The thesis which had to contain not less than a hundred points and embrace the entire field of Catholic theology, was first printed in a small quarto volume and then distributed among the friends and distinguished scholars who would be asked to the disputation. One of Wiseman's fellow-students who assisted in this friendly act was George Errington, a member of one of the old Catholic families, who had become Wiseman's friend at Ushaw and who was now his colleague among the brighter stars of the English College. They were to be associated through life, but not always so happily.

Following the distribution of the thesis, those who were invited, and any professor or doctor resident in Rome who cared to attend, assembled in a large hall where the candidate had to defend his propositions in public; being submitted, in the morning, to the onslaught of chosen examiners, and in the afternoon, to a more general attack. On the occasion of Wiseman's own examination the day was made historic by the presence of two strangely contrasted characters, both later his friends, and both destined to leave their mark on the religious life of their time, first in concert and later in bitter opposition. 'I remember well,' Wiseman writes in his *Recollections*, 'in the particular instance before my eye, that a monk clothed in white glided in and sat down in the inner circle; but though a special messenger was despatched to him by the professors, he shook his head, and declined to become an assailant. He had been sent to listen and report. It was F. Capellari, who in less than

[1] *Recollections*, p. 134.

six years was Pope Gregory XVI. Not far away from him was seated the Abbé de Lamennais, whose work he so justly and so witheringly condemned. Probably it was the only time that they were ever seated together, when they thus listened to an English youth vindicating the faith, of which one would become the oracle, and the other the bitter foe.' Wiseman was awarded his degree and the next day was received in audience by Leo XII whereon 'not only does he receive a loving paternal blessing; but his cheeks glow and his heart beats as he bends beneath the expressions of the kindest encouragement, and even words of praise'.[1]

On July 12th, the young Doctor of Divinity left Rome for France, where his mother was still living near Versailles. Despite the gravity and dignity of his new distinction Wiseman was not above enjoying himself like any other young man off on a holiday after the grind of preparing for his degree and the nervous strain of his public examination. To friends in Rome he wrote amusing accounts of his visit to Paris, where a bookseller had delighted him by referring to Boswell's famous biography as 'Bowels of Dr. Johnson', while he was himself (in a letter to George Errington) to dismiss the French with the sweeping generalizations of excessive youth: 'I think the French are the greatest political hypocrites in the world. Two-thirds of them are Liberals, and pretend to be Royalists.' Of a firework display in honour of the fête of St. Louis he comments: 'I never saw such ingenuity in my life, either in amusing people or getting money,' quoting, rather smugly, Napoleon's maxim *'Avec un violon et un spectacle on peut gouverner la France.'* On the return journey he encountered a fellow traveller 'whose conversation was elegant, and who made remarks of the most judicious nature, well read in the French classics, and possessing one of the most accurate and solid acquaintances with history, especially modern, I ever knew'. This intelligent individual turned out to be none other than the head cook to Napoleon's widow, Marie Louise, who was then living a life of far from respectable retirement as Duchess of Parma. The other occupants of the vehicle were of a less intellectual calibre: 'Opposite was a young Frenchman beginning his travels, who was astonished on entering Turin to find that the people were dressed the same as in France and not in the old Roman costume. A

[1] *Recollections*, p. 192.

rawboned, long-legged German and a tremendously snouted Tuscan cavalier with his servant completed our live-stock.'[1] Wiseman's own expansive personality and his linguistic abilities (he was fluent in both Italian and French as well as Spanish) combined with his engrossing interest in his companions and his surroundings, no doubt made him an agreeable travelling companion.

On returning to Rome Wiseman was admitted to Holy Orders. The subdiaconate was conferred on 18th December 1824, and he was made deacon the following January; on 10th March 1825, he was ordained priest. On attaining the priesthood two facts should be noted about Wiseman; his academic career had started brilliantly and promised further distinction, and he had not revisited England since he first arrived in Rome at the time of the reopening of the Venerable English College. He was quite out of touch with life at home and with the work of the English mission. His mother had been living near Paris since the time he left Ushaw so that he did not even have family ties with the country he had quitted as a youth of sixteen; indeed, such ties as he had were more with Spain and Ireland than with England. In Rome he was already beginning to enjoy an accepted position in the academic world and his oriental studies had brought him under the notice of scholars of international repute such as Monsignor Angelo Mai, later Cardinal, who was then working on his *Scriptorum Veterum Nova Collectio*, and who would allow Wiseman to work in the Vatican library at times when it was not normally open to students, and who would occasionally give him work of his own to revise and correct. In these circumstances it is not surprising that Wiseman envisaged for himself a future as a scholar and teacher in the academic world of the Roman university, rather than as a mission priest under the English Vicars Apostolic; and it was to the former of these two alternatives that he now dedicated himself with the full encouragement and approval of his superiors.

[1] Letters to Errington and Richard Gillow, quoted in Ward, Vol. I, pp. 48-49.

III

ife in papal Rome during the first half of the nineteenth
century must have been agreeable enough if one could shut
one's eyes to the political ferment in the rest of Italy and to
the maladministration of the pontifical government during the
reigns of Leo XII, Pius VIII, and Gregory XVI. Wiseman's enjoyment of life in the Eternal City was enhanced by a vivid historical
imagination and by an informed appreciation of the fine arts; and
his attitude to the political situation was softened by the fact that
two of these Popes, whose temporal administration resulted in one
of the sorriest chapters in the history of the Church, were both
known to him personally, so that his judgement of them in the
political field was mitigated by his knowledge of their characters as
devout and, in the case of Gregory, scholarly, men who received
him with fatherly affection and took a flattering personal interest in
the advancement of his career. We are not, therefore, surprised when
he tells us, in his *Recollections*, that 'the life of a student in Rome
should be one of unblended enjoyment'. Certainly this period of his
life, after the first successes had been achieved and before other
duties and responsibilities began to crowd in on him, was one of
contentment and peace. He responded with enthusiasm to the
appeal which Rome made to his imagination, an enthusiasm which
still remained when he wrote many years later of this happy period
of his life. Of the young Roman student he had once been, he wrote,
'if he loves his work, or what is the same, if he throws himself
conscientiously into it, it is sweetened to him as it can be nowhere
else. His very relaxations become at once subsidiary to it, yet most
delightfully recreative. His daily walks may be through the field of

art; his resting-place in some seat of the Muses; his wanderings along the stream of time, bordered by precious monuments. He can never be alone; a thousand memories, a thousand associations accompany him, rise up at every step, bear him along.'[1]

The years that immediately followed the taking of his degree were spent by Wiseman in collecting material for the book that was first to bring him to the notice of academic circles outside Rome and was, indeed, to give him a European reputation. This was his *Horae Syriacae*, which was published in 1827. The work is concerned with the history of the Syriac version of the Old Testament, and in particular with the Monophysite manuscript in the Vatican library known as the Karkaphesian Codex, which prior to Wiseman's investigation had been known only by name. Like many pioneer works the book has now been superseded, but at the time it was hailed as a landmark in the world of Oriental linguistic scholarship, and brought the twenty-four year old author to the notice of the scholarly world in all parts of Europe. England was not slow to recognize the merits of the book and Wiseman was elected a member of the Royal Asiatic Society and of the Royal Society of Literature. Letters poured in from many quarters in praise of the book. One, which must have particularly pleased the author, was from the Anglican Bishop of Salisbury, himself a distinguished Oriental scholar, who helped to make Wiseman's work known to English critics and sponsored his election to various learned societies. 'It would give me great pleasure,' the bishop wrote to him in 1829, 'to hear of the publication of the second volume of your very interesting *Horae Syriacae*.'

To these learned studies another duty was added in 1827, which was destined ultimately to change the direction of his life in a manner which neither he, nor his Rector, nor the Pope who was responsible for it, can have envisaged at the time. At an audience granted to Dr. Gradwell in this year, at which Wiseman was also present, Leo XII commented on the fact that there was no church in Rome where the numerous English visitors to the city could hear a sermon in their own language. As the English flocked to Rome in great numbers at this period he had decided to remedy the defect by setting aside the church of *Gesu e Maria* in the Corso for this

[1] *Recollections*, p. 183.

particular purpose. The only problem now to be settled was that of deciding to whom the task of delivering the sermons should be entrusted. The Pope had no sooner expressed his doubts on this question than Dr. Gradwell, perhaps not wishing this additional burden to fall on his own shoulders, pointed to his young companion and suggested that Dr. Wiseman was the very man, and upon the younger shoulders the burden was, as Wiseman expressed it, 'laid there and then, with peremptory kindness, by an authority that might not be gainsayed'.

The preparation of these sermons, and their delivery, caused him immense trouble and anguish. He was quite inexperienced in public speaking save for what he himself described as 'such juvenile essays as students blushingly deliver before their own companions', and it was with no feeling of confidence or hope of success that he mounted the pulpit for the first time. The Pope had gone out of his way to make an occasion of these English discourses, sending a detachment of his own choir to add distinction to the service, causing his director of music, one Canonico Baini, to compose, for their especial use, a motet with English words. And so, to the spirited falsetto of the Papal *castrati*, Wiseman found himself attempting that art in which he was later to excel so greatly; though in these early days of his career as a preacher it was only with the greatest anxiety, pain, and trouble that he was able to gain the command he considered essential to the preaching office. But these early sermons were destined to have as marked an effect upon himself as upon any of his listeners, as he recalled in his *Recollections*: 'Leo could not see,' he wrote 'what has been the influence of his commission, in merely dragging from the commerce with the dead to that of the living, one who would gladly have confined his time to the former, —from books to men, from reading to speaking. Nothing but this would have done it.'[1]

Another factor in his life this same year, while not outside his accustomed orbit of academic life, was to help still more, perhaps, in the process of turning his thoughts 'from books to men', and this was his appointment as Vice-Rector of the English College. It was a distinguished appointment for so young a man, and must have helped to establish his self-confidence by giving him an accepted position in Roman society. Certainly when we next encounter him

[1] *Recollections*, p. 218.

34

as a preacher, in the memoirs of the times, he appears in an altogether more authoritative light. The incident took place some few years later at the funeral of Cardinal Weld, when Wiseman was the preacher, and was witnessed by the future Bishop Ullathorne. 'All the best singers in Rome,' he wrote, 'had been obtained to sing Mozart's requiem, with instrumentation, and this was a rarity in Rome which attracted the artists and musicians to the audience. When, therefore, the thrilling tones of Mozart had been interrupted for some time by the monotonous and harsh tones of the English language, as read by Dr. Wiseman, however interesting the lecture was to English ears, the Italians all lost patience, and set up a sibilation and a hissing from one end of the church to the other. After a few moments Dr. Wiseman got a hearing, and a few words of grave and dignified rebuke restored silence until the lecture was completed.'[1] But this assurance which could quieten a whispering congregation unfamiliar with the language of the sermon by a few words of dignified rebuke, only came with time as the slow process took place by which the scholar and recluse was transformed into a leader and a man of action.

The acclaim which resulted from the publication of the *Horae Syriacae* decided Wiseman to aspire to the chair of Oriental Languages in the Roman (now Gregorian) University, then about to become vacant. A decree of Leo XII had recently thrown all professorships open to competition and Wiseman was encouraged by his previous teachers and professors to apply for the vacancy. As this was, however, a somewhat obscure appointment for which it was not expected that there would be any competition, it was announced that the Papal Bull would be set aside and a direct appointment made. Wiseman's hopes seemed to be dashed by this prospect of an arbitrary act on the part of the University authorities, but before giving up hope he sought an audience with Leo and laid his cause at the Pope's feet. 'Nothing could have been more affable, more encouraging,' he tells us, 'than Leo's reply. He expressed his delight at seeing that his regulation was not a dead letter, and that it had animated his petitioner to exertion. He assured him that he should have a fair chance, "a clear stage and no favour" desiring him to leave the matter in his hands.'

[1] Archbishop Ullathorne: *From Cabin Boy to Archbishop*, p. 128.

Time passed, and when the vacancy occurred Wiseman's hopes were again dashed to discover that it had been filled without any reference to himself or to the 'clear stage' which the Pope had promised. Once again he presented himself to the papal apartment to plead his cause, but the Holy Father cut him short. 'I remember it all,' the Pope announced; 'I have been surprised. I have sent for C——, through whom this has been done; I have ordered the appointment to be cancelled, and I have reproved him so sharply, that I believe it is the reason why he is laid up today with fever. You have acted fairly and boldly, and you shall not lose the fruits of your industry. I will keep my word and the provisions of my constitution.'[1] The authorities of the University gave way before the word of the Pope lest the unfortunate and un-named C's fever should become an epidemic, and Wiseman became Professor of Oriental Languages.

To all outward appearances Wiseman's career had so far been one of continual success. While still only in his twenties he had achieved his doctorate, the Vice-Rectorship of his college, and a professorship in the Roman University. His fame was already beginning to spread beyond the confines of his own Church; his future prospects seemed to hold nothing but promise; and he was clearly regarded with personal favour by the Sovereign Pontiff. All this would suggest to us that the young ecclesiastic had every reason to be satisfied and contented with his lot and that he could legitimately regard his progress in his chosen calling with some degree of complacency. This, however, was far from the case. From about the time that he took his degree, and certainly over the period during which he was writing his *Horae Syriacae*, Wiseman's mind was troubled with serious religious doubts which cast a cloud over his whole life for a period of some years.

The existence of this period of doubt he never denied; indeed, he came later to look upon it as a valuable period during which his ideals had been put to a severe test, and that in combating the sceptical notions which beset his mind he was unwittingly equipping himself for the controversial writing and lecturing in which he was subsequently to distinguish himself. But at the time the trial was real enough, and sufficient to extinguish, for the moment, the

[1] Leo's words are quoted by Wiseman in his *Recollections*, Ch. VI, p. 196.

enjoyment he felt at living in Rome and being a part of the life of that most ancient and fascinating of cities.

Though he touched on these doubts in his later writing, Wiseman always remained reticent about the actual form his doubts took. We may follow the tortuous process of Newman's mind as he thought himself from one position to another, from the fundamentalist Evangelicanism of his youth and early manhood, through Laudian High Churchmanship to the ivory tower of Anglo-Catholicism, and finally into the bosom of Rome. While every sort of doubt seems to have assailed him as to the nature of the church, and as to where the True Church was to be found, Newman's labyrinthine intellect never seems to have been confronted with the supreme doubt of the very existence of God. For Wiseman we may assume that his battle was not over the nature of the Church; there is no evidence anywhere to suppose that, given the truth of the Christian revelation, he ever called in question the supremacy of the Pope or the absolute claims of the Holy See. We must assume, though we can do so only on indirect evidence, that his problems were of a more fundamental nature. It is not unknown that the study of Biblical criticism has sometimes resulted in destroying the student's faith in the divine inspiration of the text he is criticizing, and it is possible that Wiseman's own Biblical studies, which occupied him during these years, were responsible for the sceptical thoughts which assailed him so vigorously.

Today, when we live in a climate of disbelief, our attitude to religious doubt is different from that which prevailed in the first half of the nineteenth century. The twentieth century, which has given itself many enticing but no very convincing names (among which perhaps the 'Century of the Common Man' carries least conviction of all) might more truthfully be described as an age of non-belief than an age of disbelief. We do not so much reject belief as fail to come anywhere near understanding what belief means; an attitude of mind which leaves in the public conscience a void which is often filled by the sort of fake philosophies which are possibly all that an age of mass advertising and publicity can hope to expect, but which have little to recommend themselves as an alternative to the seven devils of the parable.

The nineteenth century, on the other hand, presented a façade of conventional religious belief, whether Catholic or Protestant, so that those who had doubts saw the process as a retreat from belief, a back-sliding, however genuine, from what was the general opinion of society. In the nineteenth century one 'lost one's faith'; in the twentieth, if one is lucky, one finds it.

This should be borne in mind when considering Wiseman's attitude to his religious difficulties; he looked upon them as a disease, a plague, for which the cure would be found by perseverance, though at the cost of much anguish of soul. It was in this light that he wrote about it, twenty years later, in a letter to his nephew. 'Many and many an hour have I passed alone, in bitter tears, on the *loggia* of the English College, when everyone was reposing in the afternoon, and I was fighting with subtle thoughts and venomous suggestions of a fiend-like infidelity which I durst not confide to anyone, for there was no-one that could have sympathised with me. This lasted for years; but it made me study and think, to conquer the plague—for I can hardly call it danger—both for myself and for others. . . . But during the actual struggle the simple submission of faith is the only remedy. Thoughts against faith must be treated at times like temptations against any other virtue—put away; though in cooler moments they may be safely analysed and unravelled.'[1]

The latter part of the last sentence of Wiseman's letter gives us the key to his attitude to the 'plague' which had struck him. It must be analysed and unravelled, but just as one sets about the cure of a disease on the assumption that one will return to the state of good health from which one is temporarily removed, so Wiseman never abandoned the assumption that he would be restored to full faith or that his present troubles in any way separated him from the body of the Church; and it is typical of his intellectual energy at this period of his life, that he should make use of much of the thought and study expended in combating doubt on a series of lectures later published on 'The Connexion between Science and Revealed Religion'. He was later to have another reason to be thankful for the lesson he had learnt during these years and for the self-discipline his struggle had incurred. 'Without this training,' he was to write, 'I should not have thrown myself into the Puseyite Controversy at a later period.'

[1] Letter quoted by Ward, Vol. i, pp. 64–65.

An event of these years which may have helped to raise Wiseman from the pit of depression was the visit paid by Leo XII to the English College at their summer retreat of Monte Porzio in the Autumn of 1827. Despite the private nature of the visit a good deal of display and ceremonial was involved, and this always delighted the heart of the young Vice-Rector. Towards the end of his life he wrote of the ceremonies of the Church, 'As people in the world would go to a ball for their recreation, so I have enjoyed a great function,' and this papal visit, to which he devotes the best part of six pages of his *Recollections*, was just such an occasion as to make him forget his worries for a while and rejoice in the external splendours of the papacy and the Church.

The visit had been kept a great secret, so that even the Pope's Major Domo and Master of the Household, when ordered to drive out to Monte Porzio, had no idea why they had been sent there and showed great astonishment when told that the Holy Father was expected. Shortly afterwards the tramp of horses was heard and the papal carriage, escorted by noble guards and dragoons, galloped through the little town and drew up at the door of the English College. The Pope first went to the local church for a visit to the Blessed Sacrament and then proceeded on foot to a neighbouring house from the balcony of which he gave his blessing to the assembled population, no less astonished than the two Monsignori of the Papal Court at finding the Vicar of Christ in their midst. The Pope then received 'the more respectable villagers', after which he devoted himself to the English students.

Dinner followed, at which the Pope sat alone at a small table raised on a dais at the head of the table occupied by the students and staff of the college, and flattered them by remarking that it was seldom that a poor Pope could enjoy the pleasure of sitting down to dinner with so fine a set of young men. The Pope ate little, Wiseman tells us, 'but would employ his leisure in carving, and sending down the dishes from his own table; while his conversation was familiar, and addressed to all'. Afterwards the company retired to the Rector's sitting-room where a special golden chair of throne-like proportions had been prepared for the august visitor, but this he declined to use, seating himself instead on an ordinary chair with a rush seat, upon which he gave audience to the village clergy with a becoming modesty. This did not prevent the golden chair with its damask upholstery from becoming a treasured relic of the College, and one that was occasionally used by Wiseman himself when he succeeded Dr. Gradwell as Rector.

That Wiseman should succeed to the Rectorship was a foregone conclusion, and when Dr. Gradwell was consecrated a bishop in 1828, Wiseman stepped into his shoes to succeed in the post which he was to occupy until his own episcopal consecration twelve years later. In intellectual eminence he was foremost amongst those who had come to Rome in 1818 to reopen the college, and though he was still under thirty years of age it was clear that no one else was so well fitted as he to carry on the traditions that had been built on the ruins of the old college, left all but derelict after years of re-volution and neglect. On the academic side there can have been no doubt as to his ability for the post. But there was another side to the work of the Rector of the English College; by a tradition going back to the old days it was the custom for the Rector to act as agent in Rome for the English bishops, a difficult position not rendered any easier by the remoteness of England from the centre of the Catholic Church and by the prolonged and often unreliable means of com-munication between England and the Holy See. To this aspect of his new position Wiseman came without experience and lacking in the authority which a more mature age might have given him. Though on cordial terms with the authorities of the Congregation of the Propaganda, who governed the English Church as a missio-nary district, he was virtually unknown to the Vicars Apostolic in England whose representative in Rome he now became. How he would conduct himself in this new field remained to be seen.

IV

In the year following Wiseman's appointment as Rector of the
Venerable English College Pope Leo XII died, and was succeeded on the throne of the Apostle by Cardinal Castiglione,
who was elected on the 31st of March 1829, and took the name of
Pius VIII. His reign lasted no more than twenty months, but for
English Catholics it has an historic significance in so far as it was
during this brief pontificate that the Act of Catholic Emancipation
was passed by the British Parliament. It fell to Wiseman, in the
first month[1] of the new reign, to carry the news of the passing of this
Act to the Sovereign Pontiff, and afterwards, with Dr. George
Errington, his Vice-Rector, to celebrate the occasion in a suitable
fashion at the College. This was done in traditional manner by the
singing of a solemn *Te Deum*, after which a banquet was held, and
the College illuminated. The inhabitants of Rome were not a little
curious to see the legend *Emancipazione Cattolica* spelt out in
transparencies across the ancient façade of the building. 'In fact,
the first of the two words,' Wiseman tells us,[2] 'long and formidable
to untutored lips, was no household word in Italy; nor was there
any imaginable connection in ordinary persons' minds between it
and its adjective, nor between the two and England.' The reader
of these words will not be surprised to learn that this triumphant
message was 'read by the people with difficulty, and interpreted
by conjecture; so that many came and admired, but went away,
unenlightened by the blaze that had dazzled them, into the darkness
visible of surrounding streets'.

---

[1] This measure received the royal assent of George IV on the 23rd of April 1829.
[2] *Recollections*, Ch. IV, p. 250.

But if the inhabitants of the Papal States had still many years to wait before the word *Emancipazione* should become a reality for themselves, it was most certainly a matter of great rejoicing to the Catholics of England when this long-delayed measure put an end to the years of injustice and intolerance under which they had suffered. It is important at this point when Wiseman, as agent to the English Bishops, came into closer contact with the work of the English mission, that we should glance a little more closely at the history of the Catholic Church in England in the years immediately preceding the Act of Emancipation, and also consider the beginnings of that movement in the Established Church, known as the Oxford Movement, which was to have such a profound effect upon both Catholic and Anglican circles in the years that lay immediately ahead.

There is, fortunately, no need to dwell here on the years of active persecution which had once been the lot of Catholics in England. It is not a happy chapter in the history of a country that has always paid lip service to the idea of liberty. That for many years a priest could be condemned to death for saying Mass is but one of the penalties which professing Catholics were liable to suffer under the laws of England, and it was only in the year 1778 that the threat of life imprisonment, that could until then be enforced against Catholic bishops, priests, and schoolmasters, was repealed; and even this slight measure of toleration was denounced in a 'bigoted and inflammatory letter to the Press' from the pen of John Wesley, the founder of Methodism.[1] This act at least freed Catholics from living at the mercy of the common informer and was a first step on the road towards full emancipation, though the men who witnessed this dawn, and saw in it a great hope for the future, might have been surprised had it been revealed to them that the last marks of discrimination against them were not to be removed until the year 1926.[2]

The hostile and bigoted attitude of the average Englishman to the Catholic minority was to some extent ameliorated by the events of the French Revolution. Great numbers of *émigré* bishops and

[1] E. I. Watkin: *Roman Catholicism in England from the Reformation to 1950*, Ch. IV, p. 128.
[2] By the Catholic Relief Act of 1926 it was no longer an offence to wear the habit of a religious order in public.

clergy found refuge in this country, while the plight of Pius VII and the diplomacy of Cardinal Consalvi did much in official circles, as well as in the realm of public opinion, to soften the image of 'Giant Pope' which the seductive pen of Bunyan seemed to have etched permanently and indelibly on the imagination of the British nation. With the dawn of the nineteenth century, with its strong current in popular feeling towards liberation and reform, Catholics again took hope and with the active support of the Whig aristocracy, began the long battle for emancipation which was eventually to triumph in the Act of 1829. It may fairly be said that this Act would have become law much sooner but for one solid obstacle which stood in the way of every previous attempt to pass it. This was the conscience of King George III. Aged, infirm and mad, the old monarch stalwartly refused to give consent to an Act which he considered to be a betrayal of his coronation oath, and while he bore his Catholic subjects no malice, he found himself in this respect wholly unable to compromise with his conscience. George IV, in whom an excessive devotion to conscientious scruples must have come as something of a surprise to his ministers, also found difficulties in reconciling himself to the Act, despite the fact that his irregular marriage to a Roman Catholic subject gave a bigamous complexion to his official union with Caroline of Brunswick, and it was only the persuasion of the Duke of Wellington and Sir Robert Peel that induced him to give a tearful assent to the bill in the ninth year of his reign.

The Catholic community which found itself emancipated by the passing of this Act numbered about one per cent of the population of the country, though this number was to be increased considerably by the influx of Irish labour during the course of the century and by a flow of converts, less numerous but more influential, from the Established Church. The community was governed from Rome as a mission directed by the Congregation *de Propaganda Fide*, which derived its authority in this respect from the Constitution *Apostolicum Ministerium* of Pope Benedict XIV issued in the year 1753. Under this Constitution the English mission was organized in four Districts, each presided over by a bishop with the title of Vicar Apostolic. Each Vicar Apostolic was responsible for his own district, but was answerable to the Cardinal-Prefect of Propaganda as his superior, and did not enjoy the full authority of a diocesan bishop under a normally constituted hierarchy. The men who filled these episcopal offices were not perhaps especially outstanding as intellectual leaders, but were men of strong force of character, of an undemonstrative but deep piety, and were almost continually over-worked. We get a glimpse of the Vicar Apostolic of the London District as seen through the eyes of an Anglican clergyman about ten years after the passing of the Emancipation Act.[1] 'I just now saw the R.C. Bishop of London,' he wrote, 'get out of an omnibus in Piccadilly, seize his carpet bag, and trudge straight home with it to Golden Square. He had a blue cloak, but it hung below the skirts, and on he went. A very pleasing, venerable, episcopal-looking man, very like any other Bishop, save that none of ours would touch a carpet bag with his little finger.'

The clergy who worked under these bishops had received their education either in seminaries abroad or, since the time of the French Revolution, in the colleges which had been established at Ushaw in the north, or at St. Edmund's College, Old Hall, in the south. Though it had been legal to hold Catholic services in public chapels since the Act of 1778, these were usually built on obscure sites so as not to attract public attention, and were small and ill-adapted for the celebration of the Catholic liturgy. It was the custom for priests to dress in the simplest and plainest of clothes, the Roman collar was unknown, and even the cassock was never worn except during the actual celebration of Mass or Divine Office. It was not the custom to call a priest by the title of 'Father'. Unless he were a member of a religious order the priest would be addressed by the simple designation of 'Mr.', and it was only during the time of Cardinal Manning that it became customary to address the secular clergy by the name hitherto reserved for regulars. Even the bishops themselves were more usually referred to as 'Dr. Bramston' or 'Dr. Griffiths' than by their episcopal titles, habits of discretion surviving from the days when to hold any office in the Catholic Church was a criminal offence.

The life of the Catholic community was simple and obscure and quite lacking in that ostentation which the Protestant mind tended

<hr />

[1] The Rev. W. H. Brookfield. Quoted by Bernard Ward, *The Sequel to Catholic Emancipation*, Vol. I, p. 171.

to associate with the 'pomps of Rome'. Few English Catholics, unless they had travelled abroad, had seen the liturgy of their Church performed with anything but the minimum of ceremonial. Only in London, in churches such as the chapel of the old Sardinian embassy, was a fully musical service possible. But here again there was no very high liturgical standard, and the generous habit of visiting opera singers in offering their services on these occasions, did not necessarily add to the religious content of the ceremony. The following account from the *Orthodox Journal* of 8th June 1839, of such a service, suggests that a music critic rather than a religious correspondent, would be best fitted to describe the scene. 'A little after eleven o'clock (Signori Rubini and La Blanche being in the choir) the grand instrumental High Mass composed by the Maestro di Capella began with a sublime *Kyrie*, which finished as the priests got to the *Gloria*, when Mr. Le Jeune, the organist, commenced the splendid *Gloria* with a trumpet, well supported by the remainder of the band. It is a masterly composition, and Signor di Angeli has shown great musical talent in this piece, for it might be compared with any of Mozart's or Haydn's. Signor Rubini sang the admirable *Quoniam* with great effect. It was more like the warbling of a bird than mere singing, for it must have astonished as well as delighted the whole congregation, among whom were many Protestants. The *Gloria* was followed by the *Veni Sancte Spiritus*, most beautifully sung by Signor La Blanche. To say the most of the *Credo* in a few words, it excelled the *Gloria*, and was supported by Madame Persiani and Signor Tamburini, who came in during the sermon. The Offertory was appropriated to Madame Persiani, who certainly sang both sweetly and elegantly. The remainder of the Mass was in the same style as the beginning.'

Such a performance, even in London, was much more the exception than the rule. While Signor Rubini warbled like a bird at the grand instrumental High Mass, and seems to have carried off the musical laurels by a short head from Signor La Blanche, the average Catholic was witnessing a very different scene. For him Mass, or 'Prayers' as it was still often called by a generation not far removed from the days when the very mention of the word Mass had a danger all its own, might perhaps be celebrated in a small unostentatious chapel or in some room hired for the occasion. The priest, who probably had to travel many miles, would be clad in vestments showing all the wear and tear of much packing and un-packing, carefully mended by pious hands where age and long use had frayed them; for money was short and could not be spent on rich chasubles or embroidered copes. It is understandable that these priests of old Catholic stock should have failed to appreciate the enthusiasm for 'Gothic' vestments that was ushered in by the convert architect Pugin and his followers, or have cherished the humour of his remark to a priest whose sacerdotal dress did not come up to his medieval ideal: 'What is the use, my dear sir, in praying for the conversion of England in a cope like that?' The clergy, who were glad to wear any vestments without danger of summary arrest or being the occasion of a minor riot or brawl, took time to shake off the careful and retiring attitudes which a back-ground of persecution and proscription had bred, and did not always respond with enthusiasm to the boisterous exuberance of recent converts.

The Catholic lay population was dominated by a small group of interrelated aristocratic families, chief among whom, at this time, was John Talbot, sixteenth Earl of Shrewsbury and Waterford, a man of generous sympathies and great munificence, who extended a warm welcome to the early converts. The political affiliations of the leading Catholic families were largely to the Whig party, not necessarily from any inherent attachment to Whig principles but rather because this party, with its vaguely liberal sentiments, had long favoured Catholic emancipation. In trying to accommodate their own principles with their fellow Whigs of the Protestant faith in order to ease the passing of measures for Catholic relief, the lead-ing Catholic laymen had often found themselves opposed to the Vicars Apostolic, and for this reason had gained for themselves a largely undeserved reputation for Gallicanism, that is to say, of advocating a restriction of the prerogatives of the Holy See in favour of the immediate needs or aspirations of the local Church.

As the emphasis in the Catholic church moved from the achieve-ment of emancipation to the establishment of a national hierarchy, this accusation of Gallicanism was one which was used often, and not always scrupulously, against their opponents by the extreme papalist, or Ultramontane party. This latter point of view was to find its most vehement advocate in the person of Monsignor George Talbot, a prelate whose over-excessive zeal for the cause of ultramontanism was to prove often as much of an embarrassment as a help when in later years his enthusiasm and devotion was placed wholly at the disposal of Cardinal Wiseman. The truth is that the English Catholic laity were in no way lacking in respect and devotion to the Holy See, but an unfamiliarity with the devious ways and archaic etiquette of the Papal Court often gave to their robust recommendations the character of disrespect when no such meaning was in any way intended.

The Established Church of England presented a very different picture in comparison with the small and unimportant remnant of Catholicism which had survived into the nineteenth century. The great Evangelical revival, though it had resulted in the separation of the followers of John Wesley from the Established Church, had had a revivifying effect upon the Church of England, recalling it to its pastoral responsibilities out of the long and dignified slumber into which it had fallen. There was a move to reclaim the vast bulk of the urban working classes who had been largely lost to nonconformity, and in the period following the Napoleonic wars many new churches were built. In this tide of Evangelicalism a new current began to appear in the 1830's, recalling the Church to its supposed Catholic and medieval origins, which was supported by an appeal to the ancient Fathers and by a more exact examination and application of the rubrics of the Book of Common Prayer, in which were discovered a residue of Catholic teaching which had been overlooked or forgotten since the days of Lancelot Andrewes and Archbishop Laud.

It was in the common room of Oriel College at Oxford that these ideas began to take shape in the minds of a number of young Fellows who grouped themselves around the person of John Keble, a scholarly and saintly clergyman, who divided his time between Oxford and the curacy of his father's parish in Gloucestershire. At first, the movement confined itself to a rediscovery of liturgical devotion, a tendency towards a stricter observance of fasting and abstinence, and found an outlet in poetry more distinguished for its religious sincerity than for any literary merit. The influence of this group, under the gentle and pious leadership of Keble, might never have passed beyond the confines of the University, had it not been joined, early in the third decade of the century, by two men of outstanding character amounting, in the latter case, to something of genius: Edward Bouverie Pusey and John Henry Newman.

Pusey brought academic distinction to the movement; he had been elected at an early age to the chair of Hebrew in the University, and enjoyed a wide reputation for scholarship. He was also a man of good family, a point which in early nineteenth-century Oxford, probably counted for more than mere scholarly attainments; for this was an age when the Church of England could boast that it had a scholar and a gentleman in every parish, though it was more generally observed that so long as the latter qualification could be guaranteed the former might be overlooked. But in Pusey's case both these distinctions could be claimed with equal assurance, for not only was he a Pusey of Pusey in Berkshire and a grandson of Viscount Folkestone, he had also enjoyed the rare academic triumph of being appointed to a Regius Professorship when only twenty-eight years old. Those who had been prepared to dismiss Keble's disciples as whimsical and poetical young men capable of nothing more excessive than a tendency to have crosses embroidered on their stoles, had to take a more serious view of the movement when it was joined by the formidable Dr. Pusey, whose weighty scholarship took so little account of the mere externals of worship that even at the very end of his long life he was overheard to inquire of a more ritualistically-minded companion: 'Pray tell me, sir, what is a cope?'

In the person of John Henry Newman it may be said that the Oxford Movement gained, in the long run, considerably more than it had ever bargained for. He was a born leader in so far as he could inspire unselfish devotion in his followers, and admiration that came near, in his younger disciples, to adulation; but had those men who so eagerly welcomed his support when he first joined them been forewarned of the direction that his leadership would eventually take, they might indeed have preferred the simple devotion of Keble or the stolid scholarship of Pusey to this shooting-star intellectual, whose sublime but disquieting flights of rhetoric were to land both himself and many of his followers on a shore that seemed

48

then not only distant and dangerous, but also decidedly hostile to all that their movement stood for.

Newman had allied himself to Keble and his followers soon after his election to a Fellowship at Oriel. His religious faith, always deep and personal, had moved from the Calvinism of his upbringing, through Evangelicalism, to this new High Church position with its emphasis on dogma and the traditions of the Catholic Church. At first, these novel teachings caused little stir in the university, and even less in the world outside; the only surprise shown by Newman's less sympathetic friends was when they discovered that much of the so-called new ideas to which they took exception, had in fact been expressed in the Book of Common Prayer all the time if only they had troubled themselves to examine it in detail. It was only when Newman and Pusey began to address their ideas to a wider public in a series of tracts, which they called *Tracts for the Times*, that an opposition began to organize itself and the 'Tractarians', as the authors of the Tracts came to be called, first started to attract the unsympathetic and even alarmed attention of their diocesan bishops. It was, however, some considerable time before any positive action was taken against the new Movement, and Newman, who was appointed Vicar of the University Church of St. Mary's at Oxford in the same year in which Nicholas Wiseman was made Rector of the English College at Rome, had by then become one of the most prominent clergymen in the Established Church, famous for his oratory in the pulpit, respected for the sanctity of his personal life, and either followed with enthusiastic devotion, or held in the strongest aversion and fear, for the fascinating if dangerous beliefs which he expounded with such eloquence from the pulpit or propounded in such impeccable style with his pen.

That Wiseman, in distant Rome, should know of these happenings so many hundreds of miles away, may seem strange to the reader. But Wiseman did know, and watched the developments in Oxford with a growing interest, being kept well informed of all that happened by three converts to the Roman faith whose zeal for the conversion of England was as boundless as their observation, and the conclusions they drew from it, was so often at fault. Each one was in his own way extraordinary. Pugin, the architect, carried his enthusiasm for Gothic architecture to such a pitch that he would offer the guests at his table a gothic pudding[1] with the same enthusiasm as he would announce that his wife had presented him with a gothic baby. Equal in ardour for the faith as well as for fan-vaulting and rood-screens, was Ambrose Phillipps, before his conversion the first man to put a cross on the communion table of an Anglican Church since the Reformation, and after it one whose taste for ecclesiastical titles brought a rebuke from Dr. Poynter who, answering a letter in February 1827, had to point out 'when you write pray do not give me such high titles. I am not an Archbishop. . . .' Last in this trio came a man of remarkable spiritual life, the Hon. George Spencer, later known as Father Ignatius of the Passionist Order. If Spencer showed less of the extraordinary characteristics of the other two, the mode of his conversion was none the less unusual, for it took place during a performance of Mozart's opera *Don Giovanni* at the Paris Opera in 1820. It was these three men, at different times and under different conditions, who kept the Rector of the English College both informed and misinformed, about the religious revival which had started in Oxford, and hinted at possibilities of such great promise for the Roman Catholic Church.

[1] B. Clarke: *Church Builders of the XIX Century*, p. 60.

V

The special problems occasioned by the Oxford Movement were not the only matters coming from England which occupied the attention of Dr. Wiseman. He was to take an ever deeper interest in the affairs of the Established Church after George Spencer came as a student to the English College in 1830, but long before that date, before, even, he became Rector of the College, he came into contact with a personality whose influence in the Catholic Church was not always as helpful as it was vigorous, but whose forceful character dominated the English scene in the years before and just after the passing of the Emancipation Act. This was Peter Augustine Baines, a Benedictine monk of Ample-forth Abbey, who in 1823 had been consecrated coadjutor to the Vicar Apostolic of the Western District with the title of Bishop of Siga *in partibus infidelium*. We have noted that the Vicars Apostolic were men of simple tastes who tended to live in quiet, if not obscure, lodgings, and who avoided any ostentation or display in the exercise of their sacred office. Bishop Baines was the exception to this rule, though he was not able to indulge his taste for living *en grand seigneur* until some years after he first became a bishop, nor did his love of episcopal grandeur spring from personal ambition or lack of more worthwhile accomplishments, as is witnessed by the fact that his merits encouraged Leo XII to suggest his candidacy for a Cardinal's hat, while his own modesty prompted him to decline it.

Bishop Baines was one of the strangest men to be produced by the English Catholic Church for many generations. 'When he undertook great or magnificent works,' Wiseman wrote of him,[1]

[1] *Recollections*, Ch. VII, p. 205.

'he would stand alone: assent to his plans was a condition of being near him; any one that did not agree, or that ventured to suggest deliberation, or provoke discussion, was easily put aside; he isolated himself with his own genius; he had no counsellor but himself; and he who had, at one time, surrounded himself with men of learning, of prudence, and of devotedness to him, found himself at last alone, and fretted a noble heart to a solitary death.'

When this prelate, with his rather excessive ideas about the splendour of his office, arrived as coadjutor in his district, he could not fail to notice that in certain details the Western District might appear as inferior to the other three. In geographical extent it was of equal proportions, containing not only the entire principality of Wales, but also all the counties from Wiltshire and Gloucestershire to Land's End. In population of Catholics and in the number of missions, however, it was very much the smallest, and while the Northern and London districts had their colleges at Ushaw and Old Hall, and the Midland District supported a flourishing seminary at Oscott near Birmingham, the Western District could boast of no college or seminary at all. This defect it was Bishop Baines's ambition to remedy at once, and his imperious nature fixed upon a plan which was to involve him in disputes lasting almost until the end of his life, bringing the remote concerns of the Western District of the English Mission through the tribunals of the Congregation of Propaganda to the very feet of the Sovereign Pontiff himself, carrying Dr. Wiseman along in their wake.

Lacking, then, the prestige of a diocesan seminary of his own, the bishop's eye, as he surveyed his District, fell upon the monastery of St. Gregory the Great at Downside, and his problem seemed to be solved. Did he not himself wear the Benedictine habit, and was it not the tradition that the Western District should be ruled by a regular, either Benedictine or Franciscan? He would resolve his difficulty by making the Western District an entirely Benedictine diocese with Downside as its college. The plan seemed simplicity itself and had an impressive pre-Reformation precedent in the primatial diocese of Canterbury centred in the great Benedictine Abbey and shrine of St. Thomas à Becket, a saint with whom the Bishop of Siga may be said to have shared certain characteristics. In proclaiming the solution to his dilemma, however, Dr. Baines had

overlooked one important point, and that was obtaining the agreement of the Prior and monks of Downside Abbey to this scheme
which would so entirely change the character of their monastery.
Laying claim to the freedom of monastic institutions from episcopal
control the Downside community refused to have anything to do
with the bishop's plan. A complete deadlock was reached, and any
hope there might have been for a compromise solution was lost by
the imperious manner adopted by the Bishop which made negotiations with him almost impossible. At this critical point the whole
matter was suddenly shelved by circumstances beyond the control
of either Dr. Baines or the Prior of Downside. The Bishop of Siga's
health broke down completely and he was compelled to exchange
the enervating atmosphere of Bath for the more temperate and
tranquil skies of Italy. Neither the clergy of his District nor the
monks of Downside ever expected to see him again in this world.

The Bishop was in Italy from 1826 until 1829, in fact, just at the
time when Wiseman was promoted from Vice-Rector to Rector of
the Venerable English College. The two men met, and Wiseman,
in his *Recollections*, has described how the Italian climate soon
effected a cure. 'He came in a state of almost hopeless illness, with
an interior abscess working on an enfeebled frame and constitution,
apparently unable to expel it from the system. He came merely as
a visitor, with some private friends who had kindly accompanied
him, in hopes that change of climate might do more than medicines
or their administrators. They were not deceived. The mild climate,
the interesting recreation, and perhaps, more still, the rest from the
labour and excitement in which he had lived, did their duty; at
some due period, their interior enemy capitulated, in that Englishman's stronghold of misery and pain—the liver. . . .' After a con-
valescence spent at Assisi and Porto di Fermo he settled in Rome.

For all that his health was still fragile the Bishop of Siga was not
idle during the months he spent in the Eternal City. He improved
his acquaintanceship with Dr. Wiseman and shared with him the
duties of the English sermon which Leo XII had instituted. The
Rector of the English College, with becoming modesty, describes
his rival's success in this activity which he himself was then still
finding something of a burden: 'The church, which was nearly
empty when preachers of inferior rank occupied it, was crowded

when Bishop Baines was announced as the orator. .... The flow of his words was easy and copious, his imagery was often very elegant, and his discourses were replete with thought and solid matter. But his great power was in his delivery, in voice, in tone, in look, and gesture. His whole manner was full of pathos, sometimes more even than the matter justified. ...'[1] These qualities, both in and out of the pulpit, made a good impression in Rome. Wiseman, who was sometimes critical of the attainments of his fellow clergy, found much to admire in the Bishop, and fully shared in his enthusiasm for improving the educational standards of English Catholics, both lay and clerical. The Bishop was beginning to form ideas for an English Catholic University, and there was no more enlightened or more appreciative person with whom to discuss such plans than young Dr. Wiseman. There were also contacts to be made with the Congregation of Propaganda, and Dr. Baines soon won the confidence and support of the Prefect, Cardinal Capellari, a conquest that was to be all the more useful two years later when that prelate was to rule the Catholic Church as Gregory XVI.

Meanwhile the paternal eye of Leo XII was turned upon the proud and forceful personality of the still young bishop from England, and noted with approval his strength of character and engaging eloquence. The Pope had long wished to honour the Benedictine Order as a compliment to the memory of his predecessor, Pius VII, who had been a Benedictine monk, and it occurred to him that he might do honour both to that Order and to England by placing a Cardinal's hat on the deserving head of Bishop Baines. Had he done so he might have saved both England and his successor a good deal of trouble. Dr. Baines, however, had no ambition to remain in Rome as a member of the Sacred College, and the gracious offer of a red hat was tactfully declined. The Pope's intention to include an English voice in the secret councils of the Church was not fulfilled until March 1830,[2] when Bishop Thomas Weld was raised to the sacred purple. The appointment was unique in more ways than one, for the new Prince of the Church had lived for many years with his wife and child as Squire of Lulworth Castle, where his father had entertained King George III during that

---

[1] *Recollections*, Ch. VII, pp. 205-6.
[2] By Pius VIII.

54

monarch's visits to Weymouth. After the death of his wife and his daughter's marriage Thomas Weld renounced the world and became a priest, being ordained in 1821 by the Archbishop of Paris. Five years later he was consecrated bishop, though continuing to live in England until in 1830 the final honour of the Cardinalate was conferred upon him. Not only was he the first Englishman for many years to sit in the Senate of the Church but his position was also unique in the College of Cardinals in that he could admit, without blushing, to being both a father and a grandfather.

Perhaps one of the facts that induced Dr. Baines to decline the supreme honour of the Church was the news, which reached him in September 1829, that Bishop Collingridge, whose coadjutor he was, had died, and that he was himself now the undisputed ruler of the Western District. His health was restored, so he could return to England at once. If the monks of Downside trembled when they heard of the bishop's return, they did so with good cause, for Dr. Baines had left something in the nature of an ecclesiastical bombshell behind him in Rome.

This parting shot, aimed at the Order of which he was a member, was nothing less than the claim that the Order of St. Benedict in England was uncanonically instituted, having been founded there without formal permission from the Holy See as canon law required, and that in consequence their monastic vows were invalid. In pressing this astounding and, as it was to be proved, untenable proposition, the Bishop hoped to prove that the monks were, in fact, not monks at all, but secular priests, in which case they would come under his immediate and undisputed jurisdiction. But this time the Bishop overplayed his hand by a step which has been described as 'almost unparalleled in our ecclesiastical history, and one which alienated much sympathy from his side, as well as causing him grave trouble in Rome'.[1] The Downside monks appealed immediately to the Holy See and sent a member of the community to plead their cause before Propaganda.

One might suppose that the Bishop would now stay his hand, at least until the issue had been decided one way or another. But not Dr. Baines; he had set his heart on gaining control of Downside, and nothing, it seemed, would stop him. He addressed an ultimatum

[1] Bernard Ward: *Sequel to Catholic Emancipation*, Vol. I, pp. 23-24.

to the monks demanding that they should show within four days why they considered themselves free from episcopal control. As the matter had already been referred to Rome the monks not unnaturally refused, whereupon the Bishop withdrew all faculties from the community, that is, deprived them of canonical authority to hear confessions. The bishop's act caused the gravest scandal and was to prove fatal for his own designs, for it evaporated what influence remained to him in Rome, despite all the golden opinions he had won from Cardinal Capellari. Furthermore it prejudiced him for the future with the Holy See, for when he was later involved in controversy over the question of the converts, and the issue was referred to Rome, he was already clearly looked upon there as a potential trouble-maker.

Meanwhile peace had somehow to be restored to the Western District. Cardinal Capellari had been elected Pope in February 1831 under the name of Gregory XVI, and deputed Bishop Bramston, of the London District, to mediate in the dispute, but in this the good bishop had no success. It was then that the Pope turned to Dr. Wiseman. Gregory had often come into contact with the Rector of the English College when the business of the English Mission brought him to Propaganda, and, furthermore, he admired him as a scholar. He had, indeed, helped the young Rector to correct the proofs of a book shortly before the death of Pius VIII, so that when Wiseman went to pay his respects to the newly elected Gregory XVI he was greeted with the jovial remark: 'You must now revise your own proofs. I fear I shall not have much time in future to correct them.'[1] It was, therefore, with good knowledge of the man he was sending, that Gregory despatched Wiseman to England in September 1832 on a mission of reconciliation.

Bishop Baines's dispute had now spread from Downside to the sister community of Ampleforth in Yorkshire, where he had himself formerly been a monk, and later Prior. When it seemed clear that he would be unable to transform Downside into a seminary the Bishop had purchased Prior Park, a vast country house outside Bath, and here he hoped to establish a school and a seminary in each of the two wings, and possibly later make it the nucleus for a Catholic University. Meanwhile he installed himself in the main

[1] *Recollections*, p. 263.

part of the mansion where he proceeded to live in considerable state. To staff his college he had persuaded some of the Ampleforth monks to quit their monastery and ally themselves to his new institution at Prior Park, an act which had made him as unpopular with the remainder of the Ampleforth monks as he was already with their brethren at Downside.

Wiseman's mission as a peacemaker was not an unmitigated success. All he could do was to try to implement the compromise which he had suggested in 1830 over the status of the English Benedictine community, namely that the Holy See should issue a *Sanatio*, or decree of healing, which made good any defects which might have existed in the past, without being too specific about them, and assured that for the future there could be no shadow of doubt as to the validity of further monastic professions. His visit to England was short, for he was back in Rome by December. We may conclude that he took a charitable view of Bishop Baines's curious conduct, for he remained the enthusiastic supporter of all his activities to improve the educational standards of Catholics. The possibilities of a Catholic University were again discussed and it may well be that during this brief visit Bishop Baines first suggested, as he was soon formally to request, that Dr. Wiseman should take charge of the university and be appointed as well bishop-coadjutor of the District. Such exciting future plans, so close to the heart of the young Rector, must have compensated him for the comparative failure of his mission, for though he brought a modicum of peace to the distracted District, Dr. Baines continued, from his sumptuous surroundings at Prior Park, to harry the unfortunate monks of Downside whenever an opportunity offered. The return journey to Italy from this brief and unspectacular visit to England almost cost Wiseman his life, for near Turin his coach was overturned and he was carried, unconscious, to a nearby house. Fortunately, he suffered nothing more serious than shock and was well enough, on his return, to celebrate the feast of St. Thomas of Canterbury at a ceremony in the chapel of the English College at which eleven members of the Sacred College were present.

If Wiseman's involvement in the dramatic concerns of the Bishop of Siga had done nothing else, it had at least served to broaden his outlook and kindle his interest in the practical affairs of the English

Mission. It was now that he began to turn his attention to those religious movements in England which were outlined in the previous chapter, for in 1830 there arrived at the English College a new and interesting candidate for the priesthood in the person of the Hon. George Spencer, a convert clergyman of the Church of England.

George Spencer, the youngest son of George John, Earl Spencer, Knight of the Garter, was born at Admiralty House, London, in December 1799, during his father's tenure of office as First Lord of the Admiralty. His mother was a daughter of the Earl of Lucan and his father's family was closely related to the noble houses of Marlborough and Sunderland, so that young George, like the character in Oscar Wilde's play, may be said to have risen from the ranks of the aristocracy. He received the conventional upbringing of a member of his class passing from Eton to Trinity College, Cambridge, where he matriculated as a fellow commoner in 1817. After leaving Cambridge he travelled abroad. It was at the Paris Opera, in 1820, that the trombone chords of Mozart's *Don Giovanni* called him to repentance, and he experienced his first conversion. We have his own account of the scene.[1] 'The most remarkable impression of religion which I remember in all this period,' he recorded, 'was in a place where it might have been least expected. No other than the Italian Opera at Paris. I passed through that city . . . in my last journey to Lausanne, and on my return a month later. Both times I went to see the opera of *Don Giovanni*, which was the piece then in course of representation. . . . The last scene of it represents Don Giovanni, the hero of the piece, seized in the midst of his licentious career by a troop of devils, and hurried down to hell. As I saw this scene, I was terrified at my own state. I knew that God, who knew what was within me, must look on me as one in the same class with such as Don Giovanni, and for once this holy fear of God's judgement saved me: and this holy warning I was to find in an opera-house at Paris.'

The holy warning was taken to heart; in December 1822, George Spencer was ordained into the ministry of the Church of England by the Bishop of Peterborough and commenced his career as a Protestant clergyman. The next seven years saw him moving gradually in the direction of Rome, but the crisis did not come until

[1] Quoted by the Rev. Father Pius: *Life of Father Ignatius of St. Paul*, Ch. XI, p. 90.

1829 when he was introduced to another convert, a Cambridge man like himself, though a good many years his junior. This was Ambrose Lisle Phillipps (who later changed his name to Ambrose Phillipps de Lisle) who came of a well-to-do Leicestershire family and had been converted to the Roman faith while still a schoolboy. Under the influence of this enthusiastic young convert Spencer, already hovering on the brink, was swept across to the farther shore. A visit to Phillipps had resulted in the resolve to be received into the Catholic Church the week following, but then even so short a delay as seven days had seemed too much. 'I said to Phillipps (Father Spencer later wrote) "If this step is right for me to take next week, it is my duty to take it now. My resolution is made; tomorrow I will be received into the Church."' Thus began his career as a Catholic which was to end only with his sudden death thirty-five years later as Father Ignatius of the Passionist Order.

Ambrose Phillipps (or Phillipps de Lisle as we shall refer to him in future) had fired George Spencer with his enthusiasm for the conversion of England to the Catholic Faith. Phillipps de Lisle brought to the nineteenth century a romantic medievalism which was to find an ally in the architect Augustus Welby Pugin when he too joined the Catholic Church in 1834. He welcomed with open arms all those medieval aspects of Catholicism which many of the older Catholics had no wish to see revived and which non-Catholics regarded as no more than Popish superstition. Furthermore, he really believed that England was on the very verge of a return to the ancient faith. If one man was converted he believed that ten would soon follow; if ten were converted, a hundred would follow them; and if a hundred converts made their submission then all England would be begging Rome to receive it back. This enthusiasm was as genuine as it was misconceived. Thus, in 1837, when ten men had come for religious instruction to the Prior of the Monastery he had established on his country estate, he wrote to Lord Shrewsbury: 'In fact, I expect that in the course of a little time the majority of this neighbourhood will be Catholic,' and he was always preparing lists of Protestant bishops and clergymen whom he considered as willing to submit to Rome at a moment's notice.

It was full of these exalted but misleading notions for the conversion of England that George Spencer arrived at the English

59

College in 1830 to pursue his studies for the priesthood. Phillipps de Lisle came to Rome with him and remained long enough to impress Dr. Wiseman with his zeal. Certainly Spencer's arrival at the College was a turning point in Wiseman's career. The new student was three years older than the Rector and his position there was from the beginning rather a special one, so that he not only spent more time in the company of the Rector and Vice-Rector than was usually the case, but could also associate with them on terms of greater equality than was customary in a student. Spencer had great charm and tact, but this did not prevent him from telling Wiseman quite frankly 'that he should apply his mind to something more practical than Syrian MSS or treatises on geology, and that he would rather see him take up with what suited a priest on the English mission as it was'.[1] If the Rector was a little startled to receive such an admonition from one of his students, he took it in good part, for his discussions with Bishop Baines had been, to some extent, upon the same lines and his thoughts were turning more and more towards the possibility of returning to England. For Spencer himself he had nothing but praise; 'I think he is destined to do wonders in England,' he wrote to a friend,[2] while Spencer, like a true disciple of Phillipps de Lisle, lost no opportunity to expatiate on the great theme of the conversion of England whenever occasion offered.

To these ideas of a religious revival a new emphasis was brought in 1831 when three Frenchmen arrived in Rome and soon made themselves known to Dr. Wiseman. The most singular of these was the Abbé de Lamennais, who since the revolution of 1830 had been proclaiming the ideas of Ultramontanism in his paper *L'Avenir*, attempting to reconcile an absolutist interpretation of the papal office with the new ideas of political liberalism. With him came the Abbé Lacordaire, not yet clothed in the Dominican habit, and the Count de Montalembert, both of whom survived the eventual condemnation of their ideas by the Holy See, remaining in the Catholic body as a liberalizing influence while their elder companion became a bitter enemy of the papacy which he now exalted so highly.

As these three men waited for a decision from the Holy See on

---

[1] Quoted by Ward, Vol. I, p. 101.
[2] Letter to Dr. Husenbeth, quoted in Ward, Vol. I, p. 101.

the principles which they expounded with such effect in the pages of *L'Avenir*, a decision which the advisers of Gregory XVI seemed excessively slow and reluctant to give, they gratefully accepted the hospitality of Dr. Wiseman as one who shared in many of their hopes for a European revival of religion, and displayed more sympathy for them than some of the older and more conservative divines who seemed to increase in number and influence the nearer they got to the person of the Holy Father. The idea of trying to reconcile democracy with the Church was bound to fail under the pontificate of Gregory XVI, but Wiseman, with his English background, was less likely to identify democracy with militant atheism, as did the advisers of the Pope, and gave the Frenchmen what help and encouragement he could. With Montalembert he was to remain on friendly terms for life.

If anything were needed to encourage the hopes which Spencer's enthusiasm had kindled in Wiseman's mind with regard to the conversion of England it was the visit paid to him in 1833 by John Henry Newman and Hurrell Froude. This visit to Rome was the culmination of a European tour which the two men had made together, the latter in search of health (which was to be denied him) and the former, though unconsciously, in search of faith. To him this was to be granted, but only at the end of a long and agonizing pilgrimage. For him 'Rome is the place after all where there is most to astonish me, and of all ages, even the present,' but despite this he was still a long way from any acceptance of the claims of the Roman Church, though he could view her ecclesiastical organization with less distaste than some of his fellow-countrymen. To his sister he wrote: 'And now what can I say of Rome, but that it is the first of cities, and that all I ever saw are but as dust (even dear Oxford inclusive) compared with its majesty and glory? Is it possible that so serene and lofty a place is the cage of unclean creatures? I will not believe it till I have evidence of it.'[1]

In this spirit of cautious inquiry the two Oxford clergymen called upon the Rector of the English College. It is to be hoped that they found neither his cordial welcome nor his pleasant apartments, which Macaulay later described as 'snugly furnished in the English style, and altogether very like the rooms of a senior Fellow of Trinity',

[1] Quoted by Sir Geoffrey Faber: *Oxford Apostles*, Ch. VIII, p. 288.

as in any way suggestive of the cage of an unclean creature, though in the answers he gave to their questions the Rector must have appeared, to Froude at least, as something of a bird of ill-omen. For it is in Froude's *Remains* that we have an account, written with characteristic exuberance, of this historic encounter. 'It is really melancholy (Froude wrote) to think how little one has got for one's time and money. The only thing I can put my hand on as an acquisition is having formed an acquaintance with a man of some influence at Rome, Monsignor Wiseman, the head of the English College, who has enlightened Newman and me on the subject of our relations to the Church of Rome. We got introduced to him to find out whether they would take us in on any terms to which we could twist our consciences, and we found, to our dismay, that not one step could be gained without swallowing the Council of Trent as a whole. We made our approaches to this subject as delicately as we could. Our first notion was that terms of communion were within certain limits under the control of the Pope, or that in case he could not dispense solely, yet at any rate the acts of one council might be rescinded by another. . . . But we found, to our horror, that the doctrine of the infallibility of the Church made the Acts of each successive council obligatory for ever, that what had once been decided could never be meddled with again—in fact, that they were committed finally and irrevocably, and could not advance one step to meet us, even though the Church of England should again become what it was in Laud's time, or indeed what it may have been up to the atrocious council, for Monsignor Wiseman admitted that many things (e.g. the doctrine of the Mass) which were final then had been indeterminate before.'

If this encounter disappointed Froude (though Newman, at this time, was very much less inclined than his friend to 'twist his conscience' for the sake of an accommodation with the decrees of the Council of Trent) from a personal point of view it was a success. 'We mean to make as much as we can out of our acquaintance with Monsignor Wiseman,' he added, 'who is really too nice a person to talk nonsense about.' It was, in fact, upon Wiseman, that this meeting was to have the profounder effect. That these two men should come to his door so full of inquiry about the Catholic Church; eager, in Froude's case at least, to show their own Catholicity of spirit and outlook; so manifestly crestfallen when confronted with the unyielding exclusiveness of the Roman claims, brought a new reality to all that Spencer had told him, and impressed so strongly upon him. The interest which Spencer had aroused was now to become a dominating influence in the life of the future Cardinal. Looking back in 1847, two years after Newman's reception into the Roman Church, Wiseman wrote of their first meeting: 'From the day of Newman and Froude's visit to me, never for an instant did I waver in my conviction that a new era had commenced in England ... to this grand object I devoted myself ... the favourite studies of former years were abandoned for the pursuit of this aim alone.'

This new and absorbing interest, which was destined to change the course of his life, came at a time when Wiseman was conscious of the final triumph of faith over those doubts and suspicions which had clouded his mind at an earlier period. In 1833 he had suffered a serious chest complaint which had compelled him to reduce his activities and live, to some extent, the life of an invalid. His return to health seems to have coincided with a new spiritual serenity which he describes in a letter,[1] written in March, 1834, that shows him as having passed through the 'dark night of the soul' to a new position of spiritual strength. 'I have felt myself for some months (he writes) gradually passing into a new state of mind and heart which I can hardly describe, but which I trust is the last stage of mental progress, in which I hope I may yet much improve, but out of which I trust I may never pass. I could hardly express the calm mild frame of mind in which I have lived; company and society I have almost entirely shunned, or have moved through it as a stranger; hardly a disturbing thought, hardly a grating sensation has crossed my being, of which a great feeling of love seems to have been the principle. Whither, I am inclined to ask myself, does all this tend? Whence does it proceed? I think I could make an interesting history of my mind's religious progress, if I may use a word shockingly perverted by modern fanatics, from the hard dry struggles I used to have when first I commenced to study on my own account, to the settling down into a state of stern conviction, and so after some years to the nobler and more soothing evidences furnished by the grand harmonies and beautiful features of religion, whether considered in contact with

[1] Quoted in Ward, Vol. I, p. 123.

lower objects or viewed in her own crystal mirror. I find it curious too and interesting to trace the workings of those varied feelings upon my relations to the outward world. I remember how for years I lost all relish for the glorious ceremonies of the Church. I heeded not its venerable monuments and sacred records scattered over the city; or I studied them all with the dry eye of an antiquarian, looking in them for proofs, not for sensations, being ever actively alive to the collection of evidences and demonstrations of religious truth. But now that the time of my probation, as I hope it was, is past, I feel as though the freshness of childhood's thoughts had once more returned to me, my heart expands with renewed delights and delicious feelings every time I see the holy objects and practices around me, and I might almost say that I am leading a life of spiritual epicureanism, opening all my senses to a rich draught of religious sensations.'

This year saw Wiseman at the height of his career in Rome before his first prolonged visit to England made it clear that his future would be dedicated to that country. He was widely known and respected as a scholar, and his position as Rector and agent of the English bishops gave him an assured place in the ecclesiastical world. His genial and friendly manner made him a much sought-after personality among the many English people who frequented Rome at this time. Not only Catholic-minded clergymen like Newman and Froude, but rising young politicians like Macaulay and Gladstone paid their respects to the Rector of the Venerable English College. He was highly thought of by the Pope himself, who created him a chamberlain, a rank which carried the title of Monsignor and the rank of prelate, and who always showed him such kindness that Wiseman could claim 'innumerable favours and gracious acts, so many unexpected and unmerited manifestations of goodness' from Gregory XVI as to 'leave his memory impressed on mine as that of a father rather than a sovereign'.[1]

He was clearly a man marked out for preferment in the church, and no one could have been surprised when Bishop Baines, who had returned to Rome in 1834 in the pursuit of his vendetta against the Benedictines, formally requested to have Dr. Wiseman consecrated as his Bishop coadjutor. The request was not refused by the Holy

[1] *Recollections*, p. 335.

See, but the matter was postponed, not through any lack of confidence in the candidate but because it was thought that Wiseman was too young to be appointed a bishop and that the Bishop of Siga was scarcely old enough to require an assistant. The question was therefore *dilata*, or left over for a decision at a future date.

But meanwhile it was clear that the time had come for Monsignor Wiseman to pay a much longer visit to England than the brief one he had undertaken in 1832 at the request of Bishop Baines. Apart from anything else he needed a change. His health, though much improved, was not entirely restored, and but for this fleeting visit of 1832 he had not visited his home country since he first came to Rome as a boy of sixteen. It was important that the man who was agent for the English bishops should have some first-hand experience of the conditions under which they worked, especially as the move for the restoration of a properly constituted episcopal hierarchy was beginning to take on a more urgent form. Accordingly, in the summer of 1835, Dr. Wiseman packed his bags for the long journey from Rome to England.

VI

Just before he left Rome for England in 1835 Wiseman gave a course of lectures in the apartments of Cardinal Weld in the Palazzo Odescalchi. His subject was 'The Connexion between Science and Revealed Religion'. These lectures, which were delivered before crowded audiences at which many Protestant visitors were present, served a double purpose for Wiseman, for in them he was able to make use of much of the research which had been occasioned by the religious doubts that had been troubling his mind for so long; and also, in delivering them, he was preparing himself for the more extensive series of lectures, to be given in London, which were to be the most important and significant feature of his sojourn in England. Of these lectures Wilfrid Ward writes: 'Nothing since the appearance of the *Horae Syriacae* in 1828 had so great an effect on his reputation as the delivery of these discourses; indeed, their immediate effect in Rome itself would seem to have been greater. They dealt with exactly what learned men are most disposed to attend to—the most recent theories and discussions in various sciences, notably in comparative philology; and their bearing on Christian evidences, though less interesting to some of his auditors, was an additional attraction to others. Many of these theories are now superseded; and while in some cases Wiseman's insight anticipated discoveries of a later time, the lectures as a whole, unlike his biblical researches, are now out of date. But their interest at the moment and the respect they created, for his thorough and systematic study from original sources of the literature of the subjects dealt with, were very marked.'[1] At the very same time that

[1] Ward, Vol. I, p. 125.

Wiseman was delivering these lectures in Rome, the Lent of 1835, Lacordaire gave the first of his famous series of 'conferences' in the cathedral of Notre Dame in Paris which were to have so profound an effect upon the religious life of France. Both men, friends as they were, must have felt that they were in the vanguard of a new movement to reconcile the eternal verities of the Catholic faith with the thought and ideals of the nineteenth century. It was full of the enthusiasm which these ideas would create in the lively imagination of such a mind as his that Nicholas Wiseman began his long journey to England.

He travelled by way of Munich and Paris. In the Bavarian capital he met Dr. Döllinger, who had been professor of ecclesiastical history and law in the university there since 1826, and at this time shared in the Ultramontane views of Wiseman and Lacordaire. Wiseman and Döllinger had already been in correspondence for some time and the former had been responsible for introducing the Bavarian historian to the works of Dr. Lingard, his old master, which Döllinger greatly praised though he felt himself bound to note, in a letter which followed Wiseman to England, that it was to be regretted that Lingard did not understand German and was 'consequently incapable to profit of (*sic*) the historical works lately written in that language'.[1] In Paris Wiseman renewed his acquaintance with Lacordaire and Montalembert but not with the Abbé de Lamennais. The decision of the Holy See on the question which had brought the three men to Rome in 1831 had not been pronounced until they were already on their way home. It reached them in Munich and was nothing less than a severe condemnation of *L'Avenir* and all it stood for. The blow was a crushing one, and Lamennais was not to recover from it. He had retired into the country on their return to France, and the year previous to Wiseman's arrival there had published *Paroles d'un Croyant* which resulted in a complete break with his former friends. Soon he was to leave the Catholic Church altogether. So too, many years later, was Döllinger, but not until after Wiseman's death.

It was in Paris that Wiseman had gone to confession and had been amused by the rebuke administered to him by the priest: '*Président d'un collège à Rome? Et voyageant partout, loin de vos élèves? Mon fils,*

[1] Ibid., p. 140.

je tremble pour vous.' His trembling, in this case, was misplaced.

Wiseman reached London on 14th July 1835. He had two chief objects in view; to visit Dr. Baines at Prior Park which he hoped might soon be the scene of his own future activity in collaboration with the Bishop; and to gain first-hand knowledge of the work of the English Mission by visiting as many parts of the country as he could. With regard to the second of these two objectives he had much to learn, as he himself readily admitted. But his long residence abroad and his foreign education had, he maintained, certain distinct advantages. 'Whatever may be considered the disadvantages of a foreign education,' he was to note in his *Recollections*, 'it possessed, especially at that period, the great advantage that it reared the mind and nursed the affections beyond the reach of religious contests and their irritation. One hardly knew the bitter things that were said against what was dearest to us.'

This could not be said of his co-religionists in England. Despite six years of emancipation the past, with all its bitterness, was still very much with them. If Wiseman had expected to find the leading Catholics now taking part in the public life of their country, he was soon to be disillusioned. The reaction of Catholics to the Emancipation Act had been wary, almost timid. Dr. Bramston, the Vicar Apostolic of the London District, in his first Pastoral Letter after the passing of the Act[1] had urged upon his flock the evangelical warning: 'What will it avail a man to gain the whole world and lose his own soul?' He had advised those 'in the higher sphere of life' to avoid seeking office 'if the passion of ambition or the thirst of worldly lucre be their leading motive.' While not entirely discouraging participation in public life if the service of their country was indeed their principal object, the Pastoral warned such would-be office holders against 'the world and its vain and empty honours' which can so easily 'entirely engross the heart of man, to the dissipation, destruction, and oblivion of his religious reflections and desires'. Such a message could hardly encourage his upper-class spiritual subjects to fling themselves into the political strife of their day, to make the Catholic voice heard in the councils of state, as Wiseman would have them do. To 'others professing the Roman Catholic Religion in inferior walks of life' Bishop Bramston felt

[1] Issued on New Year's Day, 1830.

the necessity of adding a warning on the consequences of their new freedom. 'To these,' he wrote, 'will be opened various situations where many and very dangerous temptations may assail them.' Among the forbidden fruits of emancipation which he mentioned was the awful liability of being 'corrupted by bribery, and by taking, or allowing others to take, false, unlawful, and unnecessary oaths' and the condoning of these offences by 'avaricious feelings and the plea of custom'. Clearly the Bishop saw no very rosy future for the emancipated Catholic, and many of those to whom the Pastoral was addressed, be they in the higher sphere of life or merely in an inferior walk, must have wondered whether the Bishop did not look upon Catholic emancipation as about the most alarming fate that could have fallen upon them.

Nothing could have been further removed from Dr. Wiseman's attitude than Bishop Bramston's cautious view of the situation. But the Bishop was only reflecting the general opinion of the Catholics of his day. They had a long history of persecution, the last violent outbreak of which was still within the memory of many then living[1] and they did not have Wiseman's detached appraisal of their present condition. For them, having achieved peace, the thing to do was to enjoy it peacefully. They knew the depth of anti-Catholic feeling and they feared, justly, as Wiseman himself would learn in due time, lest any provocation on their part should stir it up. This was the atmosphere that prevailed in the unobtrusive house in Golden Square which served as 'bishop's palace' to Dr. Bramston and his like-minded coadjutor, Dr. Griffiths, where Wiseman was a frequent visitor until he left in August for Prior Park, where we may assume he hoped to find a spirit more congenial to his aspirations for the future of the Catholic Church in England.

His visit to Prior Park was to prove a disappointment, indeed, a complete failure. As he approached the vast Palladian mansion on the outskirts of Bath he must have looked forward to renewing his contact with the imperious and ambitious spirit of Bishop Baines after the rather damping effect of his initial experiences in London. Here was a man who lived in splendid surroundings as befitted the Roman purple and whose ideas were on the same scale as the great

---

[1] If Bishop Bramston was born in 1763 as is generally supposed (the exact date of his birth is uncertain) he would have been 17 years old at the time of the Gordon Riots.

building he chose to inhabit in such blatant contrast to the discreet obscurity of Golden Square. But Wiseman was in for a shock. At Rome the young Monsignor and the Bishop had met on terms of some equality, each paramount in his own sphere and able to exchange the ideas which both shared for the future of the English mission with uninhibited familiarity. There was no feeling of dependence on Wiseman's part, whose position in Rome was one of considerable consequence and importance. He was soon to find a change. The welcome he received was quite cordial, but his Lordship the Bishop of Siga expected every man to know his place, and that included Dr. Wiseman. They were no longer in Rome, where Wiseman might be expected as Rector of the English College and *persona grata* with the Holy Father, to advise the Bishop on his difficulties with Propaganda; they were now in the Bishop's own District where it was Dr. Wiseman's place to listen to advice and not to give it.

The cool attitude of Dr. Baines did not immediately make itself felt, though Wiseman could hardly fail to notice the Bishop's reluctance to refer to the subject of Wiseman's returning as his coadjutor. On the educational side he had nothing but praise for the college which now flourished at Prior Park, and it was understood that the Pope was agreeable to granting a charter for a Catholic university. But on the question of Wiseman's becoming President, which had been discussed in Rome, the Bishop again became hesitant, not to say frankly discouraging, making the suggestion that Wiseman should only occupy the post tentatively for one year, keeping his place in Rome open so that he could return to the English College should the scheme not work out, or, in plainer language, should Dr. Baines wish to get rid of him. The suggestion was humiliating to a man in Wiseman's position and the Bishop can hardly have been surprised when he refused to accept it. The truth was, no doubt, that Dr. Baines found Wiseman's personality too strong for the sort of collaborator he required. What he needed was a man who was ready to put his, the bishop's, ideas into practice, not a person who was constantly coming out with ideas and schemes of his own and, worse still, one who might actually dare to criticize what Dr. Baines thought right and proper. Such a man would not do at all.

To Wiseman this was a bitter rebuff and one that it was hard to bear. 'As for myself,' he wrote[1] to a friend many years later, 'I was devoted to (Dr. Baines) heart and soul, and lost favour at Rome by the manner in which I espoused his cause. I saw in Prior Park the beginning of a new era for Catholic affairs, in education, in literature, in public position, and in many things which are now realities, and then were hopes. How was all this broken off? One cause of our separation is too painful for me to recite; but the decisive one was my unfortunately presuming on what I thought confidence, and offering advice when I thought it would be most useful. This produced such a rebuff as I never received before, and never have since. It was by letter; but if my answer was preserved among the Bishop's papers, I should not mind all the world seeing it.'

As Monsignor Wiseman drove back to London his disappointment was complete. The Prior Park scheme, which had been the main reason for his coming to England, had proved a failure in so far as his own participation in it was concerned. The Bishop of Siga had proved himself to be a person with whom it was hopeless to work except upon terms which would be quite impossible of acceptance to a man of Wiseman's intellectual stature and exuberant temperament. On top of this the Vicar Apostolic of the London District and the coadjutor who would soon succeed him seemed to have no grasp of the great opportunities that awaited them. They appeared to him like prisoners still dazed by the light of day after many years of confinement in some dark dungeon. 'Their "shackles",' he wrote, 'had been removed, but not the numbness and cramp which they had produced.' They accepted their emancipation almost as though it had been forced compulsorily upon them. They were also, so far as he could gather, quite unaware of the interesting developments in Germany and France, where a Catholic revival seemed imminent, and as for the Tractarian movement in the Church of England, with all its exciting potentialities, that, so far as they were concerned, might never have happened at all. This particularly distressed Wiseman who had not ceased to follow every phase of the movement since Newman and Froude had visited him in Rome. But the English Catholics seemed wholly indifferent to it, or dismissed the Tractarian divines as of no more account than any

[1] Letter published in the *Ampleforth Journal* for May 1910.

other of those ecclesiastical eccentrics who appear from time to time to enliven the English religious scene. Later on he was to express, in the Introduction to his published Essays, how he was 'surprised on visiting England in 1835 to find how little attention (the Oxford Movement) had yet excited among Catholics, though many *Tracts for the Times* had already appeared, and Dr. Whatley had sung out to their writers, *Tendimus in Latium*'. To him it offered the Catholic Church in England one of its most tremendous opportunities since the Reformation, and to the words just quoted he added: 'For Catholics to have overlooked all this, and allowed the wonderful phenomenon to pass by, not turned to any useful purpose, but gazed at till it died out, would have been more than stupidity, it would have been wickedness.' In these first disillusioned months of his visit to England it seemed more than likely to him that it was into this very wickedness that his fellow Catholics were about to fall.

One can indeed sympathize with Wiseman. He was still young and full of enthusiasm. He had come from the very centre of the intellectual and spiritual life of the Church, where he occupied a conspicuous position, to the country wherein he hoped his future work would lie, and he was met with misunderstanding and in-difference. Dr. Baines had no longer any use for him; Dr. Bramston was aged and near the end of his life; his coadjutor and successor clearly unsympathetic. Well might Wiseman have thought of re-turning at once to Rome where there was useful work for him to do in surroundings he had never ceased to love. On the other hand one must remember that he still had only a sketchy idea of the situation in England or the sort of problems that preoccupied the Vicars Apostolic. The London District, over which Dr. Bramston presided, comprised nine counties and part of a tenth; the Midland District, ruled by Dr. Walsh, contained fourteen counties. The rest of England and Wales were provided for by the Western and Northern Districts. The ecclesiastical government of areas so vast, with a minimum of cash at their disposal and a continual shortage of priests, gave the Vicars Apostolic enough to think about without concerning themselves with what went on in intellectual circles in Munich or Paris, or what particular attitudes were being struck by High Church clergymen at Oxford. Rather did they require the help of Dr. Wiseman's well-informed mind and powerful influence at Rome in the solution to some of their own difficulties. The organization of the mission was years out of date but the over-worked bishops had little time to work out a plan for its reorganization. All were agreed that a proper hierarchy must be restored with the various districts subdivided into dioceses, and it was to this end that the Vicars Apostolic expected Wiseman to assist them as their accredited representative in Rome. Once this objective was achieved there would be time enough to explore the theological opinions of Dr. Döllinger or exploit the embarrassments of the Anglican Establishment.

Fortunately Dr. Wiseman did not return to Rome; he decided instead upon an extended tour of England which he outlined in a letter to his friend Monckton Milnes. His object was to 'set out on a species of tour, or rather *progress*, through England and Ireland, having made a resolution never to sleep in an inn or hostelry the whole way; but I intend to quarter myself on such of the nobility or gentry of the realms as can sufficiently appreciate such an honour'. The plan to visit Ireland did not materialize, nor was the whole of England taken in by his tour, but he was able to visit the Earl of Shrewsbury at Alton Towers, a man who shared to the full in his ideas and set a splendid example of how, in the eyes of Wiseman at least, a Catholic nobleman should live; and also discover one bishop who sympathized with all that he stood for and showed a proper understanding of the significance of the Tractarian movement in the Anglican Church. This was Dr. Walsh, the Vicar Apostolic of the Midland District, who governed the vast area over which he had ecclesiastical jurisdiction from the industrial centre of Birmingham. Dr. Walsh was, like Wiseman, of Irish descent, and had also been educated abroad at the seminary at Douai before that college had been disbanded at the time of the French Revolution. There he had been a fellow student of Daniel O'Connell. He was a man of wider sympathies and more cosmopolitan outlook than his fellow bishops, and he received Wiseman with open arms. As a friend of Ambrose Phillipps de Lisle, and later as a patron of Pugin (who was to design the Cathedral of St. Chad at Birmingham) Bishop Walsh understood the outlook of the new converts whose activities he welcomed and encouraged. It was fortunate, as Wiseman must have noticed with relief, that the city and university of Oxford should be in the District of this bishop who was so much more in sympathy with the movement now in progress there than were either Dr. Bramston or Dr. Griffiths. Dr. Walsh found Wiseman equally to his liking, and suggested that he should become his coadjutor, subject to the approval of Rome. This offer must have brought some consolation to Wiseman after his off-hand treatment by Bishop Baines, but once again Rome deferred the appointment on the grounds that the time was not yet ripe for him to leave Rome for good.

Wiseman returned to London in November 1835 in somewhat better spirits, and was almost at once offered a temporary post which was, as it turned out, to result in the most important event of his stay in England. Dr. Baldacconi, chaplain of the Royal Sardinian Embassy, was returning on a visit to Italy and Wiseman was offered the charge of his chapel in Lincoln's Inn Fields during his absence. The appointment was made because of Wiseman's fluency in the Italian language, in which he was expected to preach each Sunday; but while he was in charge of the chapel he took the opportunity to give a course of lectures in English designed to explain the principles of Catholicism in a non-controversial spirit intended especially to appeal to Protestant listeners. The idea was entirely novel; no such lectures had been delivered publicly in London before. He announced the course for delivery on the Sunday afternoons of Advent, and they were an immediate and sensational success. Every afternoon the church was packed to overflowing. To many Protestants it was the first occasion on which they had heard a reasoned explanation of the Catholic faith by a man of acknowledged intellectual eminence. 'He had come to England,' wrote one man,[1] then an Oxford undergraduate, who had attended the lectures, 'with a very considerable reputation for learning and ability; and this took many to the Sardinian Chapel. The lectures more than sustained his reputation, and produced an immense sensation. I date from their delivery the beginning of a serious revival of Catholicism in England.'

The last sentence may now seem a little exaggerated, but it contains more than a grain of truth. The average Protestant Englishman in the first part of the nineteenth century had only the vaguest idea of

[1] Mr. David Lewis. *Vide* Ward, Vol. I, p. 233.

what a Catholic believed, and what little he did know, or imagined himself to know, he was prepared to dismiss as being the rankest superstition. No story of Papal mummery was too grotesque for him to swallow with a credulity far surpassing that which he supposed to be the exclusive possession of Catholics. He would believe any story one liked to tell of the tyranny of priests, the indolence of monks, and the all too human frailty of nuns. As to the Pope, that unfortunate prelate he regarded as either lost in stupidity or altogether too clever by half, a Machiavellian figure dedicated to the destruction of the Church of England and the spiritual enslavement of mankind. True, more enlightened minds, like that of Macaulay, did not hold such nonsensical views, but enlightened minds have never in any age formed more than an insignificant minority; and later on, as Wiseman would discover, even minds supposedly enlightened became overcast at the mere mention of Popery, for the day was not far off when the mildest Anglican bishop would find no epithet too strong to describe the depravity of Rome.

It was against such a background of bigotry and ignorance that Wiseman spoke, and men were amazed to hear the claims of Rome put forward calmly and dispassionately and supported by reasonable argument. Even if they could not accept what Wiseman had to say they were no longer able to dismiss the Catholic case as being beneath the contemplation of reasonable individuals. The success of the lectures was a great triumph for the Church, and the lecturer's co-religionists were themselves amazed and gratified to hear the truths of their faith so publicly proclaimed after the long years of secrecy from which they had but recently emerged. Dr. Bramston was among the first to appreciate the value of what was being done and begged Wiseman to repeat his series the following Lent in the Church of St. Mary at Moorfields, which was the largest Catholic church in London. To Wiseman himself the success he had achieved did much to undo the unhappy impressions which he had formed when he first reached England, and he felt at last that he was doing some real good. Later on he was to tell the future Cardinal Vaughan how he used to shed tears in the sacristy of the Sardinian chapel 'fearing that whatever good the lectures were doing to others, they were filling me with vain-glory'.[1] Only Bishop Griffiths, who

[1] Ward, Vol. I, p. 233.

resented Wiseman's criticism of the English clergy, was unmoved by the stir which the lectures caused, noting laconically in his diary that he found the preacher 'eloquent, but not so effective as Rev. J. A. Hearne', a priest whose chief claim to fame is that he later preached at Dr. Griffith's funeral.

The second course of lectures packed the larger Church at Moorfields, drawing many distinguished men to listen to them. Lord Brougham was one of these, but history does not relate what the former Lord Chancellor and founder of the 'godless institution in Gower Street'[1] thought of what he heard. Wiseman did not spare his audience, talking from an hour and a half to as much as two hours at a time. The subjects of his lectures centred on such themes as the Authority of the Church, the Catholic Rule of Faith, the Supremacy of the Pope, and more controversial subjects such as Indulgences, the Invocation of the Saints; their Relics and Images, and finally, that perennial red rag to the Protestant bull—Transubstantiation; a doctrine of the Catholic Church which he described as that which 'perhaps of all other dogmas, has been most exposed to misrepresentation, or, at least, certainly to scorn and obloquy'.[2] He ended his course with words which clearly explain the spirit in which they were given and perhaps help to account for their success. 'I have but scattered a little seed, and it is God alone that can give the increase. It is not on those effects, for which I am grateful to your indulgence, and on which till my dying hour I must dwell with delight,—it is not on the patience and kindness with which you have so often listened to me under trying circumstances, in such numbers, and at such an hour, that I presume to vest my hopes and augury of some good effect. No, it is on the confidence which the interest exhibited gives me that you have abstracted from me individually and fixed your thoughts and attention upon the cause which I represent. Had I come before you as a champion, armed to fight against the antagonists of our faith, I might have been anxious to appear personally strong and well appointed; but the course which I have chosen needed not much prowess; a burning lamp will shine as brightly in the hands of a child, as if uplifted by a giant's arm. I have

[1] University College, London, founded by Brougham and others in 1828.
[2] *Lectures on the Principal Doctrines and Practices of the Catholic Church*, Vol. II, Lecture XIV, p. 136.

endeavoured simply to hold before you the light of Catholic truth; and to him that kindled it be all the glory!'[1]

It was this refusal to score points against his adversaries but simply to proclaim Catholic truth on its own merits that won Wiseman the respect and attention of his listeners. But those adversaries themselves were not slow to see the harm which Monsignor Wiseman's lectures were likely to do to their own cause. In an attempt to frustrate this a garbled and inaccurate version was brought out which Wiseman promptly disowned. It did, however, have the good effect of making him issue an authorized edition of the lectures 'as the only effectual means to prevent injury to myself or to my cause',[2] and this was published in two volumes in 1836. One of the results to follow from this was an article in the *British Critic* for December 1836, from the pen of John Henry Newman. The article was sympathetic in tone. 'Romanism has great truths in it,' Newman wrote, 'which we of this day have almost forgotten, and its preachers will recall numbers of Churchmen and Dissenters to an acknowledgement of them.' But while Newman considered that Romanism might 'spread among Dissenters and irregulars' and even welcomed such a possibility, he still considered that the formularies of the Church of England were proof against the blandishments of Rome. If Dr. Wiseman's lectures were to have any effect upon Anglicans, so Newman held, it would not be to win them over to Roman ideas but rather to waken them to the Catholic principles dormant in their own Church. Newman's view, however, was not representative of Anglican opinion generally, and a later issue of the *British Critic* carried a violent attack on Wiseman's lecture on the Eucharist by Dr. Turton, who combined the Deanery of Peterborough with the Professorship of Divinity at Cambridge. The worthy Dean was less kind to Dr. Wiseman. 'Plausibility,' he declared, 'is the characteristic of the learned author's labours,' and he dismissed him as being 'subtle but not sagacious . . . dexterous but not circumspect . . . learned after the manner of a controversialist, not after that of a student'.

Among Catholics all criticism of Wiseman was now silenced, and messages of praise and thanks poured in upon him from all sides.

[1] Ibid., Lecture XVI, p. 243.
[2] Ibid., Vol. I, Preface, p. vi.

Clearly he was too great an asset to be allowed to disappear for ever from the scene of his triumph, and he was urged to remain in England or, if he could not do that at once, to return as soon as his present work in Rome was completed. To mark their appreciation the Catholics presented Wiseman with a gold medal. Upon one side was a likeness of the recipient, engraved from a bust by Scipio Clint, while on the other a papal tiara, St. Peter's keys, a chalice and various other objects of devotion were depicted before a shining cross. The legend which encircled this pious design read: NICOLAO WISEMAN, AVITA RELIGIONE FORTI SUAVIQUE ELOQUIO VINDICATA, CATHOLICI LONDINENSES AN M.DCCC. XXXVI.

A more durable result of the newly awakened enthusiasm among Catholics to which Dr. Wiseman's lectures had given rise was the foundation of the *Dublin Review*. The original idea of a Catholic literary quarterly came from a Mr. Michael Quin, who with Daniel O'Connell was one of the founder members of the Reform Club, and represented the liberal Catholic outlook. He was a journalist and barrister by profession and to his experience in the former field he was soon able to add the political acumen of O'Connell and the scholarship of Wiseman; though the latter, with an eye, no doubt, to O'Connell's more fiery outbursts, stipulated 'that no extreme political views should be introduced into the Review'. Quin, who deserves the credit for the original inception of the idea, did not remain long with the review, and it was primarily to Wiseman and O'Connell that it owed its survival and ultimate success.[1] The need had long been felt for a serious quarterly review, Catholic in inspiration, but meant to appeal to a wider public outside the Church. The name *Dublin Review* was fully intended as a parallel to the redoubtable *Edinburgh Review*, contrasting the Catholic associations of the Irish capital with the Protestant and rationalistic spirit which was held to characterize the Athens of the North. Wiseman accepted the editorship of the new Review and was to remain associated with it all his life. 'From its first appearance,' writes Bishop Bernard Ward,[2] 'the *Dublin Review* always maintained a high level of literary excellence. The heart and soul of

[1] In 1961 the name of this quarterly was changed to *The Wiseman Review* in honour of the Cardinal's association with its foundation and first editorship.

[2] *The Sequel to Catholic Emancipation*, Vol. I, p. 76.

it was Dr. Wiseman, who not only wrote numerous articles himself, but also by his influence and his European reputation as a scholar, succeeded in obtaining the co-operation of many distinguished writers.'

The first issue of the Review appeared in May 1836. Wiseman remained in England until the next number was ready for publication and then made his own preparations for a return to Rome. During his last weeks in this country there occurred an event which must have brought back to him with something of a jolt the first frustrating months of his visit. On 30th May 1836, the great mansion at Prior Park was utterly destroyed by a devastating fire. Bishop Baines, however, was spared the fate which the uncharitable might have thought he deserved, and did not go up in flames with his mansion. He survived, and though all that he had fought for so relentlessly might seem to have perished in the flames he lost no time in launching an appeal for the restoration of the house, which was soon to be rebuilt, though the burden of the debt was to remain with him to the end. Whatever may be said of the Bishop of Siga, he did not lack courage.

Despite, then, the initial disappointments, Wiseman was able to return to Rome well satisfied with his visit to England, which in the end had developed into something of a triumph. His life in Rome would never be quite the same again. He realized now that sooner or later he would have to return to England and make his home there, devoting the rest of his life to the work of the Catholic Church in the English Mission. These thoughts, as time went on, became more fixed in his mind so that Rome itself, which, in fact, he loved deeply, seemed to lose its charm and hold over his imagination. Thus, by 1839 he was writing to his sister, who was now married to Count Gabrielli and living at Fano, of his impatience to get back. 'I cannot tell you how anxious I am to quit Rome,' he wrote,[1] 'only your being settled in Italy and the College stand in my way. But consider: I have been 20 years in Rome, and I have not formed one single friendship in it. I have no family in which I am welcome, or where I find any comfort in going—you know well enough the heartless and cold acquaintances which the system of society leads to in Rome, (I do not speak of the provinces); all is so full of mere

[1] Letter dated 27th April 1839. The Fano Papers.

frivolity and envy; those who are climbing up the ladder of ambition are so selfish and have so little true friendship or attachment, there is so much intrigue, and so little encouragement to any one who merely seeks to do his duty, that I can assure you I am heartily sick of it all. On the other hand I was but months in England and I have friends there that are pressing my return among them, with all the sincerity of friendship, whose arms will be open to welcome me, who I know will sympathise with me, and value any little thing I can do. But this is a trifle. What good do I at Rome? Excepting in the College, nothing to the purpose; while England is in the most interesting condition, and calls for all the exertions of those that wish her well.'

The very exaggerations of this letter show Wiseman's anxiety to return to England, for it was quite untrue to say that he had no friends in Rome, though this plea of friendlessness was to grow with the years; for Wiseman, who had a strongly affectionate nature, could never reconcile his increasing eminence in his career with the isolation which all great positions in this world impose upon those who occupy them. The letter demonstrates, however, that after his return to Rome he realized fully that his main work there was done and he must abide his soul in patience until those in authority considered that the time was ripe for him to take his place, which could not be other than a leading one, in the great undertaking which now claimed the whole of his thoughts, his work, and his prayers: the conversion of England.

VII

Wiseman's increasing enthusiasm to return permanently to work in the English Mission was to be matched by a marked deterioration in his relationship with the Vicars Apostolic and with a large section of the English clergy, a state of affairs, prompted by various misunderstandings, which marked his last years as a resident in Rome. Despite the success of his visit to England and the encouraging results of his lectures at the Sardinian Chapel and St. Mary, Moorfields, his contacts with the clergy had not always been happy, and it was known that he thought some of them to be of a poor intellectual quality and lacking in what he considered to be a proper ecclesiastical spirit. Bishop Baines had introduced members of the Italian religious order, recently established as the Institute of Charity, to work at Prior Park, and Wiseman was known to encourage the presence of these foreign missionaries and the strange Italian devotions they brought with them, and this did not add to his popularity with the English secular clergy. He was also a very shy man and this, as is often the case, was mistaken for reserve or for superiority by those who did not know or understand him. Thus Dr. Bowdon, the President of Sedgley Park College, who met him at Bishop Walsh's house in 1835, found him 'distant and formal, the result of Roman pomposity',[1] while a less reticent priest, the Rev. Thomas McDonnell, was later to give vent to an ironical description of his innocent victim whom he dismissed as 'this "celebrated" personage, this polyglot prelate, this acquaintance of the learned'.[2] The reader will not be surprised to learn that

---

[1] Denis Gwynn, *Cardinal Wiseman* (1950 edition), p. 54.
[2] Bernard Ward: *The Sequel to Catholic Emancipation*, Vol. II, p. 15.

Father McDonnell wrote under some emotional stress, but his outburst indicates the effect which Dr. Wiseman's personality could sometimes have on those less fortunately endowed, either linguistically or intellectually, than himself.

To those who knew him well he presented a very different personality; warm, generous and unaffectedly simple. Thus one of his students at the Venerable English College could write of him, as he appeared in the years 1836–37, that 'he seemed unconscious of his intellectual superiority, and would seek co-operation from minds immeasurably inferior to his own, as if on the same level with himself'. The same writer[1] gives us an interesting picture of the variety of the Rector's activities: 'In proof of Dr. Wiseman's versatility I may mention that he often acted as our organist. Indeed, he had a critical appreciation of music as well as of the other fine arts. It was he, too, who painted the scenes for the first play which we acted, in 1837. I may take this opportunity of stating what I now feel myself at liberty to mention, viz. the fact that he himself wrote a piece for us, the scene of which was America. The manuscript was handed to those of the students who officiated as managers, with instructions to take a fair copy and then to return the original to him, and on no account to divulge even to the other students the fact that he had written it.' Later, when Cardinal-Archbishop, Wiseman would delight in writing little plays to be acted by the children of his friends.[2]

This wide range of interests and activity is mentioned not merely for what it shows of Wiseman's own character, but to throw into relief some of the aspects of his personality which jarred on the narrower minds of certain of the priests who laboured on the English Mission. It was no fault of theirs that circumstances had denied them the benefits of a liberal education, but they were understandably impatient when their meagre attainments, such as they were, came under the fire of criticism from one who seemed to have enjoyed all the privileges which they themselves had been denied. In this respect Wiseman lacked sensitivity; but it should be remembered that his implied criticism of some of the English

[1] The Rev. Mr. Kyan. Reminiscences quoted by Ward, Vol. I, pp. 255–7.
[2] Manuscript copies of such plays are still preserved in the de Zulueta and Vaughan families.

clergy arose rather from his own enthusiasm for what was required for the future than from any direct censure of individuals. He had a high ideal of the priesthood, and he returned from England determined that his own students should leave the English College with as wide and cultivated an education as circumstances should permit. And what better place was there than Rome for the fulfilment of such an ideal? To achieve this end, our same informant tells us, 'he was never idle for a moment. Even recreation he made subservient to a useful purpose. On each Thursday (the weekly holiday) it was his habit to take us all to one of the catacombs, or churches, or antiquities, or picture galleries, or the museums, or the studios of artists, and on such occasions we were often accompanied by some German scholar or other friend of his interested in Christian art.' These excursions formed an essential part of his educational scheme. To gain a knowledge and understanding of art, and of Christian art in particular, was to him as important as understanding Christian philosophy or theology; indeed, they all held together as threads which formed the cord of Christian civilization. 'We have never failed to embrace any opportunity that presented itself,' he later wrote[1] on the theme of Christian Art, 'of pointing out the beauties and artistic elements of the Catholic ceremonial, as well as the poetry of our ritual, and forms of prayer, all eminently conducive to the creation of religious art.' It is agreeable to picture Dr. Wiseman in the Doria Palace before Velasquez's portrait of Innocent X, or in the Vatican museum, surrounded by his little group of students, expatiating upon the beauties of Raphael's frescoes; but to the priest struggling in some industrial slum among ignorant labourers, such educational refinements seemed the height of religious epicureanism and of little purpose in training men to win the souls of drunken mechanics or half-starved factory boys. Wiseman had a splendid vision of the future of Catholicism in England, and to make a reality of this he had to create a new atmosphere among the clergy. There can be no doubt that his view of the situation was the right one, but that it should rankle in the breasts of those who had borne the brunt of the work at home for many long years of proscription, from which they had, as yet, only recently emerged, is equally understandable.

[1] *Essays on Various Subjects*, p. 413.

The change in Wiseman's outlook after his visit to England; that is to say, the orientation of all his activities towards an eventual return to his own country; was accompanied by a change in his physical appearance. A young man[1] who heard him give his lectures in Cardinal Weld's apartments in 1835, described him as 'a tall thin priest, with a stoop and a rather frowning brow and black hair, and gold spectacles'. By the time that he was settled once more in Rome he had become, in the words of Wilfrid Ward, a 'ruddy-faced and somewhat corpulent man of action'. The corpulence was to increase with the passing years so that a visitor,[2] some ten years later when Wiseman was living in London, seeing him standing with his secretary, the portly Monsignor Searle, and another equally well-proportioned priest, was amazed at the spectacle they presented. 'They formed,' he tells us, 'a trio somewhat formidable for a timid stranger to encounter. I thought, is this, then, the effect of prayer and fasting? Three such mountains of flesh I had never before seen.' Frederick Faber was subsequently to say of the Cardinal, somewhat disrespectfully, that 'when in full tog he looked like some Japanese God',[3] a reference not only to Wiseman's considerable size but also to the rather heavy face with its broad thick-lipped mouth. It was not lack of energy that caused his growing tendency to fatness; from his middle thirties to the end of his life Wiseman was rarely in perfect health, and as he grew older he became more and more of an invalid, until diabetes eventually developed, shortening his life and undermining his intellectual activity.

This, however, is looking into the future. For the present, despite occasional breakdowns in health which would incapacitate him for brief periods, he was in good spirits, overcast only by his longing to return to England and the feeling that the major part of his work in Rome was already completed. He still acted as host to English visitors who came to the Eternal City, and his last years as a resident there brought two of considerable interest; Mr. Gladstone and Archdeacon Manning.

The visit of Manning cannot have impressed Wiseman as being

---

[1] J. L. Patterson, later Bishop of Emmaus.
[2] Fr. Edward Purbrick. *Vide* Ward, Vol. II, p. 163.
[3] R. Chapman: *Father Faber*, p. 249.

of any particular significance. Though considered a clergyman of unusual parts and clearly marked for preferment, Manning was not, at this time, actively associated with the Tractarian movement. He visited the Venerable English College with Gladstone on the feast of St. Thomas of Canterbury, and heard Mass in the Chapel. Great indeed would have been his surprise had he known that he was destined to succeed Wiseman as second Archbishop of Westminster. Gladstone had two long talks with his host; first at the English College, and afterwards when Dr. Wiseman returned his call at his rooms in the Piazza di Spagna. The subject of the Oxford Movement was of vital interest to both men and not unnaturally formed the topic of their conversation. As Gladstone was himself later to describe the interview in a conversation with Wilfrid Ward, we cannot do better than quote from Ward's account.[1]

'Mr. Gladstone was impressed (he writes) as Monckton Milnes had been, by the absence in Wiseman's demeanour of the characteristics of the "proselytizer". Wiseman appeared to take broad and comprehensive views on the subjects debated. Mr. Gladstone, full of the prospects of the Oxford Movement, maintained in the course of conversation, that the movement would tend, for the time at least, to keep people from the Roman Church by satisfying within the Anglican pale growing Catholic aspirations. Wiseman, rejoicing equally at the movement, was quite prepared to endorse this view. Mr. Gladstone appears to have been struck by Wiseman's sympathy with the spread of Catholic ideas, irrespective of immediate gains to the Catholic body and the Apostolic See. In point of fact, Wiseman's confidence that the Church of England could not be the ultimate goal of the Tractarian movement was absolute. And yet, if the movement was to secure any large band of adherents it must necessarily, in the first instance, take form on Newman's *via media*. He welcomed it as restoring to the Church of England great Catholic principles which must, with men of active minds, eventually lead to a sense of the duty of that Catholic unity which is their correlative.'

It is interesting to note that Gladstone's reaction to the Oxford Movement was exactly the same as Newman's reaction to Wiseman's London lectures; that they would 'wake up the Catholic principles

[1] Ward, Vol. I, pp. 276-7.

dormant in the Established Church'. Gladstone had himself a deep sympathy with the principles of the Movement and Wiseman, from the time of this conversation in Rome, never ceased to hope that he might one day come over; hopes which reached such a climax at the time of Manning's submission that he could write: 'I now begin to expect Gladstone to follow him.' But though, with regard to the Oxford Movement, Wiseman had adopted the policy that Rome can always afford to wait, for Mr. Gladstone Rome would wait in vain.

Meanwhile in England the Vicars Apostolic were once again engaged in forming plans for the reorganization of the Mission on a more workable basis, hoping to find a way by which its status as a missionary area could be changed for the more normal form of ecclesiastical government in line with the rest of Catholic Europe, but in such a manner as not to stir up the dormant anti-Catholic prejudices of Protestant England. Bishop Griffiths[1] had approached some of his leading clergy on this subject, and their general attitude, which corresponded with that of the Vicars Apostolic, is summed up in the reply he received from Mark Tierney, the historian, who was chaplain to the Duke of Norfolk. 'With us,' Father Tierney wrote,[2] 'I conceive the restoration of the hierarchy, or in other words the return from an extraordinary to an ordinary form of government, must in a great measure resolve itself into a mere question of time. Is the present a fit time for introducing the important change? is a question which I have often asked myself; and the more I have reflected and the more I have inquired, the more satisfied have I felt that it must be answered in the affirmative. I think that the time has arrived for reverting to the original permanent and ordinary form of Church government: and I think so (1) because there is a growing uneasiness in the minds of the clergy on the subject of our present missionary character; (2) because the same feeling is spreading among the laity, and has often, in my own hearing, been strongly, I would almost say bitterly, expressed by some of the highest of their order; and (3) because in the character and disposition of the present Government, as well as in the very

---

[1] Dr. Bramston had died in July 1836 and Dr. Griffiths was now in charge of the London District.

[2] Bernard Ward: *Sequel to Catholic Emancipation*, Vol. I, p. 130.

nature of the change I am advocating, there is everything to secure us against the consequences of external opposition.' He felt the necessity, none the less, of adding to this last clause, that 'the measure should be introduced *quietly*, not ostentatiously. There should be no public or outward demonstration. In fact it should not be so much a change, as a silent and almost imperceptible transition.'

Bishops Griffiths and Walsh had visited Rome in 1837 when they had been received by the Pope, and both the Holy Father and Propaganda had shown that they were well disposed towards the establishment of a better ecclesiastical system in England. It was left to the bishops themselves to work out the details and Wiseman, with his knowledge of the workings of the Roman *curia*, urged them to follow up their favourable reception by submitting plans to the Holy See as soon as possible after their return. The bishops left Rome in July, but it was not until the April of the following year that they met with their two colleagues in York to discuss the business upon which Mr. Tierney had meanwhile given them such sound advice. Propaganda had been slightly irritated at the delay, but the irritation of the Cardinal-Prefect changed to anger when, having heard that the meeting at York had adjourned on 4th May 1838, he was still left in complete ignorance of the bishops' decisions two months afterwards.

One or two people had accused the Vicars Apostolic of wanting in zeal, and this tactless and unnecessary delay seemed to underline such reports. Among these tale-bearers was a certain Father Gentili, of the Institute of Charity, who had fallen foul of Bishop Baines and had been dismissed from Prior Park. The Father, who had a fine turn for the dramatic, had responded to the Bishop of Siga's decree of dismissal by flinging himself on his knees before the entire student body at Prior Park and publicly demanding their forgiveness before departing to Rome, where he lost no opportunity of complaining that his plans to introduce Roman devotions and pious practices had been frustrated by the Bishop. Dr. Baines, for once in his life, had met his match. Father Gentili's complaints, and Wiseman's known opinion on the lack of 'a proper ecclesiastical spirit' among the English clergy, all helped to create an unfavourable atmosphere at Propaganda, which the bishops' apparent indifference,

87

suggested by their delay in keeping Rome informed, did nothing to dispel.

At the end of June, no word having come from England, Wiseman was compelled to write in severe terms expressing Propaganda's displeasure at the Vicars Apostolic. It was a difficult letter to write, as they were, after all, his spiritual superiors, and he managed it with considerable tact, but it is understandable that the reception of a rebuke, however veiled, did not tend to endear him in any way to the august recipients. The gist of his rebuke (as expressed in his letter to Dr. Baines) was that if Rome did not hear soon what had been decided at York, 'Propaganda would feel itself called upon to take the matter into its own hands, and proceed to the formation of a plan to be proposed to the Bishops for acceptance.'[1] He did his best to water down, for the benefit of their Lordships, the irritation of the Cardinal-Prefect of Propaganda by the suggestion that 'if the delay has arisen from the time required to draw up a full report, still some general intimation to Propaganda of the conclusion of the Conference seems to have been expected. I have felt it my duty therefore to communicate these feelings, so strongly expressed, to your Lordship, that you may be guided by the knowledge of them to such decisions or course as in your wisdom you may think fit.' The Vicars Apostolic, who each received a similar letter, began to wonder whether perhaps Dr. Wiseman was not the most sympathetic man to have as their representative in Rome, where they felt, though, in fact, without justice, that he was working against their interests.

It was not only the opinions of Dr. Wiseman and Father Gentili that seemed unsympathetic to the unfortunate Vicars Apostolic at Rome; the monastic orders in England also petitioned the Holy See against them. There had always been a certain amount of rivalry between the regular, or monastic, clergy, and the secular clergy, who came directly under episcopal control. The regulars now complained that the bishops hindered their work, and even hinted that with their longer and more comprehensive training it might solve many problems if in future the bishops were chosen from their own ranks, as had been the case in the majority of dioceses in pre-Reformation England. Certainly the case of the

[1] *Sequel to Catholic Emancipation*, Vol. I, pp. 135–6.

Vicars Apostolic was not helped by memories of the unedifying war which Dr. Baines, himself a Benedictine, had waged so relentlessly against his order, and the monastic case was assured of a sympathetic hearing at Rome where the Sovereign Pontiff was himself a monk. While the bishops still fumbled with the presentation of their proposals Rome issued two edicts in favour of the regulars, in September 1838; the first of a technical nature concerning Indulgences, and the second authorizing the monks to open missions of their own without any mention of obtaining the permission of the bishops.

The Vicars Apostolic regarded the two decrees as a direct snub to themselves, the Bishop of Siga, in particular, declaring them 'a severe reprimand to us, and an approval of the many open and anonymous attacks made upon us by pious laymen or reforming priests', and when Dr. Baines referred to reforming priests there could be little doubt that he included Dr. Wiseman in their number. Indeed, writing to Lord Shrewsbury, he declared quite plainly: 'The more I reflect on these decrees . . . the worse do I think (I grieve to say it) of the episcopal agent. . . . He ought, then, to have stood forward in our defence, stated the great inconvenience that would result from the execution of these decrees, and countered the efforts of those who have succeeded in misrepresenting all our proceedings and all our feelings towards our ecclesiastical superiors. Instead of doing this, he has fanned the flame which mistaken zeal has enkindled against us. . . .'[1] The bishops forthwith petitioned Rome, praying in dignified language that the edicts might be withdrawn, if not completely, at least for a short time, so that their provisions might be discussed. Though this request was not granted Propaganda sent a mollifying reply interpreting the decrees in such a way as to leave the situation very much as it was before. Despite this, however, the Pope summoned Dr. Wiseman to an audience at which he complained, with tears in his eyes, of the lack of respect shown to him by the English bishops, a charge which Wiseman attributed solely, and rightly, to the bishops' ignorance of the forms and etiquette of the Roman court, and not to the slightest idea of disrespect.[2] It was an embarrassing audience, none the less, and

---

[1] Ibid., p. 156.
[2] Ibid., pp. 149–50.

after it Wiseman found himself again in the unenviable position of having to write and rebuke his superiors in England. The rebuke was not well received. When their Lordships gathered for their annual meeting in April 1838, one of the resolutions which they passed read as follows: 'Resolved, that the future agent of the Bishops at Rome be unconnected with the English College, and not employed in any other office.' By a twist of irony the meeting that year was held at Prior Park, a place which already held for Wiseman a sufficiency of unpleasant associations.

The situation was doubly unfortunate in so far as Wiseman had, in actual fact, done everything in his power to help the bishops to present their case favourably in Rome, and to gloss over the errors they had made through ignorance of procedure in the Roman *curia*; for simple, devout, and straightforward as they were, the subtleties and nuances of the Roman court were beyond their experience, while he, with twenty years of training, was never more at home than in the corridors of the Vatican or the ante-room of the Cardinal-Prefect of Propaganda. But his known favour for the monastic orders, many more of which he hoped to see introduced into England, and the fact that he was considered to share in the critical opinion which certain converts and 'reforming' Catholics like Lord Shrewsbury had expressed of the standards of the secular clergy, prejudiced him in the sight of the Vicars Apostolic so that they were unable to give him their full confidence.

The clergy, too, or some of them at least, shared this opinion with their bishops, and also adopted a resolution 'That the Vicars Apostolic be requested to allow an agent in Rome independent of the English College there,' and to show that they really meant it they offered to subscribe among themselves to provide a salary for the post. It must have been a bitter blow to Wiseman who was working heart and soul for the cause of the English Mission, and it speaks well for the magnanimity of his character that never once, when in later years he was at the head of the Catholic Church in England, did he show any resentment for the ungrateful treatment he had received.

Wiseman paid another short visit to England in the autumn of 1839 in the course of which he again saw Bishop Walsh at Oscott, and was present at the consecration of St. Mary's church at Derby, which was built to a design of Pugin's. 'I have travelled', he told his mother, in a letter from Oscott, 'chiefly by railway, 1,600 miles since I came to England, and have the satisfaction of being able to say that not five of them have been travelled for the sake of amusement or temporal interests of any sort, but entirely to promote as much as was in my power the interests of God and His holy religion.' While at Oscott he was able to renew his friendship with George Spencer, whom Dr. Walsh had established there as spiritual director to the students, and the opportunity would not be missed to discuss a problem which they both had very much at heart; prayers for the conversion of England.

It might be thought that prayers for such a cause would form a natural and predominant part in the devotional life of any priest working in England, and there is no reason to suppose that they did not; but to George Spencer had occurred the idea of a European campaign of prayer to this end, and it was this aspect of the matter which now occupied their attention. The inspiration had come to him in Paris—that city which had witnessed his first conversion from a worldly to an other-worldly life. In the course of an audience with the Archbishop, Spencer had spoken of the great need in England for 'good prayers to assist our exertions' and he suggested 'that if France would unite in prayer for England, the benefit would be very great'.[1] The Archbishop of Paris took up the idea with enthusiasm, and when, a few days later, he met some seventy or eighty of his clergy at St. Sulpice, he presented Father Spencer to them, at the same time commending his request for prayers with the suggestion that they should undertake to pray for the conversion of England upon each successive Thursday. The heads of various religious orders next took up the crusade, in particular the Provincial of the Jesuits, who promised the support of his powerful order. There seemed every prospect of the campaign of prayer for the conversion of England spreading through France and from France to the rest of Europe; and when Father Spencer wrote to tell Wiseman of his success, before the latter left for England, Wiseman sent him his enthusiastic support, admitting that the subject was 'one which has long occupied my thoughts though I never contemplated the possibility of enlisting foreign churches in

[1] Letter to Bishop Baines. *Sequel to Catholic Emancipation*, Vol. I, p. 205.

prayer for it, but turned my attention more to exciting a spirit of prayer amongst ourselves'. With Wiseman's influential support the scheme received a favourable notice in those quarters most likely to forward its acceptance by Rome.

It now became necessary for Father Spencer to interest those most concerned (or so one would imagine) in the success of his scheme; that is to say, the bishops of England. Dr. Walsh gave it his enthusiastic support, and it was as a result of his encouragement for it that Spencer was appointed spiritual director at Oscott. Dr. Griffiths of the London District, and his colleague Dr. Briggs in the North, however, received the news of the crusade with only the mildest show of interest; Dr. Griffiths pointing out that he had already urged similar prayers upon his flock in two successive Pastoral letters. But it remained to Dr. Baines, the indefatigable Bishop of Siga, to apply the cold test of mathematics to the red-hot enthusiasm of Father Spencer and his convert friends. In the year 1839, the bishop computed, there had been two hundred and twenty-one converts in the Western District, that is to say, less than one-hundredth of its Catholic population. Making similar calculations for the other Districts he reckoned that to convert a million people would take, at the present rate, about two centuries, and to convert the whole country would take many thousands of years. Such being the case, Dr. Baines declined to believe that there was any sign whatsoever of the conversion of the bulk of the nation to the Catholic faith.

Such, then, was the situation with regard to the crusade of prayer while Dr. Wiseman was at Oscott. But Bishop Baines had reserved his most withering attack on the scheme for the Pastoral Letter which he issued in the Lent of 1840, by which time Dr. Wiseman had returned to Rome. Dr. Baines was careful to point out that his objection rested on the fact that the conversion of England was a contingency so uncertain that, if not exactly beyond praying for, it was certainly adequately provided for in the office of the Church when she prayed that God would purge the world of all errors, and that he saw absolutely nothing to justify any further extraordinary measures. Lest these words should have left his meaning in any doubt, the Bishop next declared his belief that the object prayed for was 'as morally impossible as the return of the negro's skin to its antediluvian whiteness'. The Pastoral ended with a solemn refusal to allow the Thursday prayers in his District. 'So far, therefore, from approving this novel and extraordinary project,' the Bishop concluded,[1] 'we disapprove it, and strictly forbid any of our clergy to offer up publicly in their churches or chapels the weekly prayer above mentioned. At the same time we earnestly exhort them to pray, as has been customary, for all spiritual and temporal blessings in favour of our country, and for the conversion of such erring souls as God, in His mercy, may be pleased so to favour, and of whom we doubt not there will be a great and continually increasing number.'

By the time that this Pastoral was issued Dr. Wiseman was already, as we have said, back in Rome, where he was continuing his uneasy task of explaining the procrastinations of the Vicars Apostolic on the difficult matter of the hierarchy to the impatient authorities at Propaganda. To say that the news of Dr. Baines's Pastoral hindered him in this work is to be guilty of a considerable understatement. It did much more, for not only did it condemn a cause to which Rome had given a warm, if unofficial, approval, but it appeared both to Dr. Wiseman and to other people such as Lord Shrewsbury and Father Gentili, both of whom had considerable influence at Rome, as a veiled attack upon the converts, and this at a time when such high hopes were entertained with regard to the possible effects of the Oxford Movement. Dr. Baines was summoned before the Holy Father himself who received him, in the bishop's own account of the interview, 'in a way which manifested great displeasure against the English Vicars Apostolic, whom he had evidently been led to consider as wanting in devotion to the Holy See, and almost as factiously disposed'. Dr. Baines's case came before a congregation of eight Cardinals and many months were passed in the exchange of documents and reports. Finally in March 1841, he submitted a declaration which disclaimed the objectionable meanings which had been read into his Pastoral, and he was restored to papal favour. He was, however, to spend the rest of his life in issuing pamphlets giving what he claimed to be his own version of the affair, and these caused such displeasure that eventually the Pope, after threatening to remove the bishop from his

[1] *Sequel to Catholic Emancipation*, Vol. I, p. 215.

District, circulated the other Vicars Apostolic with a letter warning them against accepting the Bishop of Siga's version of the affair.[1]

The history of Dr. Baines's Pastoral has a particular significance in the consideration of Wiseman's career, as it shows the beginning of that distrust, which amounted at times almost to resentment, of the converts, which was to be an unhappy feature in Catholic life for some years to come, and which was already manifesting itself before Wiseman's final return to England. There was to be a division between the converts and their friends, and the 'old Catholics'[2] or those who came from families who had never abandoned the faith. The division, of course, was not absolute; both Wiseman himself and Dr. Walsh, not to mention the Earl of Shrewsbury, all came of old Catholic families and all championed the converts from the very start, but among some of the clergy there was to develop a strong feeling against the somewhat excessive enthusiasm of certain converts and the 'foreign' or 'Italian' devotions which they seemed to encourage in preference to the more sober piety of traditional English Catholicism. The affair of Dr. Baines's Pastoral against the prayers for the conversion of England gave Wiseman a foretaste of some of the opposition he would be likely to encounter in England both as one whose whole zeal was directed towards that end, and as one who would be recognized, from the moment he settled in England, as the acknowledged champion of the increasing flow of men and women who were to make their submission to the Roman Catholic Church.

[1] *Sequel to Catholic Emancipation*, Vol. I, pp. 216–18.
[2] The term 'old Catholic' refers only to members of Catholic families as opposed to recent converts and is not to be confused with the schismatic body called the "Old Catholic Church".

VIII

The proposals and counter-proposals exchanged between England and Rome, and all the delays and misunderstandings which seemed to have effected little beyond the undermining of Dr. Wiseman's position as agent of the Vicars Apostolic, were cut short in May 1840 when Propaganda issued its own plan for the future structure of ecclesiastical government in England. The measure was a compromise between the restoration of a full hierarchy and the existing state of affairs. Since the death of Cardinal Weld in April 1837 the chief adviser to the Holy See on English questions had been Monsignor (later Cardinal) Acton. Acton was the son of that English baronet, Sir John Francis Acton, who had been Prime Minister to King Ferdinand IV of Naples, in whose capital the future Cardinal had been born. He was sent to England for his education, entering Magdalene College, Cambridge, in 1819, though as a Roman Catholic he had been prohibited from taking his degree. After leaving Cambridge he returned to Italy, joining the exclusive *Academia dei Nobili Ecclesiastici* at which celebrated 'school of Cardinals' he had studied for the priesthood and started his brief but brilliant career in the Church. Acton became the close friend and adviser of Gregory XVI, who proclaimed him a Cardinal in 1842.[1] He died five years later at the early age of forty-four.

Acton did not recommend the restoration of a hierarchy such as existed in Catholic countries with bishops-in-ordinary using the territorial titles of their sees. He did not consider that the time was

---

[1] Having been created a Cardinal *in petto*, that is to say, secretly, nearly three years previously.

ripe for the English Mission to be made entirely independent of Propaganda, declaring it as his opinion that 'the English throughout their history had been factious, and opposed to authority, and were not to be entrusted with more and more independent power',[1] an opinion not very flattering to his fellow countrymen, and one which Wiseman did not share, obtaining for his country in ten years time the independence denied it in 1840 through the influence of Acton on the mind of Gregory XVI and in the councils of Cardinal Fransoni, the Prefect of Propaganda. What in effect Acton recommended, and what was now decreed, was the creation of eight Vicariates in place of the existing four. This was achieved by separating Wales from Bishop Baines's Western District, and placing it under the rule of the Benedictine Order, a decision which can hardly have been relished by the Bishop of Siga, who was then in Rome in some disgrace for the indiscretions of his Lenten Pastoral. The Midland District was divided by the formation of a new Central District, placed under Bishop Walsh, and the Northern District was deprived of Lancashire and Yorkshire, which became independent Districts on their own. To Wiseman this new dispensation meant, at long last, that his days in Rome were ended. Bishop Walsh's request to have him as his coadjutor was now implemented, and on 8th June 1840, he was consecrated a bishop by Cardinal Fransoni in the chapel of the Venerable English College, being given the title of Bishop of Melipotamus. At the request of Dr. Walsh he was to be appointed President of St. Mary's College, Oscott, in addition to his duties as coadjutor. He did not leave Rome until the following September. The longing to quit the Eternal City which he had expressed with such impatience to his sister was softened when the time of parting came. 'It was a sorrowful evening, at the beginning of autumn,' he wrote in his *Recollections*, 'when, after a residence in Rome prolonged through twenty-two years, till affection clung to every old stone there, like the moss that grew into it, this strong but tender tie was cut, and much of future happiness had to be invested in the mournful recollections of the past.'

Wiseman's last years in Rome had been marked by a deepening of his spiritual life. In 1837, following a retreat at the English College conducted by a Jesuit Father, he had recorded various

[1] *Sequel to Catholic Emancipation*, Vol. I, p. 158.

resolutions which acknowledged his indebtedness to the Spiritual Exercises of St. Ignatius Loyola. Among the rules and resolutions made 'in the presence of the Divine and Eternal Majesty of God and of His celestial court, primarily of the Most Holy Mary, my sweet mother, of Saints Ignatius and Luigi Gonzaga, patrons and protectors of these my Exercises' was one in which he declared his resolve to 'renew the resolution already made and by His mercy kept till now determinately, to avoid studying or writing anything but what may lead to the good of souls, directly or indirectly, and always to hold this object in view in my work'.[1] This decision, recorded here with such solemnity, was, so to speak, the ratification of the new course his life had taken after the visit of Newman and Froude in 1833, which his visit to England had strengthened, and which was now to inspire his life as a bishop. His days as a scholar, pursuing scholarship for its own sake, were finished. Oriental studies were now a thing of the past, like his professorship in the Roman university, which ceased with his appointment as bishop. But though the life of active scholarship was over, Wiseman's academic attainments were still to be made use of, and the fact that his appointment as coadjutor to Bishop Walsh was to be combined with the post of President of Oscott, showed that his reputation as a scholar was not to be neglected, but redirected to a new and more useful sphere.

It was, indeed, in the character of scholar as well as apologist, that Wiseman's most decisive blow was dealt at the heart of the Oxford Movement in an article in the *Dublin Review* for July 1839, which was to have far-reaching effects after his arrival in England, which it heralded in a dramatic and timely manner. The essay was upon the Donatist heresy, which at first sight may seem a far cry from the religious preoccupations of nineteenth-century Oxford dons with High Church leanings, but Wiseman was to draw so startling a parallel between this fourth-century heresy and the claims of the Catholic party in the Anglican Church that after reading it Newman was to write to a friend 'I seriously think this is a most uncomfortable article on every account.'[2] Its effect upon Newman was like that of a man seeing a ghost. 'He who has seen a

[1] Ward, Vol. I, p. 261.
[2] Letter to Rogers. *Vide* Geoffrey Faber: *Oxford Apostles*, p. 289.

ghost,' he wrote,[1] 'cannot be as if he had never seen it. The heavens had opened and closed again. The thought for the moment had been, "The Church of Rome will be found right after all"; and then it had vanished.' The thought vanished indeed; but only to return with ever greater force.

The Donatists were a group of Christians in North Africa who had separated themselves from the main body of the Catholic Church, and yet claimed, though separate, to retain all the attributes of the true Catholic and Apostolic Church. Their theory, with its clear resemblance to the Anglican 'branch' theory, was combated by St. Augustine on the grounds that if any individual member of the Church were permitted to be the judge of whether or not he formed a part of the whole Church, then all hope of Christian unity would be lost. A church could only be regarded as belonging to Catholic unity if all the rest of Christendom recognized it as such. His argument to the Donatist bishop was simply this: can you, as a bishop, give to a member of your church letters of communion that will be recognized by every other bishop in the Christian Church? If you can, then indeed you are a part of the Universal Catholic Church; if your authority is not so recognized, then you are in schism, and outside the pale of Catholic Unity. The great strength of this argument, as Wiseman applied it to the position of the Anglican Church, was that it in no way involved the exclusive claims of the Apostolic See. St. Augustine summed up his argument in a phrase which Wiseman quoted in the course of his article, a phrase which came to Newman with such force that it made him see it clearly and inescapably as 'the first real hit from Romanism' to his cherished doctrine of the *Via Media*: '*Quapropter securus judicat orbis terrarum bonos non esse qui se dividunt ab orbe terrarum in quacumque parte orbis terrarum.*'[2] The article had been pointed out to Newman by a friend. At first he did not see much in it; 'but my friend (he recounted in his *Apologia*) an anxiously religious man . . . pointed out the palmary words of St. Augustine, which were contained in one of the extracts made in the Review, and which had escaped my observations. "*Securus judicat orbis terrarum.*" He

---

[1] Newman: *Apologia* (1864 edition), p. 213.
[2] 'For the whole world judges with assurance that they are not good who separate themselves in any part of the world from all the world.'

repeated these words again and again, and, when he was gone, they kept ringing in my ears.' Newman, who had himself been studying the Monophysite heresy, was deeply imbued in the *ethos* of the early Church and in the writings of the Fathers, upon whose authority he sought to base his own arguments in favour of the claims he and his party were urging upon their fellow Anglicans; arguments which now seemed threatened by the very authority upon which he hoped to build them: 'For a mere sentence,' he wrote later,[1] 'the words of St. Augustine, struck me with a power which I never had felt from any words before. To take a familiar instance, they were like the "Turn again Whittington" of the chime; or, to take a more serious one, they were like the '*Tolle, lege,—Tolle, lege*', of the child, which converted St. Augustine himself. "*Securus judicat orbis terrarum!*" By those great words of the ancient Father, the theory of the *Via Media* was absolutely pulverized.'

Wiseman, meanwhile, had arrived in England in complete ignorance of the stir which his article had caused in Oxford. He was received at Oscott in a manner befitting the arrival of a prelate to a new diocese. He was met at the door of the college by the staff and professors, all in full canonicals, who escorted him in procession to the Chapel, while the choir sang '*Ecce sacerdos magnus*'. Here an address of welcome was read to the new Bishop and President who, in return, imparted his blessing on his flock. That Wiseman's European reputation was then at its height is indicated by an article which appeared in the French Catholic periodical *Univers* which greeted him at the time of his consecration as one who was 'going to take his place among the new Augustines whom a new Gregory sends forth to achieve a second time the conquest of England'—a phrase which must have alarmed Bishop Baines and like-minded old Catholics (had they set eyes on it) as much as it would have rejoiced the heart of Father Spencer, of Pugin, and of Ambrose Phillipps de Lisle.

One of Bishop Wiseman's first acts after his arrival as President of Oscott was to write a long letter to his old friend and teacher Dr. Lingard in which he set out some of his hopes and aspirations in his new office. 'It had been proposed by Dr. Walsh four years ago

[1] *Apologia*, p. 212.

to me to accept my present office,' he wrote.[1] 'I replied that I would hold myself perfectly neuter, would not refuse if I was appointed, but would, of course, concur in no steps for obtaining it. Whenever the Pope spoke to me about it, generally telling me that he wished me ultimately to go to England, but wished me to remain in the (English) College some time longer, I always replied that I had no choice, but would either stay or go as he ordered me. My own wish was to return to England a simple priest, without responsibility, and for this I spoke to his Holiness, but this no one would hear of; and I had no alternative but either to renounce the strong desire I had of being in England in these stirring times, or coming over in my present capacity. Thus I have got here, and I find everything to my hand that I could desire for furthering my views—a magnificent college, with a still more magnificent library; professors some already most able, the rest qualifying themselves to raise our education to the highest standard; a united and zealous clergy; a fine opening in Birmingham for every Catholic institution. These are certainly great advantages, which, conjointly with a central position, I could hardly have found elsewhere. As to my own pursuits, if worthy of a thought or mention, I think I shall have quite as much time as I have at Rome as soon I have got all things here as I expect and wish, and have organized what seems to me to have been much neglected till now, proper regulation for the official transaction of ecclesiastical affairs. Till now the Bishops' writing desks seem to have been the only chancery and *archivium* of the districts; and the whole episcopal regimen seems to have led to a sort of nomadic life, wandering about in stage coaches or gigs from place to place. A letter to a Bishop was almost a random shot, which at most could catch him while on the wing. Provision for the immediate attention to the transaction of all business and for the regular preservation of all documents, deeds, etc. (now scattered over the missions) is making in the new residence erecting for the Bishop in Birmingham, and we are getting things into train for the due observance of such matters.'

There is a note of unintentional irony in the latter part of this letter, as Wiseman was to prove wholly unbusinesslike himself in the purely administrative side of his work, leaving letters long un-

[1] *Sequel to Catholic Emancipation*, Vol. II, pp. 5–6.

answered and (as Newman was to discover to his cost) often losing or mislaying vital and important papers due solely to his neglect for that 'immediate attention to the transaction of all business and . . . regular preservation of all documents' which he now criticizes as lacking among his fellow bishops. He was also to find that his staff did not all share in his enthusiastic hopes for the outcome of the Catholic revival in the Anglican church, but viewed his sanguine hopes for a general move towards Rome with ill-concealed scepticism. With the students, however, he soon established a happy and easy relationship. The future Lord Acton (himself a nephew of Cardinal Acton) was a student at Oscott under Wiseman and recorded his pleasant impressions of the President. 'We were proud of him,' he wrote,[1] 'we were not afraid of him; he was approachable and gracious, and no great friend of discipline, and I heard him boast that he never assigned punishment. We were conscious that he was a conspicuous, even a celebrated, man, and that he had the best of the Oxford controversy. The converts used to appear amongst us, and he seemed to exhibit their scalps.' Another man[2] who passed through the College at the same period writes of Wiseman that: 'He had a fund of genial humour, and I remember how it came out when O'Connell visited Oscott. The Celtic element in him showed itself strongly on that occasion, as O'Connell and he walked about the college arm-in-arm, telling good stories to each other and laughing heartily.' Oscott comprised a school for boys as well as a College for 'Divines' or candidates for the priesthood, and of Wiseman's relationship with the former, the same writer gives us a pleasant picture. 'With the boys he was a great favourite in recreation time. Directly he appeared in the playground they crowded round him, and he stood with his hands in his pockets telling them anecdotes, and looking on at the games, in which he took a keen interest. The slight element of pompousness in his manner quite disappeared when he was with boys, and he almost seemed like one of them in his enjoyment of their society.'

The new bishop was a tall, ugly man, six feet two in height, fat, and with a ruddy complexion. Father Edward Purbrick found him 'at first sight forbidding, his shaggy eyebrows, . . . and wide,

---

[1] *Vide* Ward, Vol. I, p. 348.
[2] Canon Bernard Smith.

thick-lipped mouth, being neither handsome nor attractive'. His physical unattractiveness, however, was forgotten when he talked, for his enthusiasm for music, art, and architecture, for the latest discoveries in science as well as contemporary literature, in which he was widely read, soon fascinated his listeners. His linguistic accomplishments were prodigious. It was one of the sights of Rome to witness a conversation between Monsignor Wiseman and the celebrated Cardinal Mezzofanti. Dispensing with European languages the two prelates would converse before an admiring audience in Arabic or Persian. Later on Newman was to record how Wiseman could 'speak with readiness and point in half a dozen languages, without being detected by a foreigner in any of them, and at ten minutes notice can address a congregation from a French pulpit or the select audience of an Italian academy'. It was this brilliance of intellect and breadth of learning that impressed strangers, rather than the bulky figure and the heavy features. Children loved him. 'We children all adored him,' wrote one[1] who had known him in her childhood: 'Once I was told that he was ugly, and I could not believe it. He was so delightful to us that I could not fancy that he was anything but handsome.' To his wide culture and happiness in the company of children must be added another characteristic perhaps less edifying but none the less human; he delighted in the pleasures of the table. A strict Anglo-Catholic who had kept the rigours of the penitential season on a diet of bread and water occasionally supplemented by herbs was surprised to learn that the Bishop offered his guests four courses of fish in Lent. 'The Cardinal,' Father Faber was later to remark, 'has a lobster salad side as well as a spiritual side.'

The exuberance and enthusiasm with which Wiseman pursued his ideals was countered by a tendency to depression and discouragement. A slight failure or misfortune would cast him down into the very depths, and at times a note of self-pity would be added to the general feeling of dejection. At such moments he would often take to his bed, which under the circumstances was perhaps the best thing to do. In later life progressive ill-health was an additional cause of wretchedness, amounting at times to prostration. Letters written to his secretary on his various visits to Rome after he became Archbishop of Westminster, apart from the actual business involved,

[1] Madame Merry del Val.

contain long passages devoted to minute accounts of his physical sufferings, entering, at times, into the most clinical of details.

As he began his episcopal life he certainly had much to discourage him in the attitude taken up by some of his fellow bishops, and a number of influential men among the clergy, who quite failed to share his high hopes for the outcome of the Oxford Movement. The extremely damping response of Bishop Baines to the prospect of any large-scale conversions has already been described, but the fact that this attitude caused an expression of marked displeasure from the Holy See made Dr. Baines's anathemas rebound in a direction he had little expected, and must have been a cause of encouragement rather than depression to Dr. Wiseman, at whose head, one may safely assume, the majority of Dr. Baines's anathemas had been aimed. But the Bishop of Siga was now a slightly discredited figure, and no longer the force he once had been. More distressing to Wiseman must have been the warning of Dr. Griffiths, of the London District, who wrote to remind him that 'scarcely shall we find in history a body of schismatics returning with sincerity to the obedience of the faith'.[1] Added to this, Dr. Lingard, Wiseman's old friend and tutor, drawing historical lessons from the times of Laud and the non-jurors, wrote to caution him against indulging in false hopes.

Wiseman, however, refused to be turned from his course, either by these grave warnings or by those among his co-religionists who refused to believe that the Tractarians were sincere, but rather held that though they might play with the notion of being Catholic they would never do it to such purpose as to endanger their enjoyment of the rich endowments of the Established Church. To those who held this view, and they were numerous among the Catholic clergy, Wiseman seemed simply to be wasting his time. Thus, in a letter to Phillipps de Lisle we find him writing: 'An Irish and an English priest, who had each engaged in controversy with the Oxonians, one with Gladstone, the other in a newspaper series of Letters, have written in great dismay at the tone which I have taken, as strongly condemnatory of the light and jeering one they had assumed, and wishing to know what I was about.'[2] Wiseman was quite clear what

[1] Ward, Vol. I, p. 378.
[2] Letter dated Good Friday 1841. E. S. Purcell: *Life of Ambrose Phillipps de Lisle*, Vol. I, p. 284.

he was about. He believed in the absolute sincerity of such men as Newman and Pusey, and in the genuine good which the Movement they led could do in infusing a Catholic spirit into the Anglican Church. He also believed that such a spirit must eventually drive those who followed it faithfully into the arms of the Roman Church, for if their spirit was truly Catholic the Anglican Church would be unable, in the final resort, to satisfy them. From his strategic position at Oscott, so near to Oxford, he would be ready to receive them when the time came. This ideal, which now seemed so near to fulfilment, he expressed in another letter to Phillipps de Lisle, written in April 1841. 'Let us have an influx of new blood, let us have but even a small number of such men as write in the Tracts, so imbued with the spirit of the early Church, so desirous to revive the image of the ancient fathers; men who have learnt to teach from Saint Augustine, to preach from Saint Chrysostom, and to feel from Saint Bernard—let even a few such men, with the high clerical feeling which I believe them to possess, enter fully into the spirit of the Catholic Religion and *we* shall be speedily reformed and England quickly converted. I am ready to acknowledge that, in all things except the happiness of possessing the truth, and being in communion with God's true Church, and enjoying the advantages and blessings that flow thence, we are their inferiors. It is not to you that I say this for the first time, I have long said it to those about me, that if the Oxford Divines entered the Church, we must be ready to fall into the shade and take up our position in the background. I will gladly say to any of them *"me oportet minui"*. I will willingly yield to them place and honour, if God's good service require it. I will be a co-operator under the greater zeal and learning and abilities of a new leader. Depend upon it, they do not know their own strength.'[1]

It was upon this note of high expectancy that Wiseman began his career as a bishop in England, and he lost no time in attempting to make personal contact with the leaders of the Oxford Movement whose aspirations he understood so clearly. It was indeed fortunate for the English Church that she should be sent a man so specially endowed to help her at this critical period in her history.

[1] E. S. Purcell: *Life of Ambrose Phillipps de Lisle*, Vol. I, p. 290.

IX

'From the end of 1841,' wrote Newman at the beginning of Part VI of his *Apologia*, 'I was on my death-bed, as regards my membership with the Anglican Church, though at the time I became aware of it only by degrees.' It was, indeed, a most protracted death agony, and one that was watched with growing impatience from the vantage point of Oscott where, as the months stretched into years, Wiseman began to lose all hope of ever receiving the celebrated Tractarian at all.

In the February of this year Newman had issued the ninetieth and, as it was to prove, the last of the 'Tracts for the Times'. It was called *Remarks on Certain Passages in the Thirty-nine Articles*, and by issuing it Newman brought the Oxford Movement to its logical conclusion. The purpose of the Tract was summed up in the phrase in the Introduction where its author claimed that he intended 'merely to show that while our Prayer Book is acknowledged on all hands to be of Catholic origin, our Articles also, the offspring of an uncatholic age, are, through God's good providence, to say the least, not uncatholic, and may be subscribed by those who aim at being Catholic in heart and doctrine'. If the majority of the Church of England had accepted such an interpretation of their Articles of Religion it is probable that Newman would never have left it; instead the Tract created a storm of indignation and was roundly condemned by the Anglican bishops. The official voice of the Established Church spoke loudly and emphatically against it, and the essential Protestantism of that institution reasserted itself. To Wiseman, as also to former Anglicans like Pugin and Phillipps de Lisle, it seemed that Newman must now make his submission to

Rome at once, but in thinking this they did not understand their man. They still had four years to wait.

Both before and after the issue of Tract XC Newman had kept himself strictly aloof from contact with Catholics, despite the disturbing effect which Wiseman's article on the Donatists had had on his mind. Thus he had been very short with Father Spencer when 'that zealous and most charitable man' (as Newman later called him) visited Oxford in January 1840. He explained his attitude in a letter to Spencer which he was later to quote in his *Apologia*;[1] 'you invite us to a union of hearts, at the same time that you are doing all you can, not to restore, not to reform, not to re-unite, but to destroy our Church. You go further than your principles require. You are leagued with our enemies.' It was the feeling that the Romans 'un-churched' him that Newman resented so strongly, and to this he added a marked antipathy to what he considered as subversive in the political activities of certain Catholics, O'Connell in particular, who was known to be on such cordial terms with Bishop Wiseman. 'I had an unspeakable aversion to the policy and acts of Mr. O'Connell,' Newman wrote,[2] 'because, as I thought, he associated himself with men of all religions and no religion against the Anglican Church, and advanced Catholicism by violence and intrigue. When I found him taken up by the English Catholics, and, as I supposed, at Rome, I considered I had a fulfilment before my eyes how the Court of Rome played fast and loose, and fulfilled the bad points which I had seen put down in books against it. Here we saw what Rome was in action, whatever she might be when quiescent. Her conduct was simply secular and political.' It is not for nothing that the Church of England has been described as the Conservative Party at prayer, and as far as politics went Newman belonged to the High Tories, just as most leading Catholics at this time were affiliated to the Whig or Liberal parties, though largely, as has been pointed out, because it was the Whig influence which had supported Catholic emancipation. It is interesting in this respect to note that in 1829 Newman had himself been opposed to Peel's policy on Catholic emancipation, which he regarded as an attack on 'the independence of the Church and of Oxford'.[3] This deep

[1] p. 225. [2] *Apologia*, pp. 223–4.
[3] Faber: *Oxford Apostles*, p. 233. Peel was then Member for Oxford University.

distrust of the political activities of Catholics he expressed forcibly in a letter sent, via John Bloxam, a Fellow of Magdalen, to Phillipps de Lisle, in February 1841, the very month of Tract XC. 'What Hildebrand did by faith and holiness they (the English Catholics) do by political intrigue. Their great object is to pull down the English Church. They join with those who are further from them in Creed to oppose those who are nearer to them. They have to do with such a man as O'Connell. Never can I think such ways the footsteps of Christ.'[1]

Both Phillipps de Lisle and Pugin had been eager to make personal contact with the leaders of the Oxford Movement, and while they were met more than half-way by the younger generation of Tractarians—men like Frederick Faber and W. G. Ward—both Newman and Pusey showed no eagerness to meet them and still less to engage themselves in controversy with them. Pugin was not perhaps the best man to recommend Roman Catholicism to these retiring dons as his extremely eccentric version of the Faith was often as alarming to his co-religionists as it was to potential converts. His outspoken criticism of fellow Catholics, and the contempt he poured upon Catholic organizations such as the Society of Jesus whose architectural notions did not come up to his own high standards, must have mystified those who heard him, as when, discussing the question of Gothic vestments with his Oxford friends, he declared: 'But after all, my dear sir, what's the use of decent vestments with such priests as we have got? a lot of blessed fellows! Why, sir, when they wear my chasubles, they don't look like priests, and what's worse, the chasubles don't look like chasubles.'[2] He was particularly touchy on the question of rood-screens, which he considered as an essential feature of Gothic architecture, and therefore of Christianity, for to his mind the two went hand in hand: 'If any man says he loves pointed architecture and hates screens,' he would remark, 'that man is a liar—avoid that man, my dear sir!' To Phillipps de Lisle such opinions did not always seem to assist in the conversion of England, as he complained to the Earl of Shrewsbury. 'I wish,' he wrote, 'when he (Pugin) goes to Oxford, he would not talk against (the Jesuits) so much.

[1] Purcell: *Life of Ambrose Phillipps de Lisle*, Vol. I, p. 205.
[2] M. Trappes-Lomax: *Pugin*, p. 129.

Several persons remarked on it to me. And he is too fond of descanting on all the little miseries of our English Catholick (*sic*) body. Doing this tends to confirm any lurking prejudices in the minds of our Oxford friends.' Phillipps de Lisle, it might be added, had caught from Pugin a rather irritating 'Gothic' orthography which made him always write 'Catholick' and 'antient', while the Gregorian chant, which was as much a question of orthodoxy with him as the rood-screen was with Pugin, must always be rendered 'chaunt'. These little affectations, however, would hardly confuse Protestants as Pugin's remark was likely to when he announced that he was unable to pray in the Church of the *Gesù* in Rome because, when looking up to the roof in the hope of seeing something which would stimulate his devotion, he declared: 'I saw only *legs* sprawling over me. I expected them to begin to kick me next, and rushed out.'[1] Such remarks, Phillipps de Lisle believed, did more harm than good, and in his letter to Lord Shrewsbury he adds, with some complacency: 'For my part, when I go there (to Oxford), I make a point of making the best of the state of things amongst ourselves, and yet without in any way deviating from truth; for instance, I gave Dr. Pusey an account of the sort of mode of going on in our more pious Catholick families, such as the Stourtons, Cliffords, etc., at which Dr. P. seemed much edified.'[2]

Through his contact with the Oxford men, and especially with Bloxam of Magdalen, Phillipps de Lisle was able to act as a link between Wiseman and the leading Tractarians. Indeed, he considered it as his chief mission in life to bring the Anglican Church back into Catholic Unity. 'My great desire and object,' he told Bloxam,[3] 'is to contribute what little so humble an individual as myself is able, towards producing a good understanding between the Catholick and the Anglican Churches, with a view to the ultimate restoration of that happy and blessed Unity which formerly existed between them for more than a thousand years, and which I am perfectly certain will one day be restored. To effect this object I will spare no effort, and with God's grace, in which alone I trust, I am ready to endure reproach, and even to sacrifice my life, should

[1] Ward, Vol. I, p. 356.
[2] Purcell: *Life of Ambrose Phillipps de Lisle*, Vol. I, pp. 259–60.
[3] Ibid., p. 203.

He require it.' Had Wiseman read this letter he would have found more to surprise him in it than the writer's edifying thirst for martyrdom. Its phrasing could clearly be made to suggest that Phillipps de Lisle accepted the Anglican theory of the continuation of their church in unbroken succession from the pre-Reformation English church; in short, that he accepted the validity of Anglican ordinations and considered that church only to be in schism.[1] Wiseman, on the other hand, was always quite clear in his mind that the Anglican Church did not possess a validly ordained priesthood in the Catholic sense, but he thought it unprofitable to argue the point, preferring to base his arguments on the all-embracing question of Authority. In this he was following the advice of Dr. Lingard, who wrote to him in 1840: 'You ask what I think of arguing the validity of their orders. I doubt its policy. It is a very irritating subject, and one on which I should not hope to persuade if it be confined to the validity of the form.'[2] Phillipps de Lisle's attitude over this question made him view the Oxford Movement in an even more optimistic light than Wiseman, for instead of looking for individual conversions he maintained that the Catholic-minded Anglicans should remain in communion with their own church until such a time as the entire Established Church was ready to come over to Rome, a position which Wiseman could never accept, not only because he did not think the Anglican Church possessed a valid ministry but because, in the last resort, a man must act for the salvation of his own individual soul, and if convinced of the Roman claim must not cut himself off from the channels of grace which only Rome could provide.

Wiseman was not aware of the extent to which his friend pressed his own views, and would certainly have dissociated himself from him had he known it. That Phillipps de Lisle did not let Wiseman fully into his confidence over his negotiations with the Oxford men is shown by the fact that, at Newman's request, and unknown to Wiseman, he (in his own words) 'effected a stoppage of the circulation of Dr. Wiseman's Tracts against the High Church claims' in the neighbourhood of Grace-Dieu Manor where he held sway

[1] This was, of course, before the Bull *Apostolicae Curae* of Leo XIII had declared Anglican Orders, from the Catholic point of view, to be null and void. This was not issued until 1896.
[2] Ward, Vol. I, p. 300.

as a country squire. 'I have no right to judge a bishop,' he added, 'but I confess I thought the publication of those Tracts ill-timed from the first moment I heard of them, and I was not aware till a few days ago that any had been circulated hereabouts; for the future it is stopped.'[1] If he indeed thought he had no right to judge a bishop one is left wondering by what authority he thought he had the right to 'effect the stoppage'. If his Anglican friends were left to suppose that all Catholics dealt with their bishops in this high-handed manner they must indeed have thought that they would feel quite at home in the Roman Communion.

To Phillipps de Lisle the whole Oxford Movement appeared as a gigantic plot to win the Church of England for Rome, and he did not hesitate to project his own interpretation of it into the writings of others, on both sides of the controversy, who would have been amazed at his reading of their thoughts. He gave a full expression to all these ideas in a long letter to Cardinal Acton, which he wrote in 1842 (dated the Feast of the Conversion of St. Mary Magdalene) in which he drew a thoroughly distorted picture of the situation in England, though it is clear that the distortion rose solely from his own over-enthusiasm and excessive optimism, for his sincerity was beyond dispute. But to say that the object of Tract XC 'was to smoothen the way towards a reconciliation of the Churches' is to go very much farther than Newman ever intended when he wrote that much misunderstood document. In another passage he describes how the 'devotion to the glorious Mother of God is rapidly increasing, great numbers of the Anglicans now keep Her blessed picture with extreme reverence'. That some Anglicans, an influential minority, did indeed feel a growing devotion to the Blessed Virgin, was true, but to describe them in terms of 'great numbers' was to create a very false impression when one considers the serried ranks of Protestants who formed the vast bulk of nineteenth-century Anglicanism—for all that de Lisle could assure the Cardinal that 'a Fellow of Exeter College at Oxford burst into tears, when speaking of this Dear Mother of our Saviour'.[2] To Lord Shrewsbury he had written the year before with equal zeal but even greater

---

[1] Purcell: *Life of Ambrose Phillipps de Lisle*, Vol. I, p. 208.
[2] The full text of de Lisle's letter to Cardinal Acton is given by Purcell in the *Life of Phillipps de Lisle*, Vol. I, pp. 230–8.

exaggeration, 'of this you may rest assured that the reunion of the Churches is certain. Mr. Newman has lately received the adhesion of *several hundreds* of the Clergy: this is publickly known, and therefore I may state it. Meanwhile the dissenting party is on the alert, and though they are by no means aware of the extent to which things have gone, they are apprehensive of something: and as they are joined, politically at least, by the Low Church Party, we find it necessary to *blind* them. . . .'[1] Such suggestion of duplicity, however innocent, on the part of Newman, could hardly have been farther from the truth, and pre-figures the attacks which were later to be made on him by Charles Kingsley. No wonder that Newman was to write to him expressing his anxiety 'lest you should be entertaining sanguine hopes in which you may be disappointed. You over-rate our exertions, our influence, our tendencies. We are but a few, and we are what we are.'[2] A few! How different was this grave assessment from the ebullient account which had been sent to Cardinal Acton. Yet to the Oxford men Phillipps de Lisle appeared as representing the opinion not only of Bishop Wiseman, but of the Catholic Church generally.

Phillipps de Lisle's hopes reached their most exaggerated form when he wrote to tell Lord Shrewsbury that 'the leading men in the Anglican Church are determined to reunite their Church to the Holy See. But in order to effect this a little time is required. The Archbishop of Canterbury and the Bishop of Oxford approve of the design, but *as yet* the other Bishops stand out, and some of them violently: to gain them requires immense management: they already see that they cannot much longer resist the movement, still they have great prejudices, and to remove these is a most laborious task.'[3] One is at a loss to imagine how de Lisle could possibly believe that the Anglican Primate and the Bishop of Oxford[4] could be secretly plotting to bring their Church over to Rome at the very time when these prelates were publicly condemning the *Tracts for the Times*, and though he goes on to assure Lord Shrewsbury that he has passed on all this highly sensational information 'to our dear friend Bishop

---

[1] Purcell: *Life of Ambrose Phillipps de Lisle*, Vol. I, p. 217.
[2] Ibid., pp. 224–5.
[3] Ibid., pp. 216–17.
[4] It was, in fact, the Bishop of Oxford who suggested that the *Tracts for the Times* should be discontinued.

Wiseman (who perfectly concurs with me in everything) for the purpose of being in the strictest secrecy forwarded to Cardinal Mai, to be by His Eminence communicated to the Holy Father . . .' there is, in fact, no evidence that Wiseman himself ever held so wild a view of the Oxford Movement, or hinted to the Holy See that the Primate of All England was busily plotting to substitute Gregory XVI for Queen Victoria as Supreme Governor of the Church of England.

Wiseman did indeed tell Phillipps de Lisle of his intention of writing to Cardinal Mai, as he felt that the time had come when 'the state of things in England ought to be made known to the Holy Father'. But rather than bandy about the names of eminent Anglican ecclesiastics he made it abundantly clear that he 'would not mention names beyond those publicly known, as Newman's, but would even suppress his name, when referring to what he has privately written'.[1] But when, shortly afterwards, Newman took him to task in a letter for vindicating the invocations of the Blessed Virgin used in the Roman Church, Wiseman's high hopes were dashed and he declared to Phillipps de Lisle that Newman's attitude had thrown him on his back and painfully dispirited him, 'so that I have kept back a long letter which I had written to Cardinal Mai, for fear I may be myself deceived and may be misguiding the Holy See'.[2] No such feelings of misgiving ever seem to have crossed the mind of de Lisle, with the result that he continued, all unintentionally, to misguide everybody else concerned in the matter.

Wiseman's immediate reaction to the publication of Tract XC had been more balanced. He appreciated the delicacy of the situation, and realized that no good purpose could be served if he pushed himself forward into the dispute at that particular moment. 'I have felt that I should only be embarrassing them by any intercourse,' he wrote to Phillipps de Lisle, 'as, should it become known, it would be immediately thrown in their faces'. An opportunity did present itself, however, when Newman's Letter to Dr. Jelf was published in the month following the appearance of the Tract, in which he explained that its purpose had not been to justify the teachings of the Church of Rome, especially in such matters as the worship of the Saints, the doctrine of Purgatory, or the vexed

[1] Ward, Vol. I, p. 387.   [2] Ibid., p. 392.

question of Indulgences, but rather to show that the Thirty-Nine Articles of the Church of England had not been directed against the decrees of the Council of Trent, but that these very decrees, taken by themselves, might be reconciled to the Articles. It was an entirely new position from that which Newman had held when, in the company of Hurrell Froude, he had visited Wiseman at the English College in 1833, and Wiseman now addressed a letter to Newman in which he drew various conclusions from this changed attitude of mind, the logic of which, he held, must sooner or later lead to a full acceptance of Rome and all that Rome stood for. 'You will remember your late amiable friend, Mr. Froude (Wiseman wrote)[1] in one of his unhappy moments of hasty censure, pronounced us, not Catholics, but "wretched Tridentines". This expression was quoted, with apparent approbation, by his editors, in their preface. It seems hard that now we should be deprived of even this 'wretched' title, and sunk by you a step lower in the scale of degradation. Still more it seems unaccountable that *you* should now court that title, and assert (as your Tract does) that while *we* have abandoned the doctrines of Trent, you, and those who take the articles in your sense, interpret them in accordance with those doctrines. I say this in a spirit, not of reproach, but rather of charitable warning. That which you once considered a heavy imputation, you seem now to consider comparatively a light blame: for you would now be glad to see us in stricter conformity (according to your views) with the decrees of that Council. You then blamed us for adhesions to them; you now blame us for departure from them. Why not suspect your judgements, if you find that they vary? If there *was* ever a time when you did not see many of our doctrines as you now view them; when you utterly rejected all comprecation with, as much as prayers to, saints; all honour, without reserve, to images and relics; when you did not practise prayers for the departed, nor turned from the congregation in your service; when you did not consider bodily mortification necessary, or the Breviary so beautiful; when, in fine, you were more remote from us in practice and feeling than your writings now show you to be, why not suspect that a further approximation may yet remain; that further discoveries of truth, in what today seems erroneous,

[1] Ibid., p. 376.

may be reserved for tomorrow, and that you may be laying up for yourself the pain and regret of having beforehand branded with opprobrious and afflicting names that which you will discover to be good and holy.'

The publication of this letter drew no reply from Newman. A certain Mr. Palmer, 'a controversialist' as Wilfrid Ward describes him, 'who was seldom embarrassed by seeing two sides to a question' did attempt an answer, but merely fell back on the old Protestant arguments against Rome, and enlivened his theme by denying the validity of Wiseman's own episcopal orders. The fact was that Newman did not wish to be drawn into further controversy. He had withdrawn to Littlemore, outside Oxford, where he intended to live a life of almost monastic simplicity and devote himself to a translation of St. Athanasius. He wished to be left in peace, both from Roman prelates eager for his submission and from the curiosity of those members of his own communion who could only imagine that if he had retired from the world it could be for no good purpose. They came in person to spy on him, expecting, no doubt, to find a Jesuit concealed on the premises. Newman could recall it with humour in later years but at the time it must have taxed his patience beyond endurance. 'One day when I entered my house,' he wrote, 'I found a flight of Undergraduates inside. Heads of Houses, as mounted patrols, walked their horses round those poor cottages. Doctors of Divinity dived into the hidden recesses of that private tenement uninvited, and drew domestic conclusions from what they saw there.'[1] One can hardly wonder that he did not reply to Bishop Wiseman.

Thus, while Wiseman waited at Oscott for some indication that Newman was ready to come over, an event which to Wiseman, knowing the depth and sincerity of the other's Catholic principles, could only be a matter of time, Newman himself desired only to be left alone. It must be remembered that Newman was never a 'Romanizer'. He was a reluctant pilgrim on the road that led him ever nearer to Rome, always looking back over his shoulder for some redeeming feature in the city which he was leaving, for any indication of hope which might enable him to retrace his steps. For this reason he determined, as he expressed in a letter to a Catholic

[1] *Apologia*, p. 289.

acquaintance in April 1841, not to be party to any agitation but to remain quiet in his own place and do all that he could to make others take the same course; and he added the stipulation that he felt it 'a painful duty to keep aloof from all Roman Catholics who came with the intention of opening negotiations for the union of the Churches'.[1] He was not to be enticed or hurried, though Phillipps de Lisle might fling out Utopian schemes for Christian re-union and Bishop Wiseman argue with Roman subtlety against the Anglican claims; he would take his time, and nothing in his nature or in his thoughts would make him take one step in the direction of Rome so long as he could find any cause, however slender, for re-maining in the church of his baptism.

Others were less slow than Newman in taking the fateful step. On Good Friday, 1841, Wiseman was able to report that 'Mr. C. Hemans, son of the poet, a charming young man, with all his feeling and inspiration, came here (Oscott) on Thursday, a Protestant, and leaves us this evening a Catholic. He is not the only *straggler* towards Rome that has come in my way; I have several most singular and interesting correspondences, with persons I have never seen, but who are most anxious to become Catholics.'[2] It was a period of both hope and disappointment; of hope because the number of individual conversions continued to increase, but of disappointment because it began to grow more and more clear that any sort of move for corporate reunion between the two churches was, except perhaps in the vivid imaginations of Pugin and Phillipps de Lisle, quite out of the question. As the official Protestant leadership of the Anglican Church began to harden against the Tractarian group, those on the Roman side who had expected such great things from it began to see that perhaps they had expected too much, and those among the old Catholics who had never approved of Wiseman's attitude to the Oxford men now began to criticize him more openly and vocifer-ously as Newman lingered on at Littlemore and the Anglican clergy remained obstinately Anglican. For Wiseman it was a time of great anxiety and nervous strain.

But there were moments of triumph if the great event itself was still anxiously awaited. Towards the end of the year Wiseman received a visit from Mr. Ralph Waldo Sibthorpe, a Fellow of

[1] Ibid., p. 311. [2] Ward, Vol. I, p. 287.

Magdalen and friend of the leading Tractarians. Mr. Sibthorpe was an impressionable young man from a respectable county family, of moderate intellectual gifts and a certain reputation as a preacher. He was enchanted by all he saw at Oscott, and somewhat unexpectedly and precipitately announced his conversion to the Roman Church. Wiseman was exultant; his hopes seemed to be justified at last; his critics silenced. Certainly there was much now at Oscott to impress the visitor. The chapel had been designed by Pugin as a fitting setting for the ritual of the Catholic Church, and Wiseman, whose liturgical scholarship was matched by his delight in splendid ceremonial, initiated here a revival in the proper celebration of the office and liturgy that was to change the character of public worship in the Catholic community. The building of new churches assisted in this reform, so that under Bishop Wiseman's guidance and encouragement, the old, rather slip-shod manners left over from penal days when Mass had to be hurried through gave place to a new dignity and correctness in the celebration of Mass and the other services of the Church. To this visible stimulant to devotion was added the powerful intellectual appeal of the Bishop-President, already known to the visitor by his writings, but now encountered for the first time with the added persuasiveness of personal contact. Wiseman was a powerful and compelling lecturer, and was in no doubt as to the challenge which the Catholic Church would be called upon to face in the modern world. 'Fifty years hence,' he told his divinity students, 'the professors of this place will be endeavouring to prove, not transubstantiation, but the existence of God.'[1] Perhaps a memory of his own period of doubt was echoed in this phrase.

Sibthorpe seems to have yielded with little or no resistance to the appeal of Oscott and its President, to whom his rapid conversion came as some consolation for the tardiness of other more distinguished candidates. The new convert was ordained priest and started work in Birmingham at the Cathedral of St. Chad which Pugin was then completing. But after a while the glamour of his new condition began to wear off; his conversion had been sudden and not reinforced by a background of solid intellectual conviction, and furthermore, the delicate and refined Sibthorpe found in the industrial

[1] Ward, Vol. I, p. 360.

atmosphere of Birmingham a contrast all too marked in comparison with the lost delights of the University of Oxford. His fellow priests, alas, were not all 'gentlemen', and their conversational powers fell far below the standards of high table at Magdalen. By October 1843, Mr. Sibthorpe had decided that he could stand it no longer and returned to the Church of England. Wiseman, overcome with mortification, took to his bed, while both old Catholics and Tractarians improved the occasion by pointing out the dangers of hasty conversions.

Sibthorpe's defection was a grave blow to Wiseman's hopes, but it was not without its lessons. Fresh from Rome, and still under the influence of the heady enthusiasm of Pugin and Phillipps de Lisle, he had much to learn about the Church of England; for though he was master of its doctrinal peculiarities, he had not all his life lived alongside it as the old Catholics had done, nor realized that the Oxford men, with their Catholic ideals, stood outside the general tradition of their Church. More and more clearly he came to see that for all the great things he prayed would result from the Oxford Movement, the likelihood of any general move towards a reunion with Rome was becoming ever more unlikely. The vast bulk of the Anglican communion, alerted by their bishops' condemnation of Tract XC to the danger from within, had reasserted in unmistakable terms their unchanged aversion from the Roman Catholic Church, and from any attempt to reconcile their own Church with it. He now began to see danger in the line which Phillipps de Lisle had advocated of leaving the Tractarians to work within the Church of England in the hope that they would achieve a general conversion, rather than make individual converts of them. While he did not lose his deep understanding of, and sympathy with, the Tractarian point of view, he now held firmly to the opinion that one could only accommodate their position up to a certain point without being disloyal to one's duties as a Catholic. 'The Catholic has the laws and commands of God and His Church for his rule, and none other,' he wrote to Phillipps de Lisle after Sibthorpe's unfortunate departure from the fold: 'Were a Catholic who had the opportunity of bringing anyone into unity, to neglect it, on the ground that Providence seemed to work by exceptions in the present state of things here, he would certainly sin; for he would be violating a clear and positive duty, in favour of his private judgement and views regarding which he had no authority from revelation or tradition. This, of course, would be most uncatholic and sinful. Our duty is clearly to bring everyone, singly or with others, as his case comes before us, into the bosom of the Church, and when God does not bless our efforts, adore His counsels, and beg of Him to continue the work as most to His glory and the salvation of souls. But we must go on according to His appointed courses, and woe to us if any speculative views lead to our departing from them.'[1] Few people required this warning more certainly than Ambrose Phillipps de Lisle.

If the Sibthorpe affair had cast Wiseman into a fit of despondency, two other events of 1843, one at the beginning of the year and one at the end, must have raised his hopes once more, but only to dash them to the ground. In February Newman, from his retreat at Littlemore, made a formal Retraction of 'all the hard things' which he had said against the Church of Rome, and in September he resigned the Living of St. Mary's at Oxford. In the Retraction he used words (which he later quoted in the *Apologia*)[2] which must have made Bishop Wiseman believe that the moment had at last come when he could welcome the long-awaited convert into the fold, though he might have taken a hint of a different sort from the fact that Newman chose to announce his recantation in the appropriately named *Conservative Journal*, a periodical, so Wilfrid Ward tells us, 'which hardly anyone ever read'. 'If you ask me how an individual could venture,' Newman wrote, 'not simply to hold, but to publish such views of a communion so ancient, so wide-spreading, so fruitful in Saints, I answer that I said to myself, "I am not speaking in my own words, I am but following almost a *consensus* of the divines of my own Church. They have ever used the strongest language against Rome, even the most able and learned of them. I wish to throw myself into their system. While I say what they say, I am safe. Such views, too, are necessary for our position." Yet I have reason to fear still, that such language is to be ascribed, in no small measure, to an impetuous temper, a hope of approving myself to persons I respect, and a wish to repel the charge of Romanism.' It would seem now that he no longer wished to repel this charge, but once again

[1] Ward, Vol. I, p. 418.   [2] pp. 325–6.

Wiseman, all expectancy, saw the weeks lengthen into months, and still no call came from Littlemore to be received into the Church; and when the Living of St. Mary's was resigned Newman gave out that his reason for this act had been caused by the general repudiation on the part of the Church of England of the views contained in Tract XC, and not on account of any impending event such as Wiseman might desire.

Frustrated by these long delays in the fulfilment of his hope (for he had not given up his hopes for Newman's eventual conversion) Wiseman left England in 1844 for a visit to his native Spain, in which country he could forget his problems in the excitement of a return to Seville where, as he told his friend Dr. Russell, the President of Maynooth: 'On all sides I meet persons, clergy and laity, who welcome me as a fellow-townsman, and who perfectly remember my family, and who overwhelm me with kindness, and do all to make my brief stay here enjoyable and interesting to me.' Thus for a few months, under the Spanish sun, the young bishop could forget his regrets over Sibthorpe or his hopes for Newman, and devote his mind to a study of ecclesiastical and religious institutions in the city of his birth, and in gathering material for an article or two in the *Dublin Review*, which he hoped might alter the ideas of some of his fellow Catholics 'respecting the character of the present Spanish Church and the dealings of a liberal government with religion'—a situation he found about as much to his liking as the present state of the leader of the Oxford Movement.

X

D espite the protracted nature of Newman's death agony with respect to his membership of the Anglican Church, Wiseman could now congratulate himself on the ever increasing flow of converts into the one true Fold, and could report to Cardinal Acton that in twelve months there had been more converts than for ten years previously. 'Recently I baptized in the Cathedral at Nottingham a Mr. Richards, a Unitarian,' he told the Cardinal, 'he is a public lecturer on astronomy, and expects that some fifteen of his pupils will take the same step. On the second Sunday of Advent I received the abjuration of thirty-six in the Cathedral before High Mass, and in a few weeks we shall receive fifty more. On Sunday next I am to go to Wolverhampton to receive twenty into the Church, and in many other places much also is being done.'[1]

Meanwhile, at Oxford, since Newman's retirement into the obscurity of Littlemore the effective leadership of the party had passed into younger and more impulsive hands. Prominent among the younger group was William George Ward, a Fellow of Balliol, whose advocacy of Roman doctrines was so vehement that many people wondered why he bothered to call himself an Anglican clergyman at all, especially as he declared quite publicly that he doubted the validity of his own Orders, and when he heard confessions would not pronounce an absolution but would kneel with the penitent and join with him in a prayer for forgiveness. His impetuosity in proclaiming 'Romish' dogmas from Anglican pulpits resulted in a stern rebuke from the Bishop of London after Ward had preached a sermon in favour of monasticism at a service in All

[1] *Dublin Review*, January 1919.

Saints', Margaret Street. 'Where,' asked the Bishop, 'is your sanction as an English clergyman and not a popish priest for preaching such doctrines? Where do you find such practices recommended in our Church, or in Scripture?' But Ward was quite unabashed in quoting Scripture to his bishop: 'One thing is wanting to thee,' he replied; 'go, sell whatever thou hast, and give to the poor, and thou shalt have treasure in heaven; and come, follow me.'[1] For this rejoinder the bishop saw fit to reprimand him but was hardly able to prevent him from preaching, though Ward's extremist attitudes were by this time as much an embarrassment to the more conservative supporters of the Oxford Movement, such as Dr. Pusey, as they were to the Bishop of London. It is no wonder that Ward's Catholic friends should press him to take the inevitable step and join them, but to their inquiries he replied with characteristic candour: 'You Catholics know what it is to have a Pope. Well—Newman is my Pope. Without his sanction I cannot move.'[2]

He was, however, in constant touch with the leading Catholics, for despite his filial devotion to Newman he saw no reason to separate himself from any form of contact with the Church he admired so openly. Pugin had met him some years previously and had been impressed to see the works of St. Thomas Aquinas open on his table, though his architectural sensibility had been slightly shocked by the uncatholic state of the windows. 'What an extraordinary thing,' he felt himself compelled to note, 'that so glorious a man as Ward should be living in a room without mullions to the window.'[3] From Pugin introduction had followed to Oscott, where the architect was Professor of Ecclesiastical Antiquities. Thus it was that Wiseman first heard that Ward was preparing a book which he hoped would vindicate his odd assertion that 'the whole cycle of Roman doctrine' could be held without disloyalty by an English Churchman. 'We have heard from Ward,' Wiseman wrote to Phillipps de Lisle, 'on the subject of his letter or book. Its object will be to show that Rome is the great exemplar to which they must study to approach, and he will not admit the existence of a single practical corruption.'[4] The book appeared in June 1844, and was called *The Ideal of a Christian Church considered in Comparison with Existing Practice*, a rather

---

[1] Wilfrid Ward: *W. G. Ward and the Oxford Movement*, p. 239.   [2] Ibid., p. 240.
[3] M. Trappes-Lomax: *Pugin*, p. 138.   [4] Ward, Vol. I, p. 423.

cumbersome title for which its author was to receive the sobriquet of 'Ideal' Ward. It was an astonishing book to come from the pen of an Anglican clergyman, and Ward could hardly expect it to pass unnoticed by authority. Indeed, it is fair to believe that he would have been acutely disappointed if authority had failed to condemn it. Ward had brilliant but narrow intellectual gifts; he had few serious interests outside theology and confessed, many years later, in a letter to Newman, 'in all such matters as literature proper, etc., etc., I am like a man deprived of some sense. I literally can no more get on with it than I can read Hebrew without having learned. I am driven to the play (except that now I am taking up chess) from sheer inability to comprehend anything intermediate between theology or philosophy and the theatre.'[1] This excessively narrow field of interest tended to distort the problems he had to deal with, so that he fell into the fault of seeing all problems in terms of black and white, and to find any sort of compromise with the views of his opponents as quite out of the question. Fortunately he was able to temper this intellectual exclusiveness with a lively sense of humour, but in matters of religious opinion he had nothing but contempt for ideas he could not agree with, and used the most intemperate language to dismiss what he found himself unable to accept. Under these circumstances it is easy to understand that *The Ideal of a Christian Church* caused acute annoyance to the great majority of its readers when their eyes fell on the phrase: 'We find, oh most joyful, most wonderful, most unexpected sight, we find the whole cycle of Roman doctrine gradually possessing numbers of English Churchmen.' Nor were they reassured to learn that Ward could boast that 'Three years have passed since I said plainly that in subscribing the (Thirty-Nine) Articles I renounce no one Roman doctrine'.

If Bishop Wiseman greeted this book as another important step towards the conversion of England, the Head of Ward's College saw it in a very different light. Wilfrid Ward has drawn an amusing picture of how the Master of Balliol reacted to the publication of his father's book: 'It is said that he was found pacing up and down his room with the book in his hand—shortly after its appearance— quoting in accents of astonishment and horror some of its strong

[1] Wilfrid Ward: *W. G. Ward and the Catholic Revival*, p. 156.

expressions. "We are a corrupted Church!" "We are in a degraded condition!" "We are to mourn our corruption in penitential abasement!" "We are to sue for pardon at the feet of Rome humbly"; and the word "*humbly*" he repeated, in a yet deeper tone of horror.[1] Horror was not confined to the Master of Balliol. The whole University, except for the extreme Tractarian faction, was up in arms. Even Dr. Pusey considered that Ward had gone too far. The Vice-Chancellor and Heads of Houses decided that the moment for action had come. A resolution was drawn up for the vote of Convocation which called for the condemnation of specific passages in *The Ideal of a Christian Church* and demanded that Ward be degraded from his degrees of Bachelor and Master of Arts. In the interval between the publication of the proposed decree and meeting of Convocation another group of senior members of the University proposed that Tract XC should also be included for condemnation, and this idea was accepted with enthusiasm by the Vice-Chancellor and the members of the Hebdomadal Board.

Convocation met on 13th February 1845. Gladstone and Manning were among the Masters of Arts who came to record their votes. The proceedings were conducted in Latin but Ward was allowed to defend his book in the language in which it was written. He refused to withdraw a single proposition, the whole purport of his speech being adequately summed up by Canon Mozley in one sentence: 'If he said once, he said twenty times in the course of his speech, "I believe all the doctrines of the Roman Church".' *The Ideal of a Christian Church* was condemned by 777 votes to 391; the proposition that Ward be degraded from his degrees was passed by 569 to 511. It then came for the resolution on Tract XC to be put to the vote, but at this point there was a dramatic intervention. The Proctors stood up and pronounced their veto. '*Nobis Procuratoribus non-placet* was heard like a trumpet and cheered enormously.'[2] Despite this set-back it was a victory for the established authority of the University and the Church, but as the procession left the Sheldonian into the heavily falling snow it was greeted by the hoots of the undergraduates and a volley of snowballs was directed at the venerable head of the Vice-Chancellor. Ward, on the other hand, was received with so loud a cheer that he missed his

[1] *W. G. Ward and the Oxford Movement*, p. 324.   [2] Ibid., p. 342.

footing and tumbled in the snow, at which the undergraduates cheered him all the louder. Ward took his degradation lightly and even joked about it later in the day when he called upon Dr. Pusey. But his gay comments were checked by an unfamiliar voice. 'The situation seems to me, Mr. Ward, to be one of the utmost gravity. It is indeed a serious crisis. Let us not at such a time give way to a spirit of levity or hilarity.'[1] It was the voice of Henry Edward Manning who had also called to pay his respects to Dr. Pusey.

Newman wrote to Ward from Littlemore in a less censorious spirit than had been shown by Manning. 'No decree of council or Convocation,' he wrote, 'unless a special divine power goes with it, can destroy opinion, or those who are the organs of it. It is impossible to anticipate things; but one may say, I trust, without presumption, that your course is only just begun.'[2] And Newman was right. Within a few days of the condemnation of his book Ward announced that he was engaged to be married. As a supporter of clerical celibacy this was as clear an indication as any that he no longer considered himself to be a clergyman. In July 1845 he and his wife were received together into the Roman Catholic Church. 'This is delightful,' Lord Shrewsbury wrote to Phillipps de Lisle, 'surely Newman cannot lag long behind.'[3] All hope now centred on the recluse of Littlemore. Wiseman was almost beside himself with impatience. With the reception of Ward the Oxford Movement had virtually come to an end; its force was spent. Wiseman had long given up hope of its infusing Catholic ideas into the whole Anglican Church and precipitating a general conversion. Individual conversions were all that now could be hoped for, but if only Newman would come over there was no knowing how many might not follow him. The delay became almost unbearable. The summer passed, and still there was no indication that Newman was ready. By now Wiseman could wait no longer. He had with him at Oscott a convert clergyman, Bernard Smith, who had once been Newman's curate. Despite his resolution not to interfere Wiseman decided to send Smith to Littlemore to see if he could gather any information as to the state of Newman's mind. The delegate was received at Littlemore with marked coldness, but later in the evening he noticed something that made him realize that the die was cast. Newman was

[1] Ibid., p. 343.   [2] Ibid., p. 345.   [3] *W. G. Ward and the Catholic Revival*, p. 1.

wearing grey trousers. To Smith this was as clear an indication as had been the announcement of Ward's engagement. Clearly Newman, who always dressed so meticulously in clerical black, now no longer considered himself as being in Holy Orders. The sequel has been described by Wilfrid Ward: 'Mr. Smith's absolute satisfaction with his visit to Littlemore was apparent to Dr. Wiseman on his return. "What did he say to make you so confident?" Wiseman asked. "He hardly spoke," was the reply. Wiseman persisted in asking for the reason of Smith's conviction and brought it forth at last. He was utterly disappointed. "I knew," was Smith's reply, "that you would think nothing of it. But I know the man, and I know what it means. He will come, and come soon"'[1]

Since the end of 1844 Newman had been writing an Essay on the Development of Doctrine which was to represent the last phase of his journey towards Rome. He worked long hours standing at his desk, breaking off only for the recitation of Divine Office, for the two daily meals, and for a walk with his companions in the afternoon. They lived a life of monastic austerity. In September two of the Community, Dalgairns and Ambrose St. John, were received into the Church. Still Newman lingered. Finally Stanton, one of his remaining companions, left Littlemore and wrote early in October to say that he had arranged to be received into the Church at Stonyhurst. Newman's reply suggested that he should come back to Littlemore. 'Why should we not be received together? Father Dominic, the Passionist, comes here on the 8th to receive me. Come back on that day.'[2] The decision had been made at last. At the end of his manuscript on the Development of Doctrine Newman wrote: 'Time is short, eternity is long,' and he added the prayer of Simeon: 'Nunc dimittus servum tuum, Domine, secundum verbum tuum in pace. Quia viderunt oculi mei salutare tuum.'

On October 31st Newman arrived at Oscott to receive the sacrament of Confirmation at the hands of Bishop Wiseman. It was an embarrassing encounter for both men. From various motives of tact and prudence both had, in the past, made so scrupulous a study of avoiding each other's company that their meeting was now all the more difficult. Their previous meetings, in Rome and Oxford, had been brief. For all the sensitiveness of Newman and the shyness

[1] Ward, Vol. I, p. 429.   [2] Ibid., p. 429.

of Wiseman both men had the instincts and characteristics of leaders of men, and such temperaments do not necessarily make the happiest of companions. There was also the ever present memory of past differences. In 1841, when Newman had heard that Wiseman and his friends were praying for him he had answered: 'May their prayers be fulfilled in their substance, that is, in God's way, though not in the way they think to be God's.'[1] What now must he have thought of these words? Wiseman, too, must have reflected on his references to Newman's 'supposed spiritual illumination' in past years when he had written to Phillipps de Lisle that 'the great danger . . . seems to me to lie in the ease with which they flatter themselves into belief of Providential declarations in their favour'.[2] The spirit of the remark is very similar to Newman's; there is a note of spiritual rivalry in them both, for all the sincerity with which the words were written, which was characteristic of both men in certain moods, and which must have added to the difficulties of this first encounter. Furthermore, Wiseman had a way, in Lord Acton's words, of 'exhibiting the scalps' of his converts, and here, at last, he had brought in the greatest convert of them all. For all the tact and restraint Wiseman must have used, Newman cannot have failed to feel his position in this respect, and to have been acutely embarrassed by it. Years later he was to write, with almost bitter memory, of the 'dreary' experience of being 'the gaze of so many eyes at Oscott, as if some wild incomprehensible beast, caught by the hunter, and a spectacle for Dr. Wiseman to exhibit to strangers, as himself being the hunter who captured it!'[3]

Viewed against such a background it should surprise no one that the first meeting was an ordeal for both men, and found them more or less speechless. It was a relief to all present when Wiseman was called away to hear the confession of one of the students, and had an excuse to leave. Next day the Confirmation took place in the chapel of Oscott College, and Wiseman could write in triumph to his friend Dr. Russell: 'On All Saints, Newman, Oakely, and the other two were confirmed, and we had *ten* quondam Anglican clergymen in the chapel. Has this ever happened before since the Reformation?'[4]

---

[1] Purcell: *Life of Ambrose Phillipps de Lisle*, Vol. I, p. 224.   [2] Ward, Vol. I, p. 216.
[3] Newman: *Autobiographical Writings*, p. 255.   [4] Ward, Vol. I, p. 433.

The reception of Newman, though it was a triumph for Wiseman and a vindication of the attitude he had adopted to the Oxford Movement, still presented him with many problems. A large number of the old Catholics were as unsympathetic to Newman and his followers inside the Church as they had been distrustful of him while still an Anglican. The deplorable episode of Sibthorpe was still fresh in the minds of Wiseman's critics. His desire to integrate the converts into Catholic life and thereby raise the general intellectual level of the Catholic body was not shared by his fellow bishops. Their welcome to the neophytes had been decidedly chilling. When Ward had visited the Vicar Apostolic of the London District, Dr. Griffiths had said: 'We are glad to welcome you, Mr. Ward,' but to this he had added: 'Of course, we have no work for you.'[1] As Ward's conversion had meant an almost complete sacrifice of income (it was some years before he inherited property from an uncle in the Isle of Wight) he must have found very little of comfort in the bishop's greeting.

The economic problem was a severe one. To married men, like Ward, there was no question of their becoming priests, though as many of the married converts had previously been clergymen the problem of finding employment for them became one of Wiseman's continual worries, while the lack of co-operation he received from so many of his fellow Catholics threw him into fits of despondency. In Ward's case he was able to get him a post as lecturer at St. Edmund's College, though in doing this he was inadvertently laying up trouble for himself in the future. Frederick Faber's conversion with eleven members of his congregation, which had occurred a month after Newman's, had meant leaving a comfortable living worth £1,400 a year, and a parish in which he had done devoted work, for a future of absolute obscurity. Wiseman was the only man on the Catholic side to whom these converts could look for help and encouragement, or from whom they could expect to find, not only a warm and cordial welcome, but also a thorough understanding of, and sympathy for, their unique predicament.

It must be admitted that Newman and Wiseman were never fully *en rapport*. There was always a certain reserve between them though they had an unfeigned admiration for each other's qualities.

[1] *W. G. Ward and the Catholic Revival*, p. 8.

Newman was to become irritated by Wiseman's indecisions and his inability to follow up some of the generous but imprecise schemes which he was later to initiate so that by the time of the latter's death Newman had come to regard him among those whom he felt had been unjust to him.[1] Perhaps both men suffered a little from a sense of persecution; certainly they were both to complain on many occasions of how they had been misunderstood, unappreciated, and abandoned by their friends. But in his early days as a Catholic, Newman had every reason to be grateful for the tact and imagination displayed by Wiseman, and the trouble he took to make the distinguished convert feel at home in his new surroundings; and if Newman, looking back in later years, saw himself then as being exhibited like a wild incomprehensible beast, he was also, in another mood, to recall how he found himself welcomed and housed at Oscott: 'the whole house, I may say, boys as well as the authorities of the place, receiving me with open arms'.[2]

Wiseman realized that Newman would not wish to be separated from his Littlemore friends, and immediately offered the converts the buildings of Old Oscott, from where the College had moved when Pugin's new buildings were ready. Newman gladly accepted this retreat, and renamed the house Maryvale; but before settling in he went, also at Wiseman's suggestion, on a round of visits to the chief Catholic educational centres, so that he could meet many of the leading Catholic personalities and get some idea of the background to the new world he was entering. Writing of this plan to Dr. Russell, Wiseman expressed the hope that Newman 'will thus soon be known to all the clergy, and become popular among them',[3] but Newman himself felt that he was received with a good deal of suspiciousness outside the sympathetic atmosphere of Oscott.

Meanwhile, it was Wiseman's determination that the new convert and his followers should go as soon as possible to Rome for a period of study. Realizing that there was still a certain amount of hostility and prejudice against them among the old Catholics he considered that they would be placed in an altogether stronger position in England if they had behind them the authority and approval of the Holy See. He also believed that they would be better able to determine what precise form their future work as Catholic priests should

[1] Newman: *Autobiographical Writings*, p. 260.   [2] Ward, Vol. I, p. 443.   [3] Ibid.

take if they could consider the problem at the very centre of Catholic life, away from the scene of their recent spiritual conflicts, in the calmer atmosphere that prevailed in the shadow of St. Peter's. Wiseman, ever since his own days in Rome, had had a devotion to St. Philip Neri and the work which the Saint had founded in the Congregation of the Oratory. It had seemed to Wiseman that a congregation of secular priests, living and working in urban surroundings, was ideally suited to the special conditions of the English Mission. St. Philip Neri, who had founded the first Oratory in 1564, used to greet the English students in the streets of Rome before those intrepid missionaries left for their own country where, as often as not, the fate of martyrdom awaited them. It seemed appropriate to Wiseman that St. Philip's Oratory should now be introduced to England by these latter-day converts from the Established Church. He warmly commended the plan to Newman, but did not press it, as he realized that Newman and his disciples must see for themselves before they were committed to any particular Order or special form of religious work. Newman and his companions left for Rome in October 1846, still undecided about their future, finding much in the Dominican and Jesuit Orders that appealed to them and seemed to offer them the opportunities they sought. But in January 1847 Wiseman received a letter which told him that his original plan had been accepted. 'My dear Lord,' Newman wrote from the *Collegio di Propaganda* in Rome, 'It is curious and very pleasant that, after all the thought we can give the matter, we must come to your Lordship's original idea, and feel we cannot do better than be Oratorians.'[1]

The news must have caused Bishop Wiseman considerable satisfaction, and the success with which the rule of St. Philip adapted itself to the conditions of the English Church in the Oratories that were subsequently founded in Birmingham and London, testifies to the soundness of his judgement in this matter. Meanwhile more and more converts flowed into the Catholic Church in the wake of Newman. In Disraeli's phrase, the Church of England reeled from the blow of Newman's secession. The whole impetus of the Catholic Movement in the Church of England seemed to have run out. Dr. Pusey wandered about Oxford in the depth of gloom, shaking his

[1] Ibid., p. 453.

head over the sad plight of those who fled to Rome. 'It is very sad,' he was heard to remark. 'And all who have left us have deteriorated so much—all, that is, with two exceptions. One exception is Newman, whose nature is so beautiful, so perfect, that nothing, not even going over to Rome, could change him. The other exception is Ward. Ward had got so bad already that with him further deterioration was impossible.'[1] As Pusey's woeful forebodings deepened Wiseman was writing to Phillipps de Lisle about the continual stream of men who came to Oscott to be received. 'Mr. Glennie, and Mr. Watts Russell, and probably Mr. Woodmason are coming to settle in Birmingham, where Mr. Faber has also formed a society of young men, his converts, who live in community. So that we shall have quite a colony of converts near us. On Sunday last Mr. Stokes, late Secretary of the Camden Society, was received at St. Chad's, and next Sunday Mr. Hutchinson of Trinity, Cambridge, will be received. He talks of seven more coming. The bishops of France are all answering to our appeal; in the Diocese of Cambrai every second Mass on Christmas night is to be offered up for England, and the faithful are requested to give their Christmas Communion for the same object.'[2]

It would seem that Wiseman's triumph was complete. Bishop Baines's damping comments in the past were now shown to have been wrong. The shame of Sibthorpe's backsliding was blotted out. But once again the feeling of despondency came surging into Wiseman's mind, clouding over the triumph he might well have felt. It was like a repetition of those days when he had spent many a long hour 'alone, in bitter tears, on the *loggia* of the English College' wrestling with his dark thoughts. 'I hardly know', he wrote in a memorandum belonging to this period, 'why I should wish to make a record of my feelings at this particular time, though I have often wished to do so before. But perhaps seldom before have I felt more completely the peculiarity of my position in my *total isolation* as regards support and counsel, as well as sympathy and concurrence in views and plans . . . In the house I have reason now to know that *not one* was working with me, thought with me, or felt with me. Many an hour of the lonely night have I passed in prayer and tears by the lamp of the Sanctuary. . . . How seldom has a word been

---

[1] *W. G. Ward and the Oxford Movement*, p. 367.   [2] Ward, Vol. I, pp. 443-4.

spoken which intimated that those who entered the College considered it as more than a mere place of boys' education or (saw in it) a great engine employed in England's conversion and regeneration.' He goes on to pour out his heart over the lack of sympathy he had received, his portion being rather 'newspaper assaults, remonstrances by letter (and from some of our most gifted Catholics), sharp rebukes by word of mouth'. He then goes on to recount a curious episode that happened to him while visiting Rome on business connected with the Church's attitude to the Oxford Movement. 'There was among the chronic sick of the hospital of S. Spirito a man who had been paralysed for many years, and whom I had directed and attended up to the time I left Rome. He was a poor, ignorant, uneducated man of the lowest class, and could not know or hear much, where he was, of what was going on in England. When I visited Rome I went to see him in the hospital. He addressed me in a most unexpected way, as far as I remember (for the impression made on me by his words was very strong), telling me not to change my mode of acting, but to go on as I had done till then, without minding what people said; this was uttered in a very marked, decided tone, as if the man knew all about it, and I felt quite amazed as to what could have led him to address me in such a manner, for I had not said a word that could have suggested his speech . . . yet the impression made on my mind was that he clearly alluded to my dealings with converts (and I think his *words* must have pointed to this subject), and that it thus pleased God to console and encourage me through the mouth of one of His poor to whom I had shown some little charity.'[1]

Did Wiseman call to mind this incident to redress the feeling of neglect and frustration which so easily overcame him, and hold on to it as a sign of divine approval for the work which received so little encouragement from his fellow bishops? Was it something he stored up in his mind for these moments of depression when all hands seemed turned against him, and all hearts closed? For in fact the situation was not nearly so black as he made out. If the majority of the bishops did not share in his enthusiasm he knew that it was he who had the support and confidence of the Holy See behind him, a strong following among the more influential laymen,

[1] Ibid., pp. 447-9.

and a growing support among the clergy; though among both clergy and laity his support was strong in influence rather than in numbers. These attacks of depression to some extent had a physical cause, for at this time he was complaining of his health to Dr. Russell, writing that 'symptoms of an unpleasant nature have again shown themselves . . . they partly consist of a total prostration for the time of all mental as well as physical energy. I cannot take up business, and things stagnate about me. I get but little sleep: last night, for instance, I did not get to sleep till five this morning. This wears me out.'[1] But this alone does not account for these black moods. There was some deep psychological cause which threw him back, in these moments, from the heights to the depths, some mild form of manic depression, perhaps, which is sometimes found in minds of a high intellectual order. Certainly there can have been few moments in his career less deserving of despondency than the months which followed the reception into the Catholic Church of John Henry Newman.

[1] Ibid., p. 450.

XI

While popular attention, in the eighteen-forties, was concentrated on the secession of the leaders of the Oxford Movement, a much greater increase in the numerical strength of the Catholic population in England was to result from the immigration of poor Irish, driven out of their own country by the famine which followed from the failure of the potato crop in 1845, and in the two succeeding years. This influx presented a great problem to the Catholic bishops who had neither the priests nor the churches to cope with the thousands of people, often destitute, who crossed over St. George's Channel in their hordes, bringing with them the dreaded infection of typhus, the 'famine fever'. Many priests were to die from this terrible plague, among them one bishop, Dr. Riddell, who was the Vicar Apostolic of the Northern District. It was in the face of this challenge that the new religious orders, the Institute of Charity, or Rosminians, and the Passionists, came into their own, who by their devoted work amongst the plague-stricken poor were able to do much to overcome the prejudice in which they were held by many of the old Catholics.

These orders had not been particularly welcome to the Vicars Apostolic, not only because of the Italian devotions which they introduced but because owing allegiance to their own superiors, they were largely independent of the bishops and tended to add to the difficulties involved in administering the Districts. In the ancient dispute between the Vicars Apostolic and the Monastic Orders, these new institutions, who were soon joined by the Redemptorists, were looked upon by the older bishops as strange and formidable opponents. Almost alone among the bishops

Wiseman had supported and encouraged these Orders from the first, with the same vision that had caused him to welcome the converts from Anglicanism, for he realized that in the growing needs of the Church there would be more and more opportunities for them and their special contribution to Catholic life. In this he had the active and enthusiastic support of Ambrose Phillipps de Lisle, who had brought Father Gentili back to England after he had been banished from Prior Park by Bishop Baines;[1] but Lord Shrewsbury was unable to agree with either Wiseman or Phillipps de Lisle, and expressed himself typically of the view generally held by the old Catholics. 'We are all against your Gentili scheme,' he wrote to Phillipps de Lisle from Rome: 'It is beginning at the wrong end. Besides which, Gentili is not suited for England. We must have a new race of zealous English missionaries, such as are now bringing up at Oscott, under the good Bishop and Pugin.'[2]

Gentili returned from Rome with a better understanding of the British character and of the problems of the English clergy than he had shown at Prior Park. The devotion he gave to the English Mission more than justified the trust which Wiseman had placed in him. He visited Ireland on three occasions to preach missions and retreats, so that when famine drove the Irish from their homes Gentili was one of the first to devote his life to their spiritual needs and was, in fact, to die from the infection of the famine fever in 1848. Both he and Father Dominic Barberi, who had received Newman into the Church, may be said to have worked themselves to death in the cause of the conversion of England, and their obvious sincerity and devotion helped greatly to create a new atmosphere among the old Catholics with regard both to the converts and the work of the monastic orders.

The idea of giving retreats for the clergy was one of the devices which Wiseman especially encouraged in his plan to improve the tone and 'ecclesiastical spirit' of the mission priests. The idea was then quite new. In the past, with the clergy scattered over vast areas, it had been almost impossible to organize anything of this kind, while in penal times any gathering together of Catholic priests

---

[1] The Bishop of Siga had died in 1843 and was succeeded in the Western District by Dr. Baggs.

[2] Gwynn: *Lord Shrewsbury, Pugin and the Catholic Revival*, p. 67.

would have invited danger. But now that the Vicariates had been increased in number, reducing the administrative areas under the control of each bishop, meetings of the clergy were easier to organize, while the increasing demands on them, due to the growing Catholic population, made such meetings all the more necessary. None the less, the idea of spending a few days in retreat did not always appeal to some of the more old-fashioned of the clergy, and Wiseman once more encountered a good deal of opposition. Dr. Bowden of Sedgley Park was one of the more outspoken critics. To this priest, who had already found Dr. Wiseman 'pompous and stiff with the dignity of a Roman prelate' the notion of a retreat was far from pleasant and he was quite aghast at the thought of 'solitary confinement for ten days in darkened rooms and reflecting seriously on the state of our interior'.[1] But despite his cry 'I do not think that I can go through with it,' Wiseman persisted, and soon the clergy began to realize the benefits of the retreats both in their work and in their own spiritual lives.

On top of these problems came others of a new sort when Newman and his companions came back from Rome with a papal Brief authorizing them to found an Oratory in Birmingham. This of course, would mean the building of a new church. 'Your Lordship recollects the Oratory here,' Newman had written to Wiseman from Rome: 'It must be a building for preaching and music; not an open roof, certainly no screen. I am afraid I shall shock Pugin.'[2] Until now the Catholic revival had been associated with the revival in Gothic architecture which is especially connected with Pugin, who held the style of the Renaissance in such distaste that after a visit to Rome he announced that 'the Sistine Chapel is a melancholy room, the Last Judgement is a painfully muscular delineation of a glorious subject, the Scala Regia a humbug, the Vatican a hideous mess, and St. Peter's is the greatest failure of all',[3] though he added, as a pious after-thought, that he did not despair of St. Peter's being rebuilt in a better style. Newman now returned from Rome determined that his Oratory should be built in the Italian style, and when Frederick Faber, with his followers, decided to join Newman's Oratory, the Italian style found an even more vociferous enthusiast.

[1] Denis Gwynn: *The Second Spring, 1818–1852*, p. 133.   [2] Ibid., p. 182.
[3] D. Gwynn: *Lord Shrewsbury, Pugin and the Catholic Revival*, p. 119.

To Pugin and Phillipps de Lisle this was nothing short of treason. Pugin had begun to have doubts about Wiseman's architectural orthodoxy some years before when the latter had ventured to criticize the screen which Pugin had designed for St. Chad's Cathedral. 'Wiseman has shown his real sentiments,' he wrote in alarm, but the Bishop tactfully withdrew in the interests of peace. Another shock came later, however, when the architect was showing his work to some Protestant friends. While indicating the rood-screen for their admiration he explained how it separated the church into two and that beyond it was the sacred precinct where only those in Holy Orders might tread. At that very moment a priest appeared in the hallowed area in the company of two ladies. Pugin had summoned the verger to demand that they be told to leave, only to learn that it was Bishop Wiseman who was showing the ladies round the church. The mortified architect had retired to a pew and burst into tears. Now came this new threat from Italy and neither Pugin nor Phillipps de Lisle felt that Bishop Wiseman, tainted by twenty years residence in the very home of 'Pagan' architecture, could be trusted to champion the Gothic cause.

Battle was soon joined. 'If Mr. Pugin persists, as I hope he will not,' Newman wrote, 'in loading with bad names the admirers of Italian architecture, he is going the very way to increase their number. Men will not be put down without authority which is infallible. And if we go to authority, I suppose Popes have given a greater sanction to Italian than to Gothic.' Pugin, meanwhile, was expressing his disgust to Phillipps de Lisle: 'The Oxford men have turned out the most disappointing people in the world. They were three times as Catholic in their ideas before they were reconciled to the Church. It is really quite lamentable'; and to the charge of architectural unorthodoxy he now added a bitter complaint against their musical tastes. 'A man may be judged by his feelings on Plain Chaunt. If he likes Mozart he is no chancel and screen man. By their music you shall know them, and I lost all faith in the Oratorians when I found they were opposed to the old song.'[1] But an uglier scene had taken place between Phillipps de Lisle, Pugin, and Father Faber. After a heated argument in which Faber had been accused of 'copying a wretched people (Italian) who are now throwing

[1] Ibid., pp. 121 and 125.

off the faith, and persecuting[1] the Church,' Phillipps de Lisle, stamping (according to Faber's account) and shaking his fists to heaven, had declared: 'Father Faber, God for your pride destroyed and brought to naught your first effort. He will curse and destroy your order, and it will perish if you go on thus.'[2]

The rumour that Phillipps de Lisle had 'cursed the Oratory' was soon being discussed among the converts, despite the fact that Faber and de Lisle had shaken hands five minutes after the outburst and Faber had expressed his intention to 'consider the words not spoken'. Faber had an impulsive temperament with a strong leaning to popular Italian devotions, while among his less happy characteristics was a habit of referring to the Blessed Virgin Mary as 'Mamma'. The unfortunate episode of the 'curse' had taken place 'Opposite Mamma's image' at Cotton Hall (a house which had been placed at the Oratorians' disposal by the generosity of Lord Shrewsbury) and it was not long before Newman, at Maryvale, had heard all about it. Phillipps de Lisle wrote to him to express the hope that Faber 'may become less violent and excessive in his ways and ideas' and assured Newman, returning the argument to its architectural origins, that he 'did not quarrel with Father Faber because he had no skreen (*sic*), but he shocked me by his awful expression in denouncing the skreen at Cheadle'. Newman replied by taking him to task (and, by imputation, Pugin also) for calling Grecian and Italian architecture 'Pagan', using the word not historically, but as a term of reproach. 'If it be Pagan,' Newman reasoned, 'it is Popish too, for I suppose the Pope has given quite as much sanction to it as he has to Gregorian music, which by the by seems to be Pagan in the same sense that Italian architecture is.'[3] Both Phillipps de Lisle and Faber were impulsive men, and Pugin, after overworking his mental and physical resources for many years, was on the edge of a complete nervous breakdown, so that left to themselves there is no knowing how this unedifying and unnecessary dispute might have ended; but Newman's intervention brought peace without any humiliating sacrifice of principle, for while holding on to his own ideas, he could be generous in his opinion of others. 'Mr. Pugin is a man of genius,' he wrote to de Lisle; 'I have

---

[1] A reference to the *Resorgimento*, then in process in Italy.
[2] R. Chapman: *Father Faber*, p. 184.   [3] Ibid., pp. 186–7.

the greatest admiration of his talents, and willingly acknowlege that Catholics owe him a great debt for what he has done in the revival of Gothic architecture among us. . . . But he has the great fault of a man of genius, as well as the merit. . . . The canons of Gothic architecture are to him points of faith, and every one is a heretic who would venture to question them.'[1] But if peace was made there was to remain a certain reserve on the part of Phillipps de Lisle in his dealings with the Oratorians, those very men whose conversion he had once believed would bring the whole Anglican Church following on their heels. 'I hear they are doing wonders,' he wrote to Lord Shrewsbury after learning that a second Oratory had been opened in London: 'there is only one thing I regret about them, their strange and unaccountable enmity to Christian art and Gothic architecture. I hear that the new Oratory is to be built, not in the old ecclesiastical architecture but in the *classical style!*'[2] The argument 'opposite Mamma's image' had shown another cleavage in Wiseman's flock in addition to that between old Catholic and new convert which it was his great hope to heal. One can understand how it was later said of the Cardinal that there were moments when he would gladly return all his converts to the Church of England.

The problems posed by the Irish immigration, by the question of ecclesiastical discipline whether in connexion with the monastic orders or the special concerns of the secular clergy, and the new difficulties and conflicts arising from the growing influence of the Tractarian converts, raised once more in an urgent form the old matter of the restoration of the hierarchy. The increase in the number of Vicariates in 1840 when, by the Apostolic Letter *Muneris Apostolici* of Gregory XVI, they had been raised from four to eight, had been clearly only a temporary measure. The time had now come when negotiations must be started once more with the authorities in Rome. In 1845, after their annual meeting, the bishops had formally petitioned the Holy See for the restoration of the hierarchy and this petition had been upheld by 'great numbers of clergy and laymen distinguished for their virtues and for their rank, as well as by the immense majority among English Catholics'.[3] But

---

[1] Gwynn: *The Second Spring*, p. 186.   [2] Ibid., p. 186.
[3] Words used in Letter Apostolic of Pius IX restoring the English Hierarchy. *Vide*: *The English Catholics 1850–1950*, p. 110.

other influences equally strong, if less numerous, had been opposed to any further change. Chief among these opponents was Cardinal Acton. Acton was heart and soul behind Wiseman in the forward policy he was pursuing, almost single-handed, in England; but he believed that the other bishops were too deeply rooted in past traditions and in the still prevailing atmosphere of pre-emancipation ways to be ready to undertake the new responsibilities which the restoration would imply. In particular he considered that Dr. Griffiths, who as Vicar Apostolic of the London District would be expected to become Archbishop and Metropolitan of the new Province, was unsuited for the duties which this office would involve. Dr. Griffiths had been unfortunate in his relations with the Holy See, where the unwelcome mantle of Bishop Baines seems to have fallen on his shoulders. His resistance to many innovations, and his known hostility to the religious orders, had prejudiced him with the authorities at Propaganda, where his ceaseless but unspectacular labours in the routine work of his District passed largely unnoticed. These unfavourable opinions were confirmed from another quarter. Father Gentili, who had previously intrigued in Rome against the Bishop of Siga, was now busily engaged in sending confidential reports to the Holy See on the various problems which would be created by the restoration of the hierarchy, and among such problems he considered that the finding of suitable candidates for the episcopal sees was more serious than the possibility of Protestant or Parliamentary opposition.[1] These views were to a great extent shared by Gregory XVI, who before his elevation to the Apostolic Throne had himself been Cardinal-Prefect of Propaganda, and so had a personal knowledge of the situation in England and of the negotiations which had so far taken place. It was unlikely that he would be prepared to make any further move in the matter.

Such, then, was the situation in 1845. On 1st June 1846, however, the papal throne became vacant with the death of Gregory, and a new era for the papacy dawned with the election, on 16th June, of Cardinal Count Giovanni Maria Mastai-Ferretti, Bishop of Imola, who assumed the name of Pius IX, and was to rule the Church for the next thirty-two years. Known to have liberal sympathies and to be likely to reverse the conservative, pro-Austrian, policy of

[1] E. E. Y. Hales: *Pio Nono*, p. 140.

Gregory XVI, the Cardinal Bishop of Imola had been particularly obnoxious to Prince Metternich whose mind had been outraged at the pernicious thought of a reforming Pope. To prevent such an evil he had dispatched the Cardinal Archbishop of Milan to the conclave armed with the Imperial veto, but this tardy prelate had only got as far as Florence when news reached him of Mastai-Ferretti's election.[1] The Austrian Chancellor at first accepted the new Pope with a good grace, but his worst fears were fulfilled when he heard that Pius had granted an amnesty to the political prisoners of the previous reign. 'God never grants amnesties,' was Metternich's chilling comment: 'God pardons, he does not forget.' But if Prince Metternich, who himself admitted that he had allowed for everything except the possibility of a liberal Pope, was filled with misgivings, the news of the election of Pius IX was greeted with joy by those who had long been striving to reconcile the Catholic religion with modern thought, and a new feeling of hope dawned in the temporal dominions of the Holy See.

The English Vicars Apostolic saw in the election of a new Pope a fresh opportunity to press for the restoration of the hierarchy, and at their first meeting of the new pontifical reign agreed to send Dr. Wiseman and Dr. Sharples, the bishop-coadjutor of the Lancastrian District, on a deputation to the Holy See to place their case before Pius IX. One of the leading obstacles to the success of their mission was removed in a tragic and unforeseen way before they reached Rome, for while the two bishops were still on their journey Cardinal Acton died suddenly at Naples at the early age of forty-four. Furthermore, when they finally reached Rome, they found that though Cardinal Fransoni, the nominee of Gregory XVI, was still Prefect of Propaganda, they had a new ally in the Secretary of that Congregation, Monsignor Barnabò, who very soon came round to their point of view and vigorously supported the scheme for a new hierarchy.

Wiseman and Sharples reached Rome in July 1847. Their first encounter was with Monsignor Palma, the special under-secretary of Propaganda charged with the conduct of English affairs, who suggested on behalf of the Pope that a new Constitution should be

[1] There is no conclusive evidence that Austria intended to use the veto against Mastai-Ferretti though the story has been widely held.

issued reforming and bringing up to date that issued by Benedict XIV in 1753, under which the English Mission was governed; but Wiseman pointed out that this could only be a temporary measure, postponing the final settlement still further, and that to prepare such an Apostolic Constitution would be so complicated a business that it would be just as simple to restore the hierarchy. 'Either the Holy See must issue another full Constitution,' he contended, 'which would supply all wants, but which would be necessarily complicated and voluminous, and, as a special provision, would necessarily be temporary; or, the real and complete code of the Church must be at once extended to the Catholic Church in England, so far as compatible with its social position; and this provision would be final. But, in order to adopt this second and more natural expedient, one condition was necessary, and that was: *the Catholics must have a Hierarchy*.'[1]

The force of this argument impressed itself on Monsignor Barnabò, and Wiseman's advocacy soon created so favourable a response that the Secretary was able to suggest to the two bishops that they should draw up a formal petition for presentation to the Pope. Pius himself had been greatly impressed by the report they had made on conditions in England, when he had required answers to various criticisms of the work of the Vicars Apostolic which the supporters of Cardinal Acton had put forward. These, as Wiseman outlined them in a letter to Bishop Ullathorne,[2] repeated the old charge of 'want of zeal and activity, as though conversions could be increased indefinitely if proper efforts were made' and suggested various faults in administration and 'arbitrary exercise of authority with regard to the clergy . . . want of fixed rules for the suspension, removal, etc., of priests . . . ' Not surprisingly, Wiseman concludes that 'much sinister influence has been exerted at Rome against the present state of things in England, and consequently against the Bishops'.[3] Wiseman's answer to these charges, and the statistics he could quote in defence of the true state of things—new missions opened, religious orders established, the flow of converts continuing —so satisfied the Pope that when, in August, news reached Rome of

[1] Ward, Vol. I, p. 476.
[2] Ullathorne had succeeded Dr. Baggs as Vicar Apostolic of the Western District in 1846.
[3] Gwynn: *The Second Spring*, p. 177.

the sudden and unexpected death of Dr. Griffiths, Pius IX appointed Dr. Wiseman to succeed him, though to emphasize that the appointment was only made pending a more final solution of the problem of the hierarchy he was created Pro-Vicar Apostolic, suggesting that the position was only of a temporary nature. One reason for this was because it was hoped to persuade Bishop Walsh, as senior English bishop, to move to London, and though Walsh declined, on grounds of age, it was still thought he might change his mind. The title was also, possibly, designed to mollify the feelings of some of the London clergy who might resent the haste and suddenness with which the vacancy had been filled without their own wishes in the matter being consulted, for it was widely known that many of them had wished to have Dr. Cox, the President of St. Edmund's College, as their next bishop. To Wiseman himself it was an indication that the favour he had enjoyed under Gregory XVI was to continue under Pius IX.

The outcome of Wiseman and Sharples's mission seemed hopeful indeed. The Pope received the bishops in audience and clearly sympathized with their views. Monsignor Palma and Monsignor Barnabò, the latter of whom was soon to be given a red hat and to succeed Cardinal Fransoni as Prefect of Propaganda, added their strong recommendations; the Vicars Apostolic in England were known, for once, to be united in their desire for the success of their representatives' petition for the restoration. The Pope considered the matter with the utmost concern, deciding to offer three Masses before he finally made up his mind. After the first two he hesitated, but after the third doubt vanished. '*Adesso sono tranquillo*,' declared the Holy Father; 'At last I am content,' and the matter appeared to be settled except for the drafting of the necessary briefs for the new sees and the issuing of Letters Apostolic to authorize the change.

But the establishment of the new hierarchy was to face yet another set-back. While Wiseman and Sharples were corresponding with the English bishops on the question, still unsettled, of the names and boundaries of the new dioceses, the political situation in Italy deteriorated so rapidly that Pius IX decided to send Wiseman back to London on a mission to Lord Palmerston, whose help he hoped to invoke against the encroachments of Austria on the Papal States.

The idea of any sort of *rapprochement* between the English Government—and a Liberal government at that—and the Holy See, would have been out of the question under the reign of any of the three previous Popes. Indeed, the last time when an English government had concerned itself with the affairs of the papacy had been in 1831, when in association with Austria, Russia, Prussia and France, England had joined in sending a memorandum to the Holy See giving various suggestions on the reform of the administration of the Papal States which was considered as necessary by those Powers; advice which Gregory XVI, then newly elected, had seen fit to ignore. With the succession of Pius IX, however, a new atmosphere prevailed. The Pope's determined efforts to liberalize the archaic government over which he presided as Sovereign of the States of the Church had won him a good deal of sympathy in England where previously the only interest shown by the masses of the people in the person of the Supreme Pontiff had been to burn him in effigy each year on the anniversary of the Gunpowder Plot. Everything that made a reforming Pope seem so deplorable to the reactionary statesmen of Vienna tended to make him a popular figure in England, especially as he compared favourably with some of his fellow Italian princes who seemed unduly reluctant to grant even the mildest forms of constitutional government to their subjects. 'What a grand fellow the new Pope seems to be,' was the opinion of Dr. Jowett, the future Master of Balliol, while the *Morning Chronicle*, going, perhaps, a little too far, referred to him as 'The most enlightened sovereign of the age.'

With the rumble of revolution growing ever louder in his ears the Austrian Chancellor decided that a move against the liberal Pope might at least quell the rising spirit of nationalism in Italy, which up till now had lacked a figurehead such as might be provided in the person of Pius IX. The idea of a political federation of Italy under the presidency of the Pope, such as was being advocated by liberal-minded clericals like the Abbé Gioberti and even, at this period, by the republican Mazzini, was utterly incompatible with the policy which Prince Metternich had been pursuing since the overthrow of Napoleon. In July 1847, while Wiseman was still in Rome, the Austrian army crossed into Papal territory with the excuse, so familiar to twentieth-century ears, that they had come to 'protect' the Pope. At once the cry of 'War against Austria' was heard everywhere in the Papal States. But Pius, caught in the dilemma of his dual role as spiritual head of the universal Catholic Church and temporal sovereign of the Papal States, was determined not to make war on a Catholic Power while at the same time he resolved not to give way to the mailed-fist policy of Austria. His only hope lay in calling in the help of some other Power capable of causing the Austrian forces to withdraw, and, his geographical position being what it was, only a strong naval power could offer this help. Thus it was that Bishop Wiseman was dispatched to London on an urgent mission to the British Foreign Secretary.

Wiseman arrived in London on September 11th and called immediately at the Foreign Office. In the absence of Lord Palmerston he was received by Mr. Addington, at whose request he drew up a memorandum which was submitted to the Foreign Secretary. Wiseman began the memorandum by emphasizing the liberal character of the new pontificate. 'It has been too notorious a fact to require repetition,' he wrote, 'that from the very beginning of his pontificate His Holiness Pius IX commenced a series of important reforms, extending to almost every department of internal government, and tending essentially to modify the system of his immediate predecessor,' and he went on to enumerate some of these reforms; the act of general amnesty, revision of the penal code, formation of a Council of Ministers, the grant of greater liberty to the press, the extension and improvement of the education of the poor, and other similar innovations like the construction of a railway from the Modenese frontier to the border of the Kingdom of Naples, a project the very thought of which had horrified Gregory XVI, who always referred to the railway as the *chemin d'enfer*. He then went on to depict the Pope's dilemma between the more extreme liberals who seemed 'impatient of every, even necessary, delay' and the 'partisans of the late order of things'—the Austrian party, in fact—of whom, at the moment, the Pope appeared to stand in greater dread. This second party, wrote Wiseman 'has clearly relied on the avowed disapprobation by Austria of the papal reforms . . . as well as the marked hostility of most of the smaller states of Italy, so as not only to thwart, by many indirect means, the effectual carrying out of His Holiness's benevolent designs, but to show themselves

144

ready to resort even to violence or tumult to effect this purpose'. The Holy See no longer possessed the confidence of the French Government as 'the remarks of M. Guizot on the subject of Austria, in the French Chamber, seem to give ground for suspicion that there is a secret understanding between the two Governments, perhaps assigning to each its sphere of unchecked interference, or at any rate precluding France from manifesting such sympathy and offering such diplomatic support as might counterbalance the decided opposition of the Austrian Cabinet'. Now that the Papal Government, of its own accord, had adopted the reforms urged upon it by Great Britain in 1831, it might legitimately hope that Britain would help it to maintain these reforms in the face of the Austrian threat. In the present state of things in Italy the return of Austrian ascendancy could only come about by force of arms: 'the rousing of the Italian spirit even in Tuscany is the strongest evidence of this truth'. Thus a conflict seemed inevitable save for the intervention such as he now solicited from Her Majesty's Government, 'that of a wise forbearance . . . with such just and admitted countenance as will serve to check the violence of parties, and preserve a balance between possibly contending interests'. The fruits of this 'fair and generous policy,' Wiseman contended, would soon be manifest, and he summed them up in terms calculated to appeal to the known sympathies of Lord Palmerston—sympathies, in this respect, which Wiseman heartily shared. 'There is every reason to hope that the enlightened views adopted and courageously pursued by the present Pope, if supported, will tend not only to secure great happiness to his own subjects, but to free Italy from a grievous danger, and to procure for it solid and enduring advantages.'[1]

The result of Wiseman's memorandum was that Lord Minto, a member of the Government, was sent to Italy as Minister Plenipotentiary, but as the state of law in England prohibited the accrediting of an ambassador from the descendant of Elizabeth I to the descendant of Pius V, his status in Rome was to be that of 'an authentic organ of the British Government, enabled to declare its views and explain its sentiments upon events which are now passing in Italy, and which, both from their local importance and from

---

[1] The full text of Wiseman's memorandum is given in Ward, Vol. I, Appendix A, and in Chapter XVI, pp. 481-4.

their bearing on the general interests of Europe, Her Majesty's Government are watching with great attention and anxiety.'[1] The presence of Lord Minto gave Pius IX an opportunity to show him the draft for the Bull restoring the hierarchy, the contents of which the Minister passed on in his reports to Lord John Russell, the Prime Minister, information which the latter appeared to receive with complete indifference. Indeed, in discussing relations with the Holy See in Parliament, the Prime Minister had declared that the spiritual authority of the Pope over English Catholics must be left unfettered. In other respects Lord Minto's mission tended to be more of an embarrassment to the Pope than a help, for he constantly associated himself with the most advanced liberals and revolutionaries, and his presence did little either to aid the Pope or deter the Austrians, but merely encouraged those forces which were destined to set the Pope in flight from Rome before the year was out.

Wiseman remained in England, and his place in Rome was taken by Bishop Ullathorne, whose previous experience in negotiating the establishment of the Catholic hierarchy in Australia admirably fitted him for the job of completing the arrangements for the restoration in England. Ullathorne reached Rome early in 1848, having witnessed, on his journey there, some of the street fighting in Paris which had followed the abdication and flight of King Louis-Philippe, and had inaugurated the fateful year of Revolutions. The situation in France was reflected in one of Wiseman's first public acts as Pro-Vicar Apostolic of the London District, when, on 4th July 1848, he opened St. George's Church at Southwark, which had been built from Pugin's designs as a Cathedral for the London District. Two hundred and forty priests and fourteen bishops attended the ceremony, including the Bishops of Tournai, Liège, Luxembourg and Trêves. It was a great demonstration of the new state of Catholicism in England, and an added significance was given to the occasion by the fact that the church, the greatest yet built for Catholic worship since the Reformation, stood on the site which had been the chief centre of the Gordon Riots sixty-eight years before. But a note of sadness was introduced into the triumph naturally felt at such an event by the absence of Monsignor Affre,

---

[1] *Vide* 'Correspondence respecting the Affairs of Italy, 1846–47, Presented to both Houses of Parliament July 1849.' Quoted by Ward, Vol. I, p. 485.

the Archbishop of Paris, whose death on the barricades, while attempting to mediate between the opposing forces in the Paris uprising, had happened only a week before.

This stark reminder was not Wiseman's first experience of the calamity which then confronted France and was soon to spread through Europe. He had already visited the exiled French royal family at their English retreat. 'Among the accidents of my position,' he wrote to his mother on 26th April 1848, 'is my being brought into contact with persons whom I certainly never expected to have met. I little thought when I entertained the Duke of Bordeaux[1] and made Louis-Philippe very angry with me, that I should have to offer *him* consolation. Yet so it is. I drove to Claremont soon after his arrival. There was not a servant in waiting; but Mad. de Montjoye's maid took us up to her bedroom, and there we saw the ex-king and queen. Poor Louis-Philippe was sadly broken down, seemed quite lost and vacant, and asked for our prayers. The Queen is certainly a saint—fully resigned, forgiving everyone. "*Je ne regrette,*" she said "*ni position, ni richesse, ni honneurs, si je puis assurer le Salut de mon âme, c'est la seule chose que je désire.*" Her only anxiety is about her children, and that for their souls only. I have seen her several times since; as I have gone to say Mass for her and given her communion as well as the Duchess of Namours, the Princess Clementina, etc. The queen says, if she is ill none shall attend her but myself; and they express themselves very grateful for my little attentions.'[2]

Meanwhile in Rome Dr. Ullathorne was bringing the negotiations for the hierarchy to their conclusion. The Pope had insisted on Bishop Walsh moving to London, despite his plea to remain in the Central District on account of his extreme age, so that he could become the first Archbishop with Wiseman as his coadjutor with right of succession, while Ullathorne was himself transferred to the important Central District. England was to be divided into twelve dioceses under Westminster as the Archiepiscopal See, forming all that part of the old London District which lay north of the Thames, while the area south of the river was to form the diocese of Southwark. With the aid of Dr. Ullathorne and Dr. Grant, the

---

[1] Charles X's son had visited Wiseman when he was President of Oscott.
[2] Fano Papers.

Rector of the English College, the Letters Apostolic were prepared by Monsignor Barnabò and Monsignor Palma, and when Ullathorne left to inform the English bishops, at their meeting at Manchester, of all that he had accomplished, the Bull only required its formal promulgation by the Holy Father. By this document, called *Universalis Ecclesiae*, normal hierarchical government was restored at last to the English Church, bringing it into line with the usual functioning of the Catholic Church throughout Europe. One clause, however, showed that the Congregation of Propaganda had not entirely relinquished its hold on the old English Mission, which it had governed for nearly three hundred years. 'We command,' the Letters Apostolic stated in the name of the Pope, 'the aforesaid Archbishop and bishops, to send, at appointed times, to the Congregation of the Propaganda, reports of the state of their churches, and to be diligent in informing Propaganda of everything which they shall think profitable for the spiritual good of their flocks. We will continue, in effect, to use the ministry of this congregation in everything which concerns the churches in England.' In this clause, which remained in force until early in the twentieth century, the voices of Gregory XVI and Cardinal Acton were heard for the last time.

If all now seemed ready at last for the long awaited establishment of the hierarchy, yet another disappointment and delay was in store for the English Catholics. Scarcely had Bishop Ullathorne left Rome than revolution broke out. Monsignor Palma, who had been so important a figure in the negotiations, was shot dead as he stood by an open window and Count Rossi, the Pope's chief minister, was assassinated on the steps of the Papal Chancellory. On the 24th of November, 1848, the Pope left his palace by a side entrance in the dress of a simple priest, and fled to safety at Gaeta in the Kingdom of Naples. The Letters Apostolic restoring the English hierarchy remained unsigned.

Until the Pope could return to Rome the English Catholics had to wait in patience for the fulfilment of their hopes. In March 1849 Bishop Walsh died, and Wiseman at last came into full possession of the London District. The death of this fine old bishop, who from the very first had given help and encouragement to the younger man when only misunderstanding and frustration seemed to emanate from other quarters, was a deep personal loss to Wiseman, and helped to contribute to the feeling of isolation he was so often to feel. 'You have heard, no doubt, of poor Dr. Walsh's holy death,' he wrote to his sister. 'It was a trying time for me; for though we might have expected such an event at any time, still it came upon us suddenly. He was so much better for some time before, that I gave him three or four more years of life, and we went on very happily together. However, we saw him begin very suddenly to break: his mind appeared to fail, and I feared rather a long protracted state of mental feebleness, than any sudden change in his bodily health. However, Providence for his happiness decreed otherwise, and a few days illness ended in a calm and holy end. I remained at his side to the last, and he was sensible nearly to the last moment.'[1] The death of Bishop Walsh meant that Wiseman would now almost certainly become the first Archbishop as soon as events made it possible for the Pope to promulgate his Bull of restoration.

Meanwhile the work of the District presented a picture of continual growth and activity. 'It is hard perhaps to describe in a letter what is going on,' Wiseman wrote to his old friend Dr. Newsham at the beginning of 1850. 'Externally something can be seen: e.g. in less than two years we have established—and, I hope, solidly—seven new communities of women and three of men, in this District; have opened two orphan-houses; have set up an excellent middle-school, or grammar-school, containing 70 boys already: have opened four new missions in the heart of the poor population, and at least seven others in different parts. This year I have a good prospect of four great establishments springing up in London. Yet all this I consider as nothing compared with what I hope is latently and spiritually being done. The vast increase of communions, the numbers of admirable conversions, the spread of devotional and charitable associations, the increased piety of the faithful in every class, are less known, though still manifest to all. I think I can safely say that in a year or little more, 15,000 persons have been reclaimed by the Retreats given in courts and alleys, etc. In one place, the very worst street of London, we boldly planted a mission among thieves and prostitutes, and, though the devil interrupted the work by causing the stairs to break, etc., the change was so visible, that a Protestant policeman asked if it would not go on again,

[1] Fano Papers.

and observed that the Government "ought to support it". But it is in the clergy that I have found my greatest consolation. You may suppose my views and thoughts were not at first well understood. Indeed, I felt almost alone. But, thank God, I believe I have now a hearty co-operation almost everywhere.' It was work of which he could indeed be proud, but in the vast, teeming, slum-ridden mass of nineteenth-century London, there were moments when the problems seemed almost beyond solution. 'I assure you,' he concluded the same letter, 'that at times I am inclined to feel low and dejected, at thinking and seeing how much there is to be done which is neglected. In one district alone we have 5,000 children to educate, and accommodation for only 400. We want a thousand things, which our wretched poverty prevents us from having. Pray for me, as your old pupil, my dear Dr. Newsham, and beg for much grace for me. For at times I feel ready to sink beneath the burthen.'[1]

But for all the moments of dejection to which he was increasingly subject, Wiseman now felt that he was at last fulfilling to the utmost the resolutions which had made him abandon an academic career and devote his life to the conversion of England. The dream so long cherished was now come true and he stood in the most influential position in the Catholic life of England; he was conscious of solid and even spectacular achievement already accomplished; he looked forward with eagerness to further triumphs when he should take his place at the head of the restored hierarchy. Pius IX had returned to Rome in April, 1850, and it could only be a matter of months before the Letters Apostolic would be published. To preside over the new hierarchy would be to Wiseman not only the fulfilment of aspirations long held by all the leading Catholics, but would be a personal triumph for himself as representing the final approval of the Holy See for all that he had done, against considerable opposition, to instil new life into the Catholic Church in England.

Thus it was with dismay that Wiseman learnt, in a letter from Cardinal Antonelli, the new Papal Secretary of State, that Pius IX had decided to raise him to the Sacred College of Cardinals, for it meant that he would have to abandon his work in England and live once more in Rome, it appearing clear that the Pope had nominated him to fill the place left by the death of Acton as English Cardinal

[1] Ward, Vol. I, pp. 516–17.

in curia. 'A painful secret' was how he described the news, which reached him in the month following the Pope's return, when he wrote to tell his friend Dr. Russell. 'The truth, then, is that I leave England (for ever) next month. In September the Consistory is to be held which binds me in golden fetters for life, and cuts off all my hopes, all my aspirations, all my life's wish to labour for England's conversion in England, in the midst of the strife with heresy, and the triumphs of the Church.'[1] He had written, he told his correspondent, 'as plainly and as strongly as one can about oneself,' to decline the great honour, but a 'peremptory answer' came that he was wanted at Rome and that a successor would be provided for him in London.

It seemed most probable that Dr. Ullathorne, the young and energetic Vicar Apostolic of the Central District, would be the successor appointed, and Wiseman went to see him where he resided at Birmingham in the house designed by Pugin, 'the most gloomy place I ever saw' as the lugubrious Dr. Bowden described it. Wiseman told the bishop that he expected to leave the shores of England for ever, and was deeply moved and distressed to think that his work in England was finished. Later on Dr. Ullathorne would refer to the interview, adding 'I have seen Dr. Wiseman in this room crying like a child.'[2] Rarely has the honour of a Cardinal's hat been accepted with such reluctance and resignation. Before leaving England for Rome Wiseman had an interview with Lord John Russell to discuss various political matters of concern between the British Government and the Holy See. It is quite clear that he then believed that he would not be returning to England again. 'He gave Lord John Russell to understand,' Lord Houghton later spoke of this interview, 'that he himself was leaving England for good, to reside for the future in Rome itself.'[3]

[1] Ibid., p. 521.
[2] C. Butler: *Life and Times of Bishop Ullathorne*, Vol. I, p. 163.
[3] Ward, Vol. I, p. 525.

XII

Wiseman's feelings on learning of his nomination to the Sacred College were summed up in his comment to Dr. Russell: 'It was only in February '49 that, by the death of good Dr. Walsh, I first became properly a free agent, acting on my own responsibility, and in May 1850 I am again thrown back into a vague and indefinite position. This is even *humiliating*; for I own that, consulting one's human feelings, to stand at the helm in the capital of this Empire, in such a crisis, while the Church is bearing all before it, is a nobler position than to be one of a Congregation in which one may have the power of giving one vote in favour of the right.'[1] To Father Faber, who had been placed in charge of the new Oratory in London, he wrote: 'My only consolation has been, and is, that, according to S. Filippo's maxims, one cannot go wrong by obedience; and that in whatever befalls one there has been nothing but thorough opposition to self and renouncing of everything dear.' To take his mind off the sad thoughts he concentrated instead on the pleasures of the journey to Rome. 'That which I look forward to at present with the greatest pleasure,' he told his Vicar-General, 'is our journey to Rome in the little open carriage Searle has bought, when we can see and enjoy the country at our leisure, and in which I can have a store of books.' His attitude was, the Vicar-General thought, very like that of a boy's anticipation of his journey home at holiday time. 'I think I said so to him plainly at the time, and we laughed together over this puzzle of his mind and heart,' Dr. Whitty afterwards remembered, adding that 'in many respects he remained a child all his life'.[2] That Wiseman did not

[1] Ward, Vol. I, p. 522. [2] Ibid., p. 523.

152

expect to return is further shown by the remark he made to his cousin Sir Charles McCarthy: 'When you have done governing the various quarters of the world, come and visit me in my Roman palazzo.'

Wiseman left London on August 16th. His journey took him through Paris where, two years previously, his friend Lacordaire, dressed in his Dominican habit, had taken his seat as a deputy of the Left in the Constituent Assembly, in the brief false dawn of Liberal Catholic hopes. That hope had faded fast and finally died when Pius IX had returned from his exile cured of his liberal leanings, while now a Bonaparte prince once more guided the destiny of France. Louis-Napoleon was then trying to gain the support of the Church by sending armed assistance to maintain the Pope in the Papal States, an act that was later to complicate his Italian policy and contribute, indirectly, to his own downfall twenty years later; while Pius's preoccupation in upholding his sovereignty in these same states was to turn him, and those who, like Wiseman, supported him in his temporal claims, from the liberalism that had marked the beginning of his reign and had seemed likely, for a moment, to place him in the vanguard of the political movement of 1848, to a conservatism that might almost have won the grudging approval of Prince Metternich. The feeling that Pius had abandoned the Liberal cause was to tell against both him and Wiseman in England in the months ahead, for the same Government was in power there as had, at Wiseman's intercession, sent Lord Minto out to assist the Pope in implementing his liberal reforms so short a time before. No longer did sympathetic Englishmen look upon Pius IX as 'the most enlightened sovereign of the age'.

But whatever Englishmen may have thought of the Pope, there is no doubt that the Catholic clergy of the London District, and, indeed, of England in general, were aghast when they realized that they were to lose Dr. Wiseman. Many of them had objected to the Roman and Italian ideas which he had introduced in the face of the old traditions of pre-emancipation days, many had resented the retreats and other new measures of discipline that he advocated, or considered that he showed too much favouritism to the converts and the monastic orders; but all were agreed that he and he only had the authority and ability to head the new hierarchy which was now clearly to be established. He stood in pre-eminence above all other candidates; his reputation as a scholar, as a controversialist, and as a figure of international repute, made him the only possible person to become the first Archbishop of the Catholic Church in England. As Wiseman crossed Europe appeals and petitions followed him begging the Pope to send him back to England to lead the Church in this critical hour in her history.

In Rome there was another powerful advocate who could be relied upon to press Wiseman's claims in the most influential quarters. This was Monsignor George Talbot, who had recently taken up his post at the Vatican as confidential advisor to the Pope on English affairs, and who had quickly won the friendship of Pius IX. Abbot Butler has described him as 'a well-meaning, fussy man ... of almost childlike simplicity, with a love of managing things and persons, from the Pope downwards',[1] which is perhaps a charitable description of one who was to become an inveterate schemer wholly incapable of appreciating any point of view but his own. Talbot was the fifth son of Lord Talbot of Malahide and had been converted to the Catholic faith by Wiseman in 1846. After being ordained to the priesthood he had worked at St. George's, Southwark, and it was while he was still there that Wiseman had suggested to him that he should go to Rome. When one considers the influence he was later to wield at the Papal Court it is interesting to note that at first he strongly opposed Wiseman's plan to send him there and only accepted in obedience to Wiseman's direct request. 'Notwithstanding your kind advice and my resolution to abide by your decision,' he had written to Wiseman at the time, 'I have since last night firmly resolved to give up my expedition to Rome *entirely*, and nothing but an express command from the *Pope* or *you* could make me change my mind. I set the example of St. Aloysius before me who was tried exactly in the same way as I have been during the past week. He was offered the highest dignities of the Church and he refused them because they endangered the success of his work. When I think, my dear Dr. Wiseman, of the good I have already been instrumental in doing under your kind direction in London, when I think of what a field there is for further exertions (only last week I have induced four educated people to submit to the Church)

[1] Butler: *Life of Ullathorne*, Vol. I, p. 227.

I think I shall have a severe threat on the day of judgement to under-go, if I relinquish my post in order to obtain a higher position in the world, or to gratify any personal ambition I may have to be on terms of intimacy with the Pope.'[1] Despite the edifying example of St. Aloysius, Talbot was persuaded to go to Rome, and there his ambition to be on terms of intimacy with the Pope was remarkably fulfilled. 'His influence,' Abbot Butler continues, 'was great—he once said he would rather not be a Cardinal, for he could, as he was, exercise more influence than any Cardinal. He surely overestimated his power over Pius, but there can be no question it was very real and very effective.' As the appeals for Wiseman's return to England began to reach the Vatican we may be sure that this real and effective influence was exerted fully in their support.

Wiseman reached Rome on September 5th, and had an audience with the Pope on the very same day, and with the Secretary of State, Cardinal Antonelli, on the day following. At these interviews Wiseman learnt for the first time that he might be returning to England after all. A week later he could write to his friend Henry Bagshawe of the possibility of a double triumph, the restoration of the hierarchy and his own return at the head of it: 'On my arrival I found the Pope, all the Cardinals, and Propaganda of the same mind, that if possible, and if compatible with the Cardinalitial dignity, I ought to return. The addresses and letters received here have done much, good Mr. Talbot still more, and the Pope had expressed himself as considering it a matter of conscience.'[2] By the end of the month all was settled. On September 29th the Pope's Brief re-establishing the hierarchy was proclaimed, and Wiseman was named Archbishop of Westminster. On the next day the Consistory was held at which he was nominated a Cardinal of the Holy Roman Church.

The next few days were taken up with the ceremonies by which a Prince of the Church is inaugurated to his high dignity. First came the bestowal of the red cap or *berretta*, on which occasion Wiseman was chosen to return thanks to the Pontiff on behalf of the newly created Cardinals. During the following three days the princes and nobility of Rome called to present their congratulations, accom-panied by their wives. 'On these occasions,' the correspondent of

---

[1] Letter dated 27th May 1850. Southwark Archives.   [2] Ward, Vol. I, p. 526.

The Times noted, 'there is generally a grand display of the diamonds of the noble Roman families, and curiosity is attracted by the brilliant jewels of the Torlonias and the splendid heirlooms of the Doria, Borghese, Rospigliosi and others.' After these compliments had been paid and received the new Cardinals returned to the Vatican for the final rites. 'At an early hour the new Cardinals take the oaths in the Sistine Chapel, whilst the other Cardinals assemble in the Sala Ducale, or hall of the Consistories, near the chapel,' ran the report in the *Times*, remarkably sympathetic in comparison with the abuse it was soon to shower on the head of the English Cardinal: 'the new Cardinals are introduced, and kneeling receive the red hat from the Pope, with an admonition that its colour is to remind them that they are to be ready if necessary to shed their blood for the Church. They are then embraced by their colleagues and take their place among them. The *Te Deum* is afterwards sung whilst the new Cardinals are prostrate on the floor.'

The elation which Wiseman felt when his return to England was assured was all the greater in comparison with the dejection he had previously felt, when the assumption of a Cardinal's hat had seemed like the end of his chosen work in England; work for the sake of which he had already once sacrificed the promise of a brilliant career in Rome. The mingled feelings of relief and triumph—relief that his work in England was not over but was to be continued with all the added authority which his new dignity conferred upon him; and triumph that at long last the restoration of the hierarchy had been achieved and his own work in England crowned with approval from the very Vicar of Christ—all this made Wiseman's ebullient nature overflow in spontaneous expressions of exultation when he thought of the new life which the Pope's action would bring to the Catholic Church in England. In this state of *hubris* he dashed off his Pastoral Letter, dated October 7th—'out of the Flaminian Gate of Rome'—to announce the restoration of the hierarchy and his own appointment as Cardinal-Archbishop to the Catholic population of his new diocese. The Pastoral was despatched at once, and five days later he himself began his slow journey back to London.

Wiseman's passage across Europe was something of a triumphal progress—to begin with. He reached Florence on October 15th, and the next day continued on to Siena where the court of the Grand Duke of Tuscany was then in residence. His reception by the royal family was nothing if not flattering. To Henry Bagshawe he wrote: 'Yesterday I went to Siena to dine with the Archduke and family, who received me with highest honours, with full Court, and placed me in the centre of the table, the Duke and Duchess on either side. This is considered a matter of some importance, as no Cardinal has ever been permitted in Tuscany (and none is remembered to have dined at Court) because of the dispute of precedence between a reigning Duke and a Cardinal. The point has now been decided, as the precedence was fully afforded to me; and today the Grand Duke has himself written to his ministers to give them a full account of what was done.'[1] Wiseman from the first was determined to keep up his state as a Cardinal, though the financial outlay which this would involve was a problem, when every penny raised in England was needed for the work of the Church. Before leaving Rome, however, he had already had some help on this point from the devoted Monsignor Talbot. 'I have had a confidential conversation with His Holiness this evening about your circumstances in a financial point of view,' Talbot had written, 'and I took the opportunity of expressing to him exactly how you stand, and what your prospects are of a contribution being made for you in London. The Holy Father in a most generous manner said that he willingly would do all in his power to assist you, and had made up his mind to allow you two thousand *scudi*[2] a year for a few years while you reside in London, and he desired me to write to you confidentially to notify to you this his intention before he speaks to you about it himself.'[3]

From Florence Wiseman continued his journey to Venice, where he dined with the Cardinal-Patriarch on October 27th, before proceeding by ship to Trieste, and thence to Vienna. At the capital of the Austrian Empire he continued to be accorded the most flattering attention. He was twice received in audience by the Emperor and dined with him on November 1st. But it was in Vienna that the feeling of a triumphal progress came to an end. The news of the Pope's action both in restoring the hierarchy and in creating Dr. Wiseman Archbishop of Westminster had by then reached England where its reception had been flattering neither to

[1] Ward, Vol. I, p. 531.   [2] A Papal *scudo* in 1850 was the approximate equivalent of one English sovereign.   [3] Southwark Archives.

the new Cardinal nor to the Sovereign Pontiff. The unpleasant news came to Wiseman like an icy wind after basking in the languorous sunshine of Italy. 'I was driving through the town, leaning back in my carriage, full of satisfaction at the events of the past month and reading my *Times*,' he later told a friend, 'when I received a rude shock as I saw my name in the leading article.'

In a malicious and vituperative attack *The Times* poured abuse upon the Cardinal and the new hierarchy. That Wiseman should have been given a red hat did not offend: 'It is no concern of ours,' the article declared, 'whether Dr. Wiseman chooses in Rome to be ranked with the Monsignori of the capital. He is simply at Rome in the position of an English subject, who has thought fit to enter the service of a foreign Power and accept its spurious dignities.' What rankled in the Protestant bosom of the Editor of *The Times* was that the Pope should have been 'pleased to erect the city of Westminster into an archbishopric and to appoint Dr. Wiseman to that see'. The thought of this liberty on the part of the Pope caused the Editor to thunder with all his guns. 'If this appointment be not intended as a clumsy joke,' he wrote, 'we confess that we can only regard it as one of the grossest acts of folly and impertinence which the Court of Rome has ventured to commit since the Crown and people of England threw off its yoke'. Having delivered himself of this invective against what was soon to be termed 'The Papal Aggression', the Editor concluded with a veiled threat against the unfortunate subject of his attack. 'The Pope and his advisers have mistaken our complete tolerance for indifference to their designs; they have mistaken the renovated zeal of the Church in this country for a return towards Romish bondage; but we are not sorry their indiscretion has led them to show the power which Rome would exercise if she could, by an act which the laws of this country will never recognize, and which the public opinion of this country will deride and disavow, whenever His Grace the titular Archbishop of Westminster thinks fit to enter his diocese.'[1]

It is difficult to imagine the effect which this article must have had upon the Cardinal. Though the injustice of it must have hurt him deeply, another thought must have risen in his mind and caused him equal pain. It was also the answer of those among the English

[1] *The Times*, Monday, 14th October 1850.

Catholic body who had always criticized him for presssing ahead too fast, for refusing to countenance the vast residue of anti-Catholic feeling dormant in the English masses, but ready at any moment to spring to life; it was the answer of those who ridiculed his belief that the Church of England had abandoned her old anti-Roman bias and was ready, as Phillipps de Lisle was always declaring, to look upon Rome with a new sympathetic understanding as a prelude to corporate reunion. The article in *The Times* came as a double blow, directly from his enemies without the fold, and indirectly from those within. The article had resulted from the anger felt at the Pope's Brief restoring the hierarchy; Wiseman's own Pastoral had not yet reached England. As he remembered the glowing terms in which that Letter was written the Cardinal must have realized that a new outburst was sure to be the result. But even had he wished to prevent the Pastoral from being published it was now too late. In fact it reached Dr. Whitty, the Vicar-General, two days after the first attack appeared in *The Times*.

Wiseman realized that his only course was to press on to England with all speed and face the situation in person. But first of all he wrote a letter to the Prime Minister whom he had left under the impression that his sojourn in Rome would be permanent. Russell had asked Wiseman to discover the feelings of the Holy See on the question of receiving a Minister from England on a special diplomatic mission, and Wiseman now made this subject the excuse for his letter. After dealing briefly with this point he referred at once to the question raised in *The Times*' inflammatory article. 'I cannot but deeply regret the erroneous and even distorted views which the English papers have presented of what the Holy See has done in regard to the spiritual government of the Catholics of England;' he wrote from Vienna on November 3rd, 'but I take the liberty of saying that the measure now promulgated was not only prepared but printed three years ago, and a copy of it was shown to Lord Minto by the Pope on occasion of an audience given to his Lordship by His Holiness. I have no right to intrude on your Lordship further in this matter beyond offering to give any explanation that your Lordship may desire, in full confidence that it will be in my power to remove particularly the offensive interpretation put upon the late act of the Holy See—that it was suggested by political views or by any hostile feelings. With regard to myself I beg to add that I am invested with a purely ecclesiastical dignity; that I have no secular or temporal delegation whatever; that my duties will be what they have ever been, to promote the morality of those committed to my charge, especially the masses of the poor; and to keep up those feelings of good-will and friendly intercommunion between Catholics and their fellow-countrymen which I flatter myself I have been the means of somewhat improving.'[1]

What Lord John Russell made of this letter is not known, but that his later exploitation of the situation was inspired by purely cynical and political motives is suggested by his calm and reassuring letter to Queen Victoria on the same question: 'Lord John Russell presents his humble duty to your Majesty: he has read with attention the letter of the Duchess of Norfolk. He has also read the Pope's Bull. It strikes him that the division into twelve territorial dioceses of eight ecclesiastical vicariates is not a matter to be alarmed at. The persons to be affected by this change must be already Roman Catholics before it can touch them. The matter to create national alarm is, as your Majesty says, the growth of Roman Catholic doctrines and practices within the bosom of the Church (of England). Dr. Arnold said very truly, "I look upon a Roman Catholic as an enemy in his uniform; I look upon a Tractarian as an enemy disguised as a spy".'[2]

Two days after the Prime Minister had written this letter to the Queen, Cardinal Wiseman's Pastoral was read in every Catholic Church in the new dioceses of Westminster and Southwark. *The Times*, meanwhile, had been keeping up its attack: 'Is it, then, here in Westminster, among ourselves and by the English throne,' the Editor demanded, 'that an Italian priest is to parcel out the spiritual dominion of this country—to employ the renegades of our National Church to restore a foreign usurpation over the consciences of men, and to sow divisions in our political society by an undisguised and systematic hostility to the institutions most nearly identified with our national freedom and our national faith? Such an intention must either be ludicrous or intolerable—either a

---

[1] Wiseman: *An Appeal to the Reason and Good Feeling of the English People*, p. 23. The letter to the Prime Minister is here quoted in full.
[2] *The Letters of Queen Victoria*, First Series, Vol. II, pp. 325-6.

delusion of some fanatical brain or treason to the Constitution.'[1] Where the Editor discovered this 'undisguised and systematic hostility' to the cherished institutions of national freedom or national faith, to neither of which there was the slightest reference in the Papal Brief, it is difficult to say, but it was in the atmosphere stirred up by this open hostility on the part of the Editor of *The Times* and the other newspapers that followed his lead, that Wiseman's Pastoral was read and widely reported. Few documents could have been worded in a manner so inappropriate to the occasion.

The language in which Wiseman announced the hierarchy to the clergy and laity of his diocese must have seemed fulsome enough to those who listened to it with sympathetic ears.[2] It began with a flourish. 'Nicholas, by the Divine mercy, of the Holy Roman Church by the title of St. Pudentiana Cardinal Priest, Archbishop of Westminster, and Administrator Apostolic of the Diocese of Southwark: To our dearly beloved in Christ, the Clergy secular and regular, and the Faithful of the said Archdiocese and Diocese: Health and Benediction in the Lord!' The Cardinal followed this by announcing his return to England; 'now do we embrace you in our Lord Jesus Christ with more tender emotions of parental love; now doth our soul yearn, and our mouth is open to you, though words must fail to express what we feel on being once again permitted to address you'. The reason for which he had been 'not so much permitted as commissioned to return' was because 'his Holiness Pope Pius IX was graciously pleased to issue his Letters Apostolic, under the Fisherman's Ring, conceived in terms of great weight and dignity, wherein he substituted for the eight Apostolic Vicariates heretofore existing, one archiepiscopal or metropolitan and twelve episcopal sees . . .' Then followed the paragraph that was to give such great offence, so much, indeed, that it was said that Queen Victoria, on reading the passage, exclaimed, 'Am I Queen of England or am I not?'[3] After describing how the Pope had been pleased to appoint him 'though most unworthy, to the archiepiscopal see of Westminster . . . giving us at the same time the administration of the episcopal see of Southwark' the Cardinal

---

[1] *The Times*, Saturday, 19th October 1850.
[2] For the full text of the Pastoral see Appendix B.
[3] Bernard Ward: *Sequel to Catholic Emancipation*, Vol. II, p. 287.

went on to add 'so that at present and till such time as the Holy See shall think fit otherwise to provide, we govern, and shall continue to govern, the Counties of Middlesex, Hertford, and Essex as ordinary thereof, and those of Surrey, Sussex, Kent, Berkshire, and Hampshire with the islands annexed, as administrator with ordinary jurisdiction'. Then, after announcing his own elevation to the rank of Cardinal, Wiseman concluded this passage of the Pastoral in the following words: 'The great work, then, is complete; what you have long desired and prayed for is granted. Your beloved country has received a place among the fair Churches, which, normally constituted, form the splendid aggregate of Catholic Communion; Catholic England has been restored to its orbit in the ecclesiastical firmament, from which its light had long vanished, and begins now anew its course of regularly adjusted action round the centre of unity, the source of jurisdiction, of light, and of vigour.' Then, after various instructions for the offering of thanksgiving, the Cardinal concluded his Pastoral Letter with a flourish similar to that with which it had opened: 'Given out of the Flaminian Gate of Rome, this seventh day of October in the year of our Lord MDCCCL.'

If the Editor of *The Times* had wanted more fuel for his fire he could scarcely have desired a more inflammable morsel nor have received it from so unexpected a quarter. The Pastoral was published in full in his newspaper on the Tuesday after it was delivered. On Wednesday, October 30th, the Editor expressed his opinion of it in no uncertain terms. The passage to which he took particular exception was that in which the Cardinal had referred to the Church in England as being 'restored to its orbit in the ecclesiastical firmament'. 'We are at a loss,' the leader proclaimed, 'for an appropriate term to characterize as it deserves such a mixture of blasphemy and absurdity, and we prefer to leave our readers to pass their own judgement on such a passage, and on the creed which dictated it. It assumes that England as a nation (and this, too, is the language of an Englishman!) once vanished from the ecclesiastical firmament, and rejected the religion of God; it affirms with equal arrogance that because a Cardinal Priest by the title of St. Pudentiana has usurped an imaginary see of Westminster, England as a nation is restored to Christian Existence, and that Christ himself is coming out of the grave. We are not aware that the misuse of language ever reached a more frightful perversion.'

When Wiseman had gone, with a deputation of English residents, to take leave of the Pope before returning to England, Pius IX had addressed them in these words: 'I had not intended sending the new Cardinal back to England; I had thought of retaining him near my own person, and of profiting by his counsels. But I perceived that the proper moment was come for executing the great enterprise for which you have come to return me thanks. I do not think there will be anything to apprehend in consequence. I spoke of it at the time to Lord Minto, and I understood that the English government would not oppose the execution of my design. I send back, therefore, to England the eminent Cardinal, and I invite you all to pray unceasingly, that the Lord will remove all difficulties, and that he will lead in to the Church a million—three millions of your fellow-countrymen still separated from us, to the end that he may cause them all to enter, even to the last man.'[1] Wiseman had set out with those calm and reasonable words ringing in his ears. How little can either he or Pius have imagined at that solemn moment what a storm their words would create in the land to which he was returning.

[1] Bernard Ward: *Sequel to Catholic Emancipation*, Vol. II, p. 284.

XIII

There can be no doubt that the ugly situation which resulted from the hostile reaction to the Pope's Bull was made considerably worse by the publication of Wiseman's Pastoral. It would clearly have been wiser to have held it up until the Cardinal returned, when it could have been rephrased in tone with the prevailing atmosphere of anti-Catholic feeling which, as will be shown, the Government was doing its best to encourage. Unfortunately Dr. Whitty, to whom, as Vicar-General, the Pastoral had been sent, was lacking in experience and, if he was to obey the instructions contained in it and cause it to be read on the Sunday after it reached England, had no time in which to consult his more experienced colleagues. 'A mere glance through it created a most perplexing question whether it should be published then or not,' he later wrote: 'It was evidently written by the Cardinal in the exulting joy of his Catholic heart, without a thought of Protestant readers, and without the faintest suspicion of the terrific storm of Protestant feeling which the news of the hierarchy would create. Every day symptoms of the coming storm were speedily becoming more unmistakable. It was then impossible to communicate with the Cardinal. . . . Thus the publication of the Pastoral or its postponement till the arrival of the Cardinal himself, became an enormous difficulty. On the one hand, the Pastoral had reached me in the legitimate way, and Catholics throughout England were daily expecting some word from the Cardinal, especially in face of the hostility which the news of the Pope's action had aroused. I felt sure I could not withhold it without a clear obligation of duty. Still less could I dare suppress or tamper with any of its expressions at my own discretion. On the

164

other hand, not a few were beginning to apprehend a repetition of the Gordon riots, and no one could say what occasion might be seized upon. I was alone and had no one whom I could consult, and the decision had to be come to at once. After a short prayer for light I decided on publishing the Pastoral just as it was.'[1]

Among those on the Catholic side who considered the publication most inopportune was Dr. Ullathorne, who, under the new hierarchy, had been named Bishop of Birmingham. As soon as he read it he came up to London and interviewed the Vicar-General. 'I asked him: "How could you publish that Pastoral?" ' the Bishop wrote in his memoirs,[2] ' "You must have known that Cardinal Wiseman never contemplated the state of things amidst which it was destined to appear; and that, had he known what was going on, he would not have written in that style." He said: "I am young and inexperienced, and in my perplexity did not know what to do, so I thought it best to obey the instruction within it, that it should be read in the churches on the Sunday following its arrival." I asked him why, in an affair of such importance which involved our common interests, he had not taken the advice of some of the senior Bishops before doing so. He said he had not thought of that.'

Dr. Ullathorne might have added that the Cardinal should have known all along that the tone and language of his Pastoral would be bound to antagonize Protestant opinion, even if the Papal Bull had not already done so. It was a fatal miscalculation on Wiseman's part. Other Catholics went even further in criticism of him. From Naples, where it might be thought he was a little out of touch with the situation in England, Lord Shrewsbury wrote in a critical spirit of the whole business of restoring a Catholic hierarchy, and in particular of the part played in it by Wiseman. 'It was, I fear,' he wrote to Phillipps de Lisle, 'and *every one* thinks, very ill-judged of Cardinal Wiseman to return *as Cardinal*. It was enough for him to be Archbishop of Westminster. It was, I fancy, all his own doing, for certainly the Pope intended him to remain at Rome. It has added to the excitement very considerably.'[3]

As the feeling against Wiseman and against the 'Papal aggression'

[1] Ward, Vol. I, pp. 541–2.
[2] W. B. Ullathorne: *From Cabin Boy to Archbishop*, p. 296.
[3] Purcell: *Life of Ambrose Phillipps de Lisle*, Vol. I, p. 327.

began to grow the Prime Minister's attitude of Olympian detachment, which had characterized his letter to Queen Victoria, underwent a complete change. The Bishop of Durham had written a letter protesting to him against the 'aggression' of the Pope and in his reply Lord John Russell used language which he must have known would excite public feeling still more and could be paralleled for irresponsibility, if a parallel were required, only by the language of Wiseman's Pastoral itself:

'There is an assumption of power in all the documents which have come from Rome,' Lord John replied to the Bishop of Durham on November 4th, 'a pretension to supremacy over the realm of England, and a claim to sole and undivided sway, which is inconsistent with the Queen's supremacy, with the rights of our bishops and clergy, and with the spiritual independence of the nation, as asserted even in Roman Catholic times. I confess, however, that my alarm is not equal to my indignation.

'Even if it shall appear that the ministers and servants of the Pope in this country have not transgressed the law, I feel persuaded that we are strong enough to repel any outward attacks. The liberty of Protestantism has been enjoyed too long in England to allow of any successful attempt to impose a foreign yoke upon our minds and consciences. No foreign prince or potentate will be permitted to fasten his fetters upon a nation which has so long and so nobly vindicated its rights to freedom of opinion, civil, political and religious.

'Upon this subject, then, I will only say that the present state of the law shall be carefully examined, and the propriety of adopting any proceedings with reference to the recent assumptions of power deliberately considered.'

The Prime Minister concluded his letter with an attack on Tractarian practices in the Anglican Church, declaring, rather surprisingly after the emphasis he had given to 'Papal aggression'—'what, then, is the danger to be apprehended from a foreign prince of no great power, compared to the danger within the gates from the unworthy sons of the Church of England herself?'[1]

One must remember, when reading this letter, that Lord John Russell had known of the Pope's intention to restore the Catholic

[1] Ward, Vol. I, p. 547.

hierarchy for at least three years, and that the Brief of Restoration had been shown to Lord Minto, who had reported its contents to the Prime Minister; yet only now did he see fit to talk in terms of 'a pretension to supremacy over the realm of England' which, in fact, nothing in the Papal Brief, addressed solely to Catholics, could possibly imply. Nor is it easy to understand how he could hope to vindicate freedom of opinion 'civil, political and religious' when the last of these freedoms, the right to organize their own religious body according to its own known laws, should be denied to Catholics whose intentions in this regard had been known to the Government since Lord Minto's mission to the Pope. The matter was, in fact, one of domestic concern to the Catholic community, to whom, and only to whom, both Bull and Pastoral were addressed. The press, led by *The Times*, had distorted this into a national issue, and the Prime Minister now condoned the distortion by accepting, in his letter to the Bishop of Durham, the notion of 'Papal aggression' which the popular press had fostered.

It is difficult to discover Lord John Russell's exact motive in thus deliberately stirring up public opinion against the Roman Catholic community. It is true that, with other Liberals, he shared in the disappointment felt in the abandonment of the cause of political liberalism by Pius IX, and he may also have believed that Wiseman had consciously misled him into supposing that he would not be returning from Rome; and that his reappearance now, clothed in the Roman purple and at the head of a new hierarchy, took on the nature of a plot of which he, the Prime Minister, had been the dupe. But to view the matter in the nature of a personal quarrel between the two men is plainly out of the question; though the thought of such a clash of personalities between the diminutive Prime Minister who, after espousing the widow of Lord Ribblesdale, had been dubbed by the London wits as the Widow's Mite, and the tall, obese Cardinal to whom an Irish servant was later to give the title of 'Your Immense', is entertaining if not realistic.

That Russell regarded himself as the champion of Protestantism can also be dismissed, for if this had been the case he would surely have opposed the restoration of the hierarchy long before this; whereas, in actual fact, his public statements had previously been quite favourable to the Catholic Church, as Wiseman was later to show. But to seek either consistency or altruism in a professional statesman at a time of political crisis is perhaps to expect too much, for at the end of this year 1850 Lord John Russell's government was in such a low state that anything that would direct the gaze of the public away from itself must have been considered as most welcome. In the agitation over 'Papal aggression' the Prime Minister must have grasped at the chance to turn the tide of opinion in his favour by posing as the champion of Church and State against the demon of foreign domination. If this was indeed his hope, he was disappointed in it, for next year his Government fell.

Meanwhile his cry of a Papist plot was taken up by the Anglican episcopate who petitioned the Queen against 'this attempt to subject our people to a spiritual tyranny from which they were freed at the Reformation', while the same idea ran through their public pronouncements. 'We trace in some of the phrases,' Wilfrid Ward wrote,[1] 'the surviving conception of the plotting Jesuit which had existed in full force since the days of Elizabeth. The Archbishop of Canterbury describes the Catholic priesthood as "subtle, skilful, and insinuating". "We are not so degenerate," wrote the Archbishop of York, "as to be beguiled by the snare which (Rome's) ever-wakeful ambition is plotting for our captivity and ruin." The Bishop of London characterized the Roman Catholic priesthood as "emissaries of darkness". Sentiments never extinguished since the days of the Armada reappear in such expressions as "foreign bondage", used by the Bishop of Salisbury, or "foreign intruders" by the Bishop of Oxford; "a foreign prince insolent in his degradation" by the Bishop of Bangor.' The word 'aggression', which *The Times* had first used, was pounced upon with enthusiasm, and a host of episcopal pens vied with each other in the choice of epithets to describe it. Thus to his Lordship of Gloucester it was 'revolting and frightful'; the northern Primate, with some lack of imagination, contented himself with 'unparalleled'; the Bishop of London considered the aggression to be 'subtle', the Bishop of Oxford 'indecent', and the Bishop of Chichester 'audacious'. The Bishop of Hereford found the Pope's Bull 'a frivolous and contemptible document'. One is only left to wonder what this last prelate would have thought of 'Ideal' Ward's opinion when that robust convert announced: 'I should

[1] Ward, Vol. I, p. 549.

like a new Papal Bull every morning with my *Times* at breakfast.'[1]

The Prime Minister addressed his letter to the Bishop of Durham on November 4th. The next day was the anniversary of the Gunpowder Plot and it was made the occasion for violent outbreaks against the Catholics, and in particular against Cardinal Wiseman and the Pope, whose effigies were burnt at ceremonies all over the country. The account of the evening as it was celebrated at Ware is typical of what occurred in many other places. 'His Holiness Pio Nono was burnt in effigy on an eminence overlooking the town. The figure was dressed in full pontificals, with the triple crown on its head, and the addition of a large pair of ram's horns. In the wagon was a donkey, to represent his Excellency the Cardinal Archbishop of Westminster. After solemnly parading the streets, the effigy was escorted by a large concourse of people to Musley Hill, where it was solemnly suspended by the neck on a gallows erected over a huge pile of faggot-wood and tar-barrels, and then burnt amid the roars and execrations of the multitude.'[2] Lest official condonement should be lacking for these expressions of mob violence, the Lord Chancellor took the opportunity at a public meeting four days later to quote, amid wild applause, the highly inflammatory lines:

> Under our feet we'll stamp the Cardinal's hat,
> In spite of Pope or dignities of Church.

To the wilder excesses of the mob, who pelted Catholic priests and later threw stones at the windows of Wiseman's carriage, and to the encouragement which the Lord Chancellor's unhappily apt quotation would seem to give to such excesses, must be added the innumerable meetings of protest that were held in all parts of the country. One of these meetings was addressed by Mazzini, whose Republic had driven Pius from Rome and who himself had fled before the returning Pope. 'There exists great agitation at the present moment in Protestant England on account of the attempted encroachment of Catholicism,' he declared. 'Think you that these attempts would have taken place if the people's banner were still floating at Rome? Think you that the Pope would have sent his Catholic hierarchy from Gaeta?'[3] Russell was not the only man to

[1] *W. G. Ward and the Catholic Revival*, p. 14.   [2] Ward, Vol. I, p. 552.
[3] E. E. Y. Hales: *Pio Nono*, p. 106.

make political capital out of Wiseman and the Pope. In the peroration to his address at another such meeting, at which Admiral
Vernon Harcourt was in the chair, Dr. Cumming, a Presbyterian
divine, suggested his own solution to the problem which, if not
lacking in novelty, did little to calm the anger and panic to which the
exaggerated notion of 'Papal aggression' had given rise. 'What is it,
then, we are to do?' Dr. Cumming asked. 'Here is my proposal;
and I hope it may be taken down in the papers. Let our Queen and
our statesmen and our Parliament (and I think they will be pretty
united upon this), say to Pope Pius IX. "Take back your Bull."
I have looked into the whole system, and in proposing this I speak
with great caution and from clear knowledge. Let England's Queen
and Parliament and people say, "You, Pope Pius IX, are a foreign
sovereign. You have sent into this country a certain Bull, parcelling
it out (I don't care a fig what you call it, ecclesiastical, or spiritual,
or what); and you have divided it into districts. You have sent a
Bull for doing this. You take back that Bull; we bid you do so; or
as sure as you are alive, if you do not take it back, then every Bishop
that that Bull constitutes shall be put on board a 120-gun ship, with
Admiral Harcourt on the quarter-deck, and delivered to Italy duty
free. I am asking and suggesting what is reasonable." '[1] It was to face
this sort of 'reasonableness' that Cardinal Wiseman returned to
England on November 11th, to a country which had so far lost its
sense of reason in the hysteria of the moment that it was not considered shocking when one Anglican clergyman went so far as to
suggest that the death penalty should be invoked for the crime of
hearing a confession.[2]

The Cardinal's friends had at first thought of begging him to
remain abroad until the hostile feeling against him had died down,
others thought it advisable for him to return to Rome and discuss
the situation with the Pope and Cardinal Antonelli; but Wiseman
himself never for one moment doubted that his duty was to continue
his journey back to England with all haste. His first act was to send
Sir George Bowyer to explain the situation in its true light to a
member of the Government, in the hope that this might better
clear up the misunderstandings than had his letter written to Lord

[1] J. Cumming: *Cardinal Wiseman, his Oath and its Obligation*, p. 27.
[2] *W. G. Ward and the Catholic Revival*, p. 3.

John Russell from Vienna. Sir George was received by Lord Lansdowne, the Lord President of the Council, whom he found 'deeply distressed at the state of things in the country'. He assured Sir George that the Prime Minister had published the Durham Letter without first communicating with his colleagues and that he himself very much regretted it. 'I had three or four long interviews with Lord Lansdowne' Sir George later told Wilfrid Ward,[1] 'and I believe the explanations I offered were so far satisfactory that the noble lord was convinced that the conduct of Cardinal Wiseman had been perfectly fair and honest, and that there was not the slightest idea of aggression or of doing anything offensive to public opinion in this country.' None the less Lord Lansdowne warned his visitor that the torrent of popular feeling was such that the Government could not ignore it, and hinted at the possibility of legislation, which was later to take effect in the Ecclesiastical Titles Act.

Meanwhile the Cardinal took up residence in the clergy house attached to St. George's Cathedral, Southwark, as his own house was in the hands of painters and decorators. Crowds of curious people gathered to see him 'enveloped in a large blue cloak' when he arrived at this house, but there was no demonstration, though later on he had to suffer the indignity of having stones hurled at his carriage. Having realized that he could expect little help from official quarters in presenting a true and unbiased account of the real purpose of the Pope's act and of his own Pastoral, the Cardinal decided to lay his case fairly before the British public in the form of an Appeal, which he began to write on the very day he reached England. This document was ready for the press within the week and was one of the most remarkable to come from his pen.

The pamphlet, which ran to thirty-two pages, was called *An Appeal to the Reason and Good Feeling of the English People on the subject of the Catholic Hierarchy*. Its style was direct, its reasoning clear, and its language precise; in fact, it was in every respect in marked contrast to the flowery verbiage and profuse hyperbole of the Pastoral from the Flaminian Gate, so that *The Times*, which published the *Appeal* in full, added the rather pert comment: 'We congratulate Dr. Wiseman on his recovery of the use of the English language.'[2] It could not be denied, however, that in the strength of

[1] Ward, Vol. I, p. 555.   [2] *The Times*, Tuesday, 21st November 1850.

his case and in the mastery of its presentation the Cardinal scored a decisive victory for his cause, and that from the publication of the *Appeal* can be dated the virtual collapse of the agitation against 'Papal aggression' and the acceptance by the public of the right of Catholics to organize their religion in freedom according to the traditional customs of their Church.

Before answering, point by point, the accusations made against him, Wiseman began his pamphlet by delivering a smart rebuke to the Prime Minister. 'At the present crisis,' he wrote, 'the Catholics of England had no right to expect any co-operation from the Government of the country—they asked for none; but they had the right of every citizen to impartiality. They naturally might have expected that he, to whom was entrusted the helm of the State would keep himself above those influences of party feeling which disqualify the mind for grave and generous counsels; would preserve himself uncommitted by any hasty or unofficial expression of opinion; would remain on the neutral ground of his public responsibility, to check excess on every side, and moderate dangerous tendencies in any party. Instead of this, the Head of her Majesty's Government has astonished, not this country alone, but all Europe, by a letter which leaves us but little hope that any appeal to the high authority which rules over the empire would be received, to say the least, with favour.'[1] It was to another tribunal that the Cardinal's appeal was now directed: 'There still remain the manly sense and honest heart of a generous people; that love of honourable dealing and fair play, which, in joke or in earnest, is equally the instinct of an Englishman; that hatred of all mean advantage taken, of all base tricks and paltry clap-traps and party cries employed to hunt down even a rival or a foe. To this open-fronted, and warm-hearted tribunal I make my appeal, and claim, on behalf of myself and my fellow Catholics, a fair, free, and impartial hearing.'[2]

Wiseman began his rebuttal of the attack made against the Papal Brief by denying the charge that it was an assault upon the royal supremacy. After briefly tracing the legal position of Catholics before 1829, he went on to show how their situation had been changed by the passage of the Catholic Emancipation Act. Before that Act was passed, he pointed out, a Catholic, in the eyes of the law, 'was a

[1] *Appeal*, p. 8.   [2] Ibid., p. 9.

person who did not admit the royal supremacy, and therefore was excluded from full enjoyment of civil privileges. A Catholic after 1829, and therefore in 1850, is a person who still continues not to admit the royal supremacy, and nevertheless is admitted to full enjoyment of these privileges,' and in this respect is in exactly the same condition as the members of the Church of Scotland, Baptists, Methodists, Quakers, Independents, Presbyterians, Unitarians and all other nonconformists, none of whom 'recognize in the Queen any authority to interfere in their religious concerns, to appoint their ministers for them, or to mark the limits of their separate districts in which authority has to be exercised'. What applied to the Queen applied also to the Bishops whom she appointed. 'None of these (the nonconformists) any more than Catholics, recognize in the Bishops appointed by our gracious Queen, in virtue of her supremacy, any authority to teach them, or rule them.'[1] He then went on to quote the authority of Lord Chancellor Lyndhurst, who had told the House of Lords on 11th May 1846, that 'it was no crime in the Roman Catholic to maintain and defend the supremacy of the Pope',[2] and he ended this section by a warning against the real danger which the country faced—not from aggression by the Pope, but from the twisting and misrepresenting of the innocent acts of British subjects for the ends of political expediency. 'Believe me, at this moment, the danger to the religious and civil liberties of Englishmen is not from any infringement on them by the Pope, in granting to English Catholics what I hope to show you they had full right to obtain from him, but from those who are taking advantage of the occurrences to go back a step, if they can, in the legislation of toleration, and take away from a large body of Englishmen, what at present is lawful to them in regard to the free exercise of their religion.'[3]

In the next section Wiseman was at pains to point out that the Anglican hierarchy was in no sense attacked by the restoration of normal diocesan government to the Catholic Church. 'The appointment of a Catholic Hierarchy does not in any way deprive the English Establishment of a single advantage it now possesses,' he wrote, adding that nothing the Catholic Church could do would alter the rank, social position, or pre-eminence of the Anglican

<hr>

[1] Ibid., p. 10.   [2] Ibid., p. 12.   [3] Ibid., p. 14.

prelates who could retain for ever, for all it concerned Catholics, 'their domestic comforts, their palaces, their lands, their incomes, without diminution or alteration. Whatever satisfaction it has been to you till now to see them so elevated above their Catholic rivals, and to have their wants so amply provided for, you will still enjoy as much as hitherto.' To this picture of the state-appointed prelate luxuriating in his palace and his princely income, Wiseman contrasted his 'Catholic rival', for the outward aspect of the two Churches would remain unchanged by the Papal Bull. 'The Catholic episcopacy and the Catholic priesthood will remain no doubt poor, unnoticed by the great, and by the powerful (so soon as the present commotion shall have subsided), without social rank or pre-eminence. If there be no security for the English Church, in this overwhelming balance in its favour of worldly advantages, surely the exclusion of Catholics from the possession of local sees will not save it.' To this parallel, hardly flattering to the Church of England, he added a note of rebuke: 'The new Bishops will not have occasion to cross the path of the prelates of the Anglican establishment in their sphere of duty; they will find plenty to do, besides their official duties, in attending to the wants of their poor spiritual children, especially the multitudes of poor Irish, whose peaceful and truly Catholic conduct, under the whirlwind of contumely which has just assailed them, proves that they have not forgotten the teaching of their Church—not to revile when reviled, and when they suffer, not to threaten.'[1]

In showing that, if Catholics were legally entitled to govern themselves in accordance with known customs of their church, that is, by an episcopal hierarchy, and such a hierarchy could only be established by an act of the Pope, Cardinal Wiseman was able to quote the authority of the Prime Minister himself in a statement which Lord John must have forgotten when he wrote his untimely reply to the Bishop of Durham. Speaking in the House of Commons on 6th August 1846, Russell had said: 'There is another offence of introducing a Bull of the Pope into the country. The question is, whether it is desirable to keep up that, or any other penalty for such an offence. It does not appear to me, that we can possibly attempt to prevent the introduction of the Pope's Bulls into this country. There

[1] Ibid., pp. 17-18.

174

are certain Bulls of the Pope which are absolutely necessary for the appointment of Bishops and pastors belonging to the Roman Catholic Church. It would be quite impossible to prevent the introduction of such Bulls.' Yet it was against precisely such a Bull that Russell was now so busily stirring up opposition and revolt. Lord Lyndhurst had made a speech similar to Russell's in the House of Lords, and after quoting from it, Wiseman showed that both quotations proved that 'in both Houses of Parliament the principle has been clearly laid down, that if Catholics are to have Bishops at all, the Pope, and the Pope alone, can make them for them. Then it enters as completely into the principles of religious liberty that the Pope should name the Hierarchy, as that Catholics should have the right to possess one—a right as necessary for them, as is for the Wesleyans that of having Conferences with Superintendents.'[1]

Wiseman next answered the accusation that the creation of a Catholic hierarchy in England by the Pope was an interference with the undoubted prerogative of the British Crown—a point made by the Anglican bishops in their address to the Queen, in which they declared that 'the Bishop of Rome has pretended to exercise spiritual dominion over the people of this country; and, in nominating certain Romish ecclesiastics to particular places or sees in England, has reasserted his claim of supremacy over the kingdom, and has interfered with a prerogative constitutionally belonging to your Majesty alone'. 'Has this assumption of titles been within the terms of the law?' the Cardinal asked in reply. 'Is there any law forbidding the assumption of the title of Bishop? A certain Dr. Dillon[2] assumed it, and ordained what he called Presbyters, and no one thought of prosecuting him. The Moravians have Bishops all over England; and so have the Irvingites or Apostolicals; yet no one taxes them with illegality. Then our taking the title of Bishops merely, constitutes no illegality. Is there any law that forbids our taking the title from any place not being the see of an Anglican Bishop? No one can say that there is.

[1] Ibid., p. 19.
[2] Robert Crawford Dillon, D.D. (1797–1845) was suspended from his ministry in the Church of England in 1840 owing to the scandalous nature of his private life, whereupon he appointed himself 'bishop' or 'first presbyter' of a 'Reformed English Church' and ordained ministers to serve in it. According to the *Dictionary of National Biography* he enjoyed a considerable reputation as a popular preacher and was 'much run after, especially by ladies'.

'Then I ask those more learned in the law than myself, can an act of a subject of Her Most Gracious Majesty, which by law he is perfectly competent to do, be an infringement of her Royal prerogative? If not, then I trust we may conclude, that by this new creation of Catholic Bishops that prerogative has not been violated. No one doubts that the Bishops so appointed are Roman Catholic Bishops, to rule over Roman Catholic flocks. Does the Crown claim the right, under its prerogative, of naming such Bishops?'[1]

Wiseman concluded his *Appeal* with a passage dealing with the title of Westminster, which had been assigned to the metropolitan see of the new hierarchy, and which had given rise to so much angry abuse and hostile comment. The Dean and Chapter of Westminster Abbey had strongly protested against it. Wiseman assured them that he had no designs upon their Abbey, their temporal rights, or their possession of any dignity or title. The splendid Abbey, 'its treasures of art, and its fitting endowments, form not the part of Westminster which will concern me', he wrote, and in the only passage in the *Appeal* in which he allowed his emotional feelings for a moment to dominate, he described the Westminster in which he hoped to labour as pastor and bishop. 'For there is another part which stands in frightful contrast, though in immediate contact, with this magnificence. In ancient times, the existence of an Abbey on any spot, with a large staff of clergy, and ample revenues, would have sufficed to create round it a little paradise of comfort, cheerfulness, and ease. This, however, is not now the case. Close under the Abbey of Westminster there lie concealed labyrinths of lanes and courts, and alleys and slums, nests of ignorance, vice, depravity, and crime, as well as of squalor, wretchedness, and disease; whose atmosphere is typhus, whose ventilation is cholera; in which swarms a huge and almost countless population, in great measure, nominally at least, Catholic; haunts of filth, which no sewage committee can reach—dark corners, which no lighting-board can brighten. This is the part of Westminster which alone I covet, and which I shall be glad to claim and visit, as a blessed pasture in which sheep of holy Church are to be tended, in which a Bishop's godly work has to be done, of consoling, converting, and preserving. And if, as I humbly trust in God, it

---

[1] *Appeal*, pp. 21–22.

shall be seen, that this special culture, arising from the establishment of our Hierarchy, bears fruits of order, peacefulness, decency, religion, and virtue, it may be that the Holy See shall not be thought to have acted unwisely, when it bound up the very soul and salvation of a chief pastor with those of a city, whereof the name indeed is glorious, but the purlieus infamous—in which the very grandeur of its public edifices is as a shadow, to screen from the public eye sin and misery the most appalling. If the wealth of the Abbey be stagnant and not diffusive, if it in no way rescue the neighbouring population from the depths in which it is sunk, let there be no jealousy of any one who, by whatever name, is ready to make the latter his care, without interfering with the former.'[1]

Wiseman had formed two immediate impressions about the situation in England even before he had returned, when the news of the 'tremendous commotion which *The Times* has excited' reached him in Vienna. This he outlined in a letter to Talbot. 'I have every hope that a most favourable reaction, from shame and remorse, will set in,' he wrote from Liège on November 9th. 'Moreover, you will see that the apple of discord has been fully thrown into the Church of England and the Puseyites must be driven out of it, or must neutralize the agitation in it. But the most important thing is, do not let our Holy Father be alarmed in the least; the storm has been violent, but so shamefully so, that it can neither last, nor leave any impression.'[2] In the hope that the Puseyites would be driven out of the English Church Wiseman was over-optimistic, but his hope of a favourable reaction 'from shame and remorse' was not only fulfilled, but was in large measure brought about by the new atmosphere created by his *Appeal*, which did as much to calm overheated tempers as his Pastoral had done in the opposite direction.

Some thirty thousand copies of the *Appeal* were sold in the first week of its publication, and various newspapers, including *The Times*, published it in full. Its effect upon minds still open to reason was immediate in calming the fears and stilling the passions which his Pastoral had raised. 'It is so temperate and logical.' the *London News* wrote on November 23rd, 'as to increase public regret that it did not appear a month ago, before the mischief was done, and before

---

[1] Ibid., pp. 30–31.   [2] Rome, English College Archives. Talbot Correspondence.

this angry flood of theological bitterness was let loose over the land.'
The *Weekly News*, in its issue of the same date declared that: 'Our
anti-Papacy zealots hardly knew that Dr. Wiseman had left the
Flaminian Gate when lo, he appears, and issues a Manifesto in which
he certainly deals slashing blows among his assailants right and left,
even if he does not succeed in parrying all those that have been
aimed at his own party. We have seldom read an abler specimen of
controversial writing than this document.'

The Editor of *The Times* clearly felt called upon to offer some
explanation as being the person most responsible for raising the cry
of 'No Popery' and appealing to certain mob instincts which in the
nineteenth century, no less than the twentieth, are not readily
associated with the readers of that newspaper. 'If we have pronounced an opinion against the Pope and the Cardinal unheard,'
he wrote in the issue of November 21st, 'it has not been from any
wish to deny them fair play, but because they did not condescend
to give us any more tangible explanation of their acts than was to be
gathered from empty gasconades and pompous manifestoes, the
very sweepings of a literary wardrobe now nearly worn out, and
never very tastefully selected.' Having thus moved its target from
the Cardinal's ideas to his English, the leader continued in a rather
heavy-handed parody of his style: 'We hear no more in the "Appeal"
of the planetary system either of Cullen or Copernicus; suns,
planets, and comets dance no more in the mazes of metaphorical
confusion. England is suffered to remain where she is, and is no
longer forced, to the great discomfiture of the Continent, to revolve
round the Eternal City. The golden chain of St. Peter rings no
longer in our ears, and the adjacent islands to the Doctor's diocese,
Thanet, Dogs, and all, do not once appear on the horizon. Grateful
for the relief from the constant strain on our imaginative faculties,
we can only express a wish that it were consistent with the rules of
orthodoxy and infallibility that the Church of Rome, as she has one
head, one faith, one code of morality, one system of politics, would
be pleased to add to these multifarious unities the unity of language,
so that her advocates might be spared the necessity of writing long
arguments to prove that her public and authorized documents mean
exactly the reverse of what they say.' And in the two long paragraphs
that followed the leader continued in the same style to show the

writer's ability to construe from such documents the exact opposite of what he read.

If *The Times* was only prepared to climb down slowly, other publicists showed even less respect for the author of the *Appeal*. 'I beg leave to say at the outset,' wrote Samuel Warren of the Cardinal in a pamphlet called *The Queen or The Pope*, 'that I regard him as disentitled to gentle or ceremonious handling; for his manifesto, as it has been called and was intended to be, is in every respect one of the most offensive documents ever laid before the British public: calculated to irritate and inflame, instead of soothe and propitiate, a country deeming, and loudly declaring itself, insulted, its confidence and liberality treacherously abused, and its national religion menaced and endangered. . . . His "Appeal" disclosed swelling ambition and intense malignity, painfully compressed and tortured into a semblance of disarming meekness and resignation; yet so successfully, as to exhibit an image of Satan *in the act* of transforming himself into an angel of light.' This writer took particular exception to Wiseman's description of the slums of Westminster. 'What are "slums"?' he asked in a furious footnote, 'and where is the word to be found explained? Is it Roman, or Spanish? There is not such a word in our language,' and having dismissed the hunger and degradation of the poor as a mere problem in etymology he seemed to think that he had scored a point in the debate. The example of *The Times*, in suddenly finding the Cardinal's use of language the real point at issue, had gained its first disciple.

Wiseman received many expressions of thanks from his fellow-Catholics for the 'Appeal', and for the way in which he had stood up to the attack. 'Highly as I put his gifts,' Newman wrote to a friend, 'I was not prepared for such a display of vigour, power, judgement, sustained energy as the last two months have brought. I heard a dear friend of his say before he had got to England, that the news of the opposition would kill him. How has he been out. It is the event of the time. In my own remembrance there has been nothing like it.'[1] From Paris the Count de Montalembert wrote to the Cardinal: 'Nothing can exceed my interest and my sympathy for what you and your fellow Bishops and flock are going through in England. You

[1] Ward, Vol. I, p. 534.

were the constant object of my preoccupations and conversation, during my late sojourn in Rome, with Cardinal Antonelli, Cardinal Fransoni, Mgr. Talbot, and even poor Lord Shrewsbury, the great antagonist of the Hierarchy.'[1]

Wiseman's own feelings were expressed in a long letter to Monsignor Talbot. 'I consider the hubbub as nearly at an end,' he wrote on December 30th, shortly after delivering a series of public lectures on the hierarchy at St. George's, Southwark. 'The papers are giving it up: and people on all sides are getting heartily ashamed of it. Cobden at Leeds expressed his fear lest the reaction in our favour should go too far, and popery triumph, which he would consider dangerous to liberty. The interest and curiosity about us remain unimpaired, or rather increase. I have finished my course of three lectures on the hierarchy: I have sent you two, which I hope you have received; the third I must send by post. St. George's was crowded beyond precedent on the third night. The lecture was on Monday morning, on Friday there was not a copy left of 30,000. This is quite unprecedented.' Meanwhile the ordinary work of the Church must continue, and more converts must be made. Wiseman was expecting further conversions to the Catholic Church as a result of the decision of the Judicial Committee of the Privy Council on the Gorham case, of which more will be said later, especially as he had heard that Archdeacon Manning had just resigned his living. He was, Wiseman believed, 'only waiting for a short time, as he is always very cautious. I believe he is waiting for Gladstone to return. I now begin to expect Gladstone to follow him, especially if James Hope does, which seems very certain.' These hopeful signs renewed the Cardinal's confidence, and he looked forward to a bright future after the present storm had spent itself; indeed, his tendency to over-enthusiasm appeared again as he assured Talbot: 'I am convinced we have now quite the upper hand, and that glorious days are coming. I doubt if Lord John will venture any new bills, if he does he will have a hard battle to fight; and no one expects more than a ridiculous law, which will do us more good than harm.' Wiseman's buoyant nature expressed itself in a final note of satisfaction: 'I now drive about everywhere with my Cardinal's arms on the carriage, and it is known by everyone; but I meet

[1] Westminster Diocesan Archives.

180

with nothing but respect.'[1] The stones and insults which had first greeted those same Cardinal's arms were quickly forgotten.

Lord John Russell's 'ridiculous law' was, in fact, introduced into the House of Commons on 7th February 1851. By then the public outcry against 'Papal aggression' had cooled considerably and a certain feeling of embarrassment surrounded the passing of the Ecclesiastical Titles Act, as the bill was to be called. While the bill was still being drafted people were beginning to think that the best thing would be to let the matter quietly die of its own accord, but the Government felt that some measure was necessary, and in this they had the support of the Anglican Establishment. The general state of public opinion by the end of the year was admirably expressed by Queen Victoria in a letter addressed to the Prime Minister on 8th December 1850. 'The Queen is glad to hear of what passed between the Archbishop[2] and Lord John. She trusts that something may be done, as the desire for it seems to be so great. On the other hand, the Queen deeply regrets the great abuse of the Roman Catholic religion which takes place at all these meetings, etc. She thinks it unchristian and unwise, and trusts that it will soon cease.'[3] It is a pity, indeed, that the Queen's tolerant attitude had not been adopted from the beginning by more of her subjects, not least her Prime Minister. Two days after writing to Lord John she expressed herself with equal emphasis in a letter to her aunt, the Duchess of Gloucester. 'Sincerely Protestant as I always have been and always shall be, and indignant as I am at those who *call themselves Protestant*, while they in fact *are* quite the *contrary*, I much regret the unchristian and intolerant spirit exhibited by many people at the public meetings. I cannot bear to hear the violent abuse of the Catholic religion, which is so painful and cruel towards the many good and innocent Roman Catholics.'[4] If Lord John Russell had adopted his Sovereign's more liberal point of view when he replied to the Bishop of Durham's letter, the whole question of the establishment of a Catholic hierarchy in England might have passed off in a manner more creditable to the reputation of a civilized country.

As it was the Ecclesiastical Titles Act became the law of the land

[1] Rome, English College Archives. Talbot Correspondence.
[2] The Archbishop of Canterbury.
[3] Letters of Queen Victoria, First Series, Vol. II, p. 334.   [4] Ibid., p. 336.

on 1st August 1851, having been violently assailed by Gladstone in the House of Commons, who described it contemptuously as 'this little miniature of a penal law'. The Act declared all ecclesiastical titles assumed in the United Kingdom, other than those of the Established Church, to be unlawful and void, and imposed a fine of a hundred pounds on any person who pretended to any such title or see. As such a law would also apply to the titles used by the bishops of the Episcopal Church of Scotland, they were exempt in a special clause, which merely served to emphasize the injustice of the whole measure, as Gladstone was quick to point out. 'If the appointment of Bishops is a spiritual act,' he asked, 'why interfere with it? If temporal, why exempt the Scotch Bishops?'[1] In effect the Act was a dead letter from the day it was passed. The fine was never imposed. Twenty years later Gladstone was to repeal it.

What may be considered a final opinion on the whole episode of 'Papal aggression' came from the pen of Ambrose Phillipps de Lisle, if one allows for that convert's peculiar enthusiasms. In a letter to Lord Shrewsbury of 5th March 1851, he wrote: 'The Pastoral from the *Flaminian Gate* was a very *flaming* affair; but then how nobly the Cardinal redeemed it by his "Appeal to the good sense of the People of England", and after all we must remember every one has his own peculiarities of style and manner, and so we must let the Cardinal have his. He certainly is a most able person, and I cannot help thinking that all this outbreak will tend to good by making our religion more thought of and talked about. If the hierarchy had come in quite quietly, it would not have done so much good by a great deal; now as it is, Catholicism is the great subject of conversation from one end of England to the other.'[2] None the less, the cost which the Catholics had had to pay in abuse and contumely, in the fear of violence, and in the knowledge of the bitter and bigoted prejudice with which they were still viewed by so many of their fellow countrymen, was a high price for the sake of having their religion discussed by so many over so vast an area. The more conservative of them were confirmed in their suspicion of the dangers that lurked in the Cardinal's many schemes for the propagation of the Faith, and greeted his every pronouncement with

[1] Ward, Vol. II, p. 25.
[2] Purcell: *Life of Ambrose Phillipps de Lisle*, Vol. I, pp. 329–30.

renewed anxiety. On the Protestant side, Wiseman's Pastoral from the Flaminian Gate was to lose him the confidence of the official and Government circles with whom, as head of the Catholic Church in England, he would have had to deal. This confidence he did not regain. In future another bishop had to be deputed to undertake all official business with the Government.

XIV

The attitude adopted by the Catholic Church to Russell's Ecclesiastical Titles Act could only take one form, and this was expressed by Dr. Ullathorne, the Bishop of Birmingham, in an 'open letter' to the Prime Minister which appeared in *The Times* on 11th February 1851. 'The Hierarchy is established;' he wrote, 'therefore it cannot be abolished, except through the physical extermination of the Catholic Church in these realms; or, which God, forbid, through universal apostasy. How can you deal with this fact? Is it wise and in the spirit of a profound legislation, to put the religious teachers of a large body of Her Majesty's subjects in conscientious opposition to the law—to force them to put the principle of divine law in opposition to a human enactment? Will it aid the sanctions of the State to force us into a position where, standing, as we are bound to do, upon the law of God and our conscience, we are compelled to count for nothing enactments which we can only consider as assaults upon the cause of Heaven and of our souls— enactments which, in fact, come from no divine fountain of justice, but are the offspring of party contests and sectarian dislikes?'[1] This letter caused another outburst of indignation, as might have been expected, but, as might also have been expected, it expressed the only possible line that Catholics could take, and the fact that the penal provisions of the Act were never enforced showed that even the Government came to recognize, once tempers had cooled and reason had been restored, the illogicality and injustice of their campaign against the hierarchy.[2]

[1] C. Butler: *Life of Ullathorne*, Vol. I, p. 194.
[2] The return to a more tolerant view was expressed by Thackeray in a letter to William Allingham (Nov. 29/30 1850): 'After making a great noise myself I begin to wonder why we have made so much to do about the Cardinal. Why shouldn't he come and set up a winking Virgin in the Strand?'

The Catholics rallied bravely in support of the Cardinal, though in private some of them had misgivings as to the readiness of the Church for the new form of government, and even Wiseman found some difficulty in finding the right men to fill the vacant sees. 'If our body is not strengthened,' he wrote to Talbot,[1] 'and if the choice of bishops is not made with reference to this consideration as well as with regard to local wants and personal claims, not rising higher than being good and respectable people, we shall never be equal to the wants of the times. If soft, good persons are put in, I do not know what will become of us. I know there is little choice, but in that let us have the best.' He was soon to discover how strongly the old Catholic tradition held among the men appointed, and how little many of them sympathized with the Roman spirit he hoped to introduce.

Newman, too, expressed in private his fears about the restoration: 'We are not ripe ourselves for a Hierarchy,' he told a friend. 'Now they have got one, they can't fill up the sees, positively can't.'[2] It was, in fact, about a year before all the vacancies were filled. Despite these misgivings Newman was ready to come to the defence of the Church, and in the summer of 1851 delivered a course of lectures in the Birmingham Corn Exchange on the *Present Position of Catholics in England*. These received a good deal of notice and were attended by large crowds of a very different sort from those who had flocked to hear the lecturer preach in the days when he was Vicar of St. Mary's at Oxford or who now came to his Oratory in Birmingham. For this reason he adopted a more popular style in these discourses, and allowed full play to the spirit of irony in the expression of which he displayed such mastery.

The principal target for Newman's ironical shafts was a certain 'Cavaliere' Achilli, who also aspired to the title of Doctor in Divinity and had once been content with the designation of Father, a spiritual title from the use of which he had been deprived by the Holy Inquisition. The Inquisition had, indeed, taken so unfavourable a view of the manner in which Dr. Achilli chose to exercise his paternal duties, which had resulted in his native Italy in a paternity of an altogether earthly character, that it had even deprived him of his

---

[1] *Dublin Review*, January 1919, p. 18.
[2] Wilfrid Ward: *Life of Newman*, Vol. I, p. 260.

liberty as well as his sacerdotal orders. When this prisoner was released he went to Corfu, then under the British flag, and from Corfu to Malta. In these islands he adopted the Protestant faith, and as his scandalous reputation had not yet caught up with him he was able to proceed to England where, as a former prisoner of the Inquisition, he was received with acclaim in Protestant circles; all the more so, as his arrival coincided with the anti-Catholic agitation following the restoration of the hierarchy. Such was the enthusiasm that greeted Dr. Achilli's denunciations of his former faith that at one meeting he was greeted by the singing of a hymn, specially composed in his honour by the Rev. J. R. Leichfield, the refrain of which ran:

> Hail! Roman prisoner, hail!
> No more a prisoner now.
> Truth, Justice, Freedom *shall* prevail,
> And priests before them bow.[1]

One priest who was not prepared to bow before the sensational revelations of Dr. Achilli was the new Cardinal Archbishop of Westminster. In an article in the *Dublin Review* Wiseman exposed the Protestant convert in his true colours and disclosed to his English admirers the real reasons why he had fallen foul of the Inquisition. He was able to show that Achilli's career as a Dominican friar had been one of such a shocking nature that had he not been dealt with by the ecclesiastical courts of the papal administration his crimes would have entitled him to equally rigorous treatment from the civil arm. Twenty years before his appearance in England as the champion of Protestantism Achilli had been proved to have caused the ruin of a girl of eighteen, and had repeated the crime a second time with a person of twenty-eight, and a third time with one of twenty-four years. But this was only the beginning. In the town of Capua he had, Wiseman wrote, 'committed the same crime of seduction, and, unfortunately, made use of the facilities which his religious character gave him, of access to establishments of female education.'[2] Given his record, we may consider the Cardinal's use of the word 'unfortunately' in this context as being excessively

---

[1] See J. Lewis May: *Cardinal Newman, A Study*, p. 117.
[2] *Dublin Review*, June 1850, p. 485.

mild. Such, and much more, was the man who now stood forth to denounce, in a spirit of moral and righteous indignation, the Church which had seen fit to eject him from its sacred ministry.

No reply or action for libel followed the publication of Wiseman's damning disclosures. But the *Dublin Review* was not widely read and to the general public Achilli's reputation was not seriously damaged. Thus it was, in the fifth of his lectures, that Newman decided on a public denunciation of Achilli, exposing in detail his degraded past, and drawing fully, for his material, on Cardinal Wiseman's article. Legal advisers had assured him that an action for libel was unlikely, as the *Dublin* article had not been challenged, and so Newman gave full rein to his powers of invective. 'The Protestant world flocks to hear him,' Newman told his audience, 'because he has something to tell of the Catholic Church. He has something to tell, it is true; he *has* a scandal to reveal, he *has* an argument to exhibit. It is a simple one, and a powerful one, as far as it goes—and it is *one*. That one argument is himself; it is his presence which is the triumph of the Protestants; it is the sight of him which is a Catholic's confusion. It is indeed our great confusion, that our Holy Mother could have had a priest like him.'[1] Then followed a long and detailed list of the offences which had blotted the career of the former Dominican, the seducer of young girls and author of crimes 'which the authorities cannot get themselves to describe', such as Wiseman had already given in the *Dublin Review*, upon which the passage in Newman's address was clearly founded. If the career which he exposed was one of singular brutality and disgrace, Newman could feel safe in the fact that each foul episode he named could be verified and proved from the material upon which the Cardinal's article had been based, and such, no doubt, was his feeling when, within a month, Achilli did, in fact, bring an action for libel against him.

Newman at once wrote to Wiseman for the necessary documents to prove his case. The Cardinal was notoriously slow in answering letters, but considering the urgency of the issue Newman grew a little alarmed when he received no reply, and wrote again in pressing terms. Still Wiseman did not answer. Newman could only imagine that the Cardinal had not bothered to search for the documents,

[1] Wilfrid Ward: *Life of Newman*, Vol. I, p. 279.

and wrote in distress to Father Gordon of the London Oratory who went at once to the Archbishop and urged on him the gravity of the situation, explaining Father Newman's understandable surprise at having had no reply to his letter. The Cardinal expressed the greatest possible embarrassment and distress, declaring that he dared not write to Newman as he had lost the vital papers. The scene was later told to Wilfrid Ward by Father Gordon himself. ' "Father Newman is surprised not to have heard from you." "I dare not write to him," was the reply; "I have hunted in vain and cannot find the documents." And then (according to Father Gordon's description) the Cardinal, unwieldy and huge, knelt down amid the heap of papers which he had been sorting and examining, and once more hunted for the missing papers without success.'[1]

The papers were not found in time. Furthermore, when Newman had inquiries made in Italy, the Cardinal again let him down. Newman could never believe that this was not due to lack of sympathy on the part of Wiseman, as he expressed strongly in a letter to W. G. Ward, when he listed first among what he described as the *origines mali,* 'the Cardinal, *who did not look* for his documents till the hour when the Rule (for the trial) was made absolute, and it was too late. In that hour he looked and found. Father Hutchinson brought them to me. I took up my hat and went to Lewis. He had just returned from Westminster. It was all over.' And second in his list was again the Cardinal 'who sent our dear Fathers to Naples with introductions not *strong enough* to open the Police books. They were told there that everything could have been done had the Cardinal been more alive'.[2]

Newman stood his trial in June 1852. Achilli appeared wearing a black wig which, according to a newspaper, 'gives to his appearance a certain air of the conventicle'. Some of the charges against Achilli were established, but not all, so that the unproved accusations constituted a libel. The judge summed up, according to Newman's biographer, with 'an obvious and flagrant bias'[3] against him, which is, indeed, borne out by the leading article which appeared in *The Times.* In the midst of the strongly anti-Catholic campaign which it was itself waging *The Times* described the proceedings as 'indecorous

[1] Ward, Vol. II, pp. 39-40.   [2] W. Ward: *Life of Newman,* Vol. I, p. 283.
[3] Ibid., p. 292.

in their nature, unsatisfactory in their result, and little calculated to increase the respect of the people for the administration of justice or the estimation by foreign nations of the English name and character'. The article then made some amends for the newspaper's own previous attitude to the Catholic community by adding: 'We consider that a great blow has been given to the administration of justice in this country, and that Roman Catholics will henceforth have only too good reason for asserting that there is no justice for them in cases tending to arouse the Protestant feelings of judges and juries.' Fortunately, Newman's counsel were able to get a fresh trial in January 1853, when a purely nominal fine was imposed.

The Achilli episode was unfortunate in that it put a strain on the relations between Wiseman and his most distinguished convert, a relationship which had, from the first, been slightly uneasy. Newman's shy and introverted nature was not of the type that responded very readily to Wiseman's more effusive geniality, and while he shared in enthusiasm for the Cardinal's wide schemes for the improvement of the Catholic Church in England, he was wholly unsympathetic to his inattention to detail and to the vagueness which tended more and more to characterize his projects. Newman was by nature touchy and almost excessively sensitive and tended to take as a personal slight what was, in fact, no more than a distressing, but characteristic, trait in the Cardinal's personality, a total disregard for the finer points of organization (which he was content to leave to others) while he concerned himself only with the broad outlines of his plans. Wiseman also suffered from a constitutional dislike for denying requests or refusing petitions, and his unwillingness to disappoint Newman in this instance no doubt contributed to the misunderstanding. From the time of Wiseman's failure to discover the papers in the Achilli case one may date Newman's growing feeling that he was neglected by the authorities of his new Church, that his abilities were not given their full scope, and that his plans were destined for continual frustration. This feeling he undoubtedly associated with Cardinal Wiseman. At the time of Wiseman's death thirteen years later Newman coupled him with Faber as 'the two chief persons, whom I felt to be unjust to me',[1] and though their place had been taken, in his estimation, by

[1] Newman: *Autobiographical Writings*, p. 260.

Ward and Manning, Newman added that he had not 'that sense of their cruelty' which he associated with the former.

The estrangement between Wiseman and Newman was only gradual, and might, indeed, easily have been healed after this initial rupture, had not other influences been brought to bear later on which were hostile to Newman and all that he stood for. As it was, at the time in question, Wiseman did all in his power to repair the damage. He organized a subscription to defray the considerable expenses involved in the case. For this Newman readily expressed his gratitude. 'Your Eminence knows, I suppose,' he wrote, 'the great success of the subscriptions, which is chiefly owing to your own exertions.' Had both men been less complicated in temperament the matter would have ended there; as it was, more misunderstandings and more difficult situations were to mar their relations with each other in the years ahead.

With the establishment of the hierarchy Wiseman believed that a new era had started for the Church which would bring forth fruit in an ever increasing flow of converts. The year 1851 was indeed to see another great secession from the Anglican Establishment but this was due not so much to the restoration of the Catholic hierarchy as to a major crisis in the Church of England itself, which had come to a head six months before the Cardinal issued his notorious Pastoral. This was the case of Mr. Gorham, an evangelical clergyman whom the Bishop of Exeter had refused to institute into his parish because he believed him to entertain heretical views on the question of baptismal regeneration. Mr. Gorham had brought a case against his bishop in the Court of Arches but had lost his action. He then appealed against the decision of the ecclesiastical court to the Judicial Committee of the Privy Council which declared in his favour and ordered the Bishop to institute him into his living whatever might be his views on the question of baptismal regeneration. This decision came as a mortal blow to the 'Catholic' party in the Church of England, for it meant that the final judgement in matters of heresy lay not with the bishops, or even with the Church courts, but with an entirely lay body, the Judicial Committee of the Privy Council, whose members would certainly always be laymen and might not necessarily even be Christians. The shock of this judgement had scarcely struck them when the agitation against

'Papal aggression' swept the country and forced them into a cruel dilemma; for while on one hand they found themselves faced with a judgement which seemed to undermine the spiritual independence of their Church, and by its interpretation of the Royal supremacy in religious matters to question their belief in the Anglican Establishment as a branch of the Catholic Church; on the other hand they were called upon to condemn at public meetings the establishment of a hierarchy which they could not but acknowledge as being of the True Church, and, if their worst fears for their own Church proved to be correct, the only succession of true bishops in this country.

To no one did this dilemma present itself with more force than to the Archdeacon of Chichester, Henry Edward Manning, who since the secession of Newman had gradually come to occupy a leading place among the remnant of the Tractarians. Unlike his former leader his life had not been spent in academic surroundings but in pastoral work in Sussex, where he had for many years been Rector of Lavington. But though Lavington was an obscure village and though there are dizzier pinnacles in the scale of preferment than the post of Archdeacon, Manning was an influential and important figure in the ecclesiastical world. He was on intimate terms with Mr. Gladstone and other rising men in the field of politics. He had been offered, and had declined, the post of Sub-Almoner to Queen Victoria, a court appointment that almost always led to a bishopric. Though Manning had come to accept the teachings of the *Tracts for the Times* he had never been in the extreme wing of the movement. He had visited Rome in 1847, and though this was two years after Newman had joined the Roman Church, Manning still held tenaciously to the theory that the Church of England was a 'branch' of the Catholic Church. When Pius IX received him in audience the Pope had declared to the Anglican Archdeacon: 'The English do many good works, and when men do good God gives them grace: and my poor prayers are offered day by day for England.' Manning's own thoughts were recorded later. 'I remember the pain I felt at seeing how unknown we (the Anglicans) were to the Vicar of Jesus Christ. It made me feel our isolation.'[1] Despite the papal audience, and his kneeling on the ground when he saw Pius pass in his carriage through the Piazza di Spagna, there

---

[1] *Manning: Anglican and Catholic*, p. 25

is no evidence to show that Manning had any leanings towards the Roman Church during this visit to the Eternal City. He only felt grief that his own 'branch' of the Church should be so unknown and her position so isolated.

After his return to England Manning retired once more to Sussex and to the busy work of his parish and diocese. But gradually the claims of Rome became more and more insistently presented to his mind. Wiseman had for some time had his eye on the Archdeacon of Chichester, waiting, as he had previously waited for Newman, for the moment when circumstances would force a final decision upon him, and as the Cardinal waited and hoped for Manning he believed that Gladstone would follow where the other led. But when, ten days after the verdict of the Judicial Committee had been announced, Manning and his friends gathered at Gladstone's house to decide upon their line of action, Gladstone himself thought it prudent not to be present. Manning decided on one last test. He drew up a resolution on the Royal Supremacy, 'admitting it in all civil matters, but rejecting it in all spiritual and mixed matters', and sent it to all clergymen and laymen who had signed the Oath of Supremacy, asking those who accepted his resolution to sign their names. Twenty thousand clergymen each received a copy of Manning's resolution; only eighteen hundred signed. 'I saw that the game was up,' Manning wrote; 'It was a fair test fully applied, and it received next to no response.'[1]

Then came the outcry against the new Catholic hierarchy. Meetings of clergymen were held all over the country to protest against 'Papal Aggression', and Chichester was no exception. On 22nd November 1850, the clergy gathered in the library of the Cathedral.[2] Manning, as Archdeacon, was present, but took no part in the protests against the Pope and the hierarchy. Those present realized that they were probably seeing their Archdeacon for the last time. At the end of the meeting Manning told them that 'it was the first and only time in ten years in which I had been separated in conviction and action from them: that I had no choice'. The meeting then passed a vote of thanks, an expression of all they owed to the Archdeacon who was now clearly destined to leave them; Manning thanked them in moving terms; it was an occasion of deep

---

[1] Ibid., pp. 33–34.　　　　　　　　　　　　　[2] Now the Lady Chapel.

emotion and many present, including the Dean, gave way freely to tears. 'So we ended and parted,' Manning later wrote: 'It was our last meeting, and the end of my work in the Church of England.'[1]

Owing to the legal formalities necessary in resigning his living and his office as Archdeacon it was some months before Manning was free to take the final step. The last time he went to an Anglican service was in a church off Buckingham Palace Road. He and Gladstone attended the service together but before the Communion began Manning decided to leave, feeling that he could no longer receive the Sacrament in the Church of England. The scene remained vividly in his mind thirty years later. 'I rose up,' he then wrote, 'and laying my hand on Mr. Gladstone's shoulder, said "come". It was the parting of the ways. Mr. Gladstone remained; and I went my way. Mr. Gladstone still remains where I left him.' On 5th April 1851, Manning was received into the Roman Catholic Church at the Jesuit Church in Farm Street with his friend James Hope, a distinguished barrister. As he left the church he turned to his friend and said: 'Now my career is ended.' Here he was mistaken; fourteen years later he would be Archbishop of Westminster in succession to Cardinal Wiseman; and later still would himself wear the red hat of a Cardinal of the Holy Roman Church.

The news of Manning's reception into the Church was particularly welcome to Wiseman, and though the other conversions that followed it, less numerous than those of 1845, were due more to the Gorham judgement than to anything else, to the Cardinal they came as a confirmation of the wisdom of the restoration of the Hierarchy and as an earnest of the good that would flow from it. He seemed, indeed, in almost unnecessary haste to have the new convert hurried through the minor orders and raised to the priesthood. To Monsignor Talbot he wrote on 14th April 1851: 'Yesterday I confirmed Manning, Hope, and Baddeley. . . . But I did more. I knew how much Manning would feel the *ignominia saecularis habitus*, the being an *Esquire*, with a most clerical appearance and leading a most strict life; so I did not hesitate to give him the tonsure at once, and so admit him into the clergy. His wish is to remain near me and study rapidly, so as to help many who are hanging on him and will follow him. He has been studying nothing but Catholic theology

[1] Ibid., p. 36.

for years, and reading our ascetic books. He will at once begin with moral theology, and I will carry him rapidly to the priesthood to satisfy his own earnest devotion and enable him to serve others; but not to undertake any public ministry for some time . . .' So spectacular a submission found the Cardinal at his most rapturous and the old vision of the conversion of England swam once more before his eyes. 'No conversion yet has produced the effect of his,' he continued in his letter to Talbot; 'nor has caused such deep regret through all the "Divided House", as I call the Anglican Establishment. The Queen, it is said, is quite struck and moved; and one clergyman observed that the Church of England had only one great man left now (Dr. Pusey).'[1] Manning was ordained to the priesthood within a few months of being received into the Church, an action on the Cardinal's part which caused a good deal of adverse comment among the old Catholics. If the name of Sibthorpe was not mentioned, it was certainly not forgotten. When Manning left England shortly afterwards to join the *Accademia Ecclesiastica* in Rome, the *Tablet* made the acid remark that Mr. Manning, having been ordained, was now proceeding to Rome 'for the commencement of his ecclesiastical studies'.

In Rome Manning was received with the greatest cordiality. The Pope gave him audience, dismissing him with the appropriate words: 'I bless you with all my heart "in your going out and your coming in".'[2] Unlike Newman, whom the Roman ecclesiastics always found difficult to understand and with whom Newman himself showed little sympathy, Manning lost no time in making himself *persona gratissima* in the highest possible circles. He remained in Rome from 1851 until 1854, returning to England only for the summer months. 'During those three years I received from Pius IX a fatherly kindness,' he recorded in his Journal more than twenty years later. 'I saw him nearly every month, and he spoke with me freely on many things, and gave me freedom to speak to him. It was the beginning of the confidence which was never broken. I owe to Cardinal Wiseman and to Pius IX all that has befallen me in my Catholic life.'[3] To these two names he might have added that of

---

[1] *Dublin Review*, January 1919.
[2] 'Vi benedico con tutto il mio cuore, *in tuo egressu, et ingressu.*' Purcell: *Life of Manning*, Vol. II, p. 10.   [3] Ibid., p. 19.

Monsignor Talbot, for the two men became friends at once, finding an identity of opinion on all the questions which were later to disturb the tranquillity of the new hierarchy, and a mutual devotion to Cardinal Wiseman and all that he represented. In Talbot Manning was to have a fanatical ally at the Court of Rome who would watch his interests and encourage his schemes until, two years after Wiseman's death, a mental breakdown brought his career to an end. Talbot's complete devotion to the interests of Wiseman and, after 1851, of Manning, left little room in his mind, which could fairly be described as narrow, for the affairs of other people; least of all for that other distinguished convert, John Henry Newman.

Newman, indeed, was to fade into the background of the Cardinal's life after Manning's return from Rome in 1854. Newman belonged essentially to his earlier period, the period of his greatest intellectual vigour, when his sympathies lay with such men as Döllinger, Montalembert and Lacordaire, the period of his controversial lectures and his theological essays in the *Dublin Review*. Wiseman's respect for Newman remained unchanged, but in his later years, when ill-health weighed down on him, he found himself less sympathetic to Newman's continuous and often startling intellectual activity, and was distressed when differing attitudes to the question of the Pope's temporal power, threatened by the unification of Italy in the years between 1848 and 1861, separated them still further. Newman was hurt by what often appeared as coldness on the Cardinal's part; Wiseman was no less unhappy at his uneasy relations with his greatest convert.

Manning was not an intellectual in so far as his mind was more concerned with facts than ideas. Having once accepted the Catholic faith he seemed to have put doubt behind him for ever. This gave him little sympathy with less arbitrary temperaments but also gave him great strength, and it was upon this strength that Wiseman was to rely more and more as problems and disputes clouded his closing years, while health rapidly declined. That Manning came to exercise considerable ascendancy over the Cardinal cannot be denied, but that he insinuated himself into the good graces of the Archbishop from motives of ambition, as some have suggested, is to misunderstand both his temperament and the circumstances of his rise to power. Manning was only ambitious for the triumph of the 'Roman spirit' which Wiseman had introduced into England and which Manning, as his disciple, was to maintain. But the extent to which he identified his own ideas, or those of the Cardinal whose champion he became, with absolute truth gave to his career the character of personal ambition. In fact, his two great achievements, his appointment first as Provost of the Westminster Chapter, and secondly as Wiseman's successor as Archbishop, were the result of direct acts of the Pope, unsolicited by Wiseman in either case. The fact that Manning's nomination to succeed the Cardinal as second Archbishop of Westminster came as a surprise even to Monsignor Talbot, who considered himself as Manning's chief ambassador in Rome, shows how little personal ambition had to do with it. Manning could truly claim, as he did in 1878, 'All that has come upon me has come without any seeking. I was made a rector without being a curate, archdeacon without being a canon, provost without being a canon also, and archbishop without being a bishop.'[1] As to Wiseman's opinion of his worth, nine years after confirming him as a Catholic he told Cardinal Barnabò: 'I do not hesitate to say that in all England there is not another priest who in double the time has done what Dr. Manning has for the advantage of the Catholic Church,'[2] If such was his opinion it is hardly surprising that he chose to share with Manning the ever increasing burdens of his position as head of the hierarchy.

[1] Ibid., p. 19.   [2] Ward, Vol. II, p. 358.

XV

For some time after the 'Papal aggression' outcry Catholics found themselves ostracized by their fellow citizens; priests who had once been greeted in a friendly manner by their Protestant neighbours now found themselves cut, and the Cardinal himself was less welcome than he had formerly been in general society. He was subjected to a further reminder of public hostility when he visited the island of Jersey in 1851. When he drove to the Catholic church a howling mob followed his carriage which they made the target for a volley of brickbats and other missiles, so that when he reached his destination the windows were all shattered. A crowd of Protestants came to hear him preach. If their intention had been to jeer at the Roman prelate they soon discovered that they had misjudged their man. The directness of his style, his solid English common sense, and his genial character which seemed quite un-abashed by the ill-mannered nature of his reception, soon won the hearts of the islanders. He was given a courteous hearing and remained several days in the island without being molested any further; and finally left after dining with the Lieutenant-Governor, leaving behind him an atmosphere of friendliness in complete contrast to the hysteria which had greeted his arrival.

Wherever there had been an outbreak of anti-Catholic feeling the presence of the Cardinal could generally be relied upon to put things right and restore a modicum of common sense. It was this particularly English quality which impressed itself upon his critics and traducers when they were brought face to face with the Cardinal in person. It was thus when he visited Bath in May 1852. He came to refute a number of sensational accusations made against 'Romish' nunneries by a Protestant clergyman of the name of Seymour, who had lectured upon the subject in the same town. The theme of Catholic nunneries has always been one to excite the imagination of Rome's less erudite critics, and the Rev. Hobart Seymour seems to have been no exception. We get a hint of the style of his attack in a letter which Wiseman wrote to Monsignor Talbot after his own lecture had been delivered. 'I send you a pamphlet which has been published on nunneries, by Mr. Hobart Seymour. I have answered it in a lecture delivered at Bath, where he gave his. But it would be most important to get (as you can) authentic answers to what he says about the Roman convents, e.g., that almost all the nuns die of madness before 25—that one threw herself into the Tyber (*sic*) in 1845, publicly (in his *Pilgrimage to Rome* he says it was an abbess) that another stabbed herself, etc. I have given the lie to these statements, but should much like to have an authentic *confutation*. The police could give it—and any residents of the time. He speaks of a married man attending the Cardinal Vicar's visitations, and in an answer to questions sent to him, he says that the man had married since, therefore he could not have been a priest. Now is it possible that anyone not a priest can have formed part of the Cardinal Vicar's staff, in visiting convents? Any information which you can get me towards more and more exposing this lying and slandering parson the better.'[1]

Once again the Cardinal impressed his hearers by the solid English qualities of his personality. Fortunately a reporter from the *Bath Chronicle* was present when Wiseman delivered his lecture, so we have an eyewitness account of the scene. 'His Eminence entered the chapel,' we are told, 'preceded and followed by some of the officials of the place, soon after seven o-clock, and took his seat in a chair placed for him in front of the high altar. He is a portly and "comfortable" looking man, with little of the appearance or the expression conventionally attributed to the priesthood of his Church; he is thoroughly English in feature and in accent, with a good deal of curling brown hair descending from his head. He was dressed in the scarlet robes of his office, including a small skull-cap of that colour on the crown of his head, which remains after he removes his many-cornered hat. After a few sentences from the Romish Liturgy

[1] Rome, English College Archives. The Talbot Papers.

had been chanted, the Cardinal advanced a few paces, and commenced—"In the Name of the Father, and of the Son, and of the Holy Ghost, Amen". The exordium of his address he delivered standing: when he addressed himself to the matter of Mr. Seymour's pamphlet, he took his seat in the chair, and remained sitting until the close of his lecture, which occupied nearly two hours and a quarter in the delivery.' Despite the obviously favourable impression which Wiseman's presence made on the reporter, it is only fair to add that the readers of the *Bath Chronicle* were treated to a display of anti-Catholic acerbity characteristic of the period which they, no doubt, considered as their due. 'No one would have dreamt,' the report later declares, 'that so soft-spoken, mild-mannered, and insinuating a gentleman was the audacious violator not merely of the law, but, what is more, of the political and religious feeling of this realm. No one would have dreamt that the Church which he insinuated was so meek, holy, and long-suffering had kindled the fires of Smithfield, commemorated the horrible massacre of St. Bartholomew, and gloried in the unspeakable atrocities of the Inquisition.' To the readers of these lines it would appear that not a single Catholic martyr had ever suffered at the stake in England or that the two Tudor Queens, those extraordinary examples of womanhood, had not vied with each other in sending their religious opponents to the rack, the gallows, and the block.

By lecturing in various parts of the country and demonstrating the peaceful intentions of what Lord John Russell had so misguidedly stigmatized as an aggression, Cardinal Wiseman did much to reconcile the country to the presence of a Roman Catholic hierarchy in its midst. Despite the harm he had done and the misery and chaos he had caused, Russell's campaign against the Church had petered out, and in the end *Punch* was to caricature him as the naughty little boy who chalked 'No Popery' on Wiseman's door and then ran away. But useful as Wiseman's lectures were, and helpful as his obviously English temperament was in calming Protestant fears, his real work lay in these years immediately following the establishment of the hierarchy in organizing the transition from the old to the new form of ecclesiastical government among the Catholics themselves, not all of whom had welcomed the hierarchy with open arms. It was to this end that he called, in the summer of 1852, a Synod of the new Province of Westminster, to draw up the decrees which would form the constitution by which the Church in England would henceforth be governed. Upon the successful outcome of this meeting he set great store; 'I hope,' he wrote to Talbot,[1] 'to make the Synod a new and stronger bond between the English Church and the Holy See.'

The Synod met at Oscott, its sessions lasting from the 6th to the 17th of July. It was attended by the twelve bishops of the new hierarchy with their theologians, representatives of the diocesan Chapters, heads of religious Orders, and others specially invited; numbering in all about fifty persons. The Cardinal, as Metropolitan of the Province, presided, and was largely responsible for drawing up the various decrees. Both Newman and Manning were present; something of the feelings of the latter was expressed in a letter written to Robert Wilberforce on July 11th: 'It is a majestic sight to see the Church after centuries taking up its work again with all the calm and ease as if it were resuming the sessions of yesterday. I have no words to express what is the divine life and divine reality of the Church and its acts.'[2]

Certainly everything had been done to give dignity to the occasion. All the prescribed ceremonial was followed in its elaborate detail; the scarlet and ermine of the Cardinal's robes, the purple of the bishops, and the different coloured habits of the religious Orders were set off against the splendid background of Pugin's Gothic chapel, in which the meetings of the Synod were held. It was fitting that those ceremonies, which would have so delighted his heart, should have taken place in the last months of the architect's life. But Pugin was not there to witness this medieval scene. His mind deranged by overwork, this most eccentric and unpredictable of converts was confined to his house at Ramsgate where he died, two months later, quite insane and only forty years of age. It was a tragic end for one who had brought such enthusiasm and beauty into the life of the Catholic Church, which he had championed with untiring zeal from the moment he had first entered her fold.

It was another convert who gave to this first Provincial Synod its particular distinction in a sermon preached on July 13th,

---

[1] Letter of 27th May 1852. Rome, English College Archives. The Talbot Papers.
[2] Purcell: *Life of Manning*, Vol. II, p. 29.

following the Mass of the Holy Spirit which opened the second session; for it was upon this occasion that Newman addressed the fathers of the Synod in what is, perhaps, the most famous sermon he was to deliver as a Catholic, that which was to be known by the name of *The Second Spring*. Contrasting the way in which the fallen year renews itself in each successive Spring while the works of man, like his own life, are mortal, 'they die, and they have no power of renovation', he pointed to the unique position in which they, as the heirs of the ancient English Church, found themselves on that day; for having once possessed the land and then been cast out, they now found themselves once more returning to their inheritance. 'We should judge rightly in our curiosity about a phenomenon like this;' he declared, 'it must be a portentous event, and it is. It is an innovation, a miracle, I may say, in the course of human events. The physical world revolves year by year, and begins again; but the political order of things does not renew itself, does not return; it continues, but it proceeds; there is no retrogression. This is so well understood by men of the day, that with them progress is idolized as another name for good. The past never returns—it is never good;—if we are to escape existing ills, it must be by going forward. The past is out of date; the past is dead. As well may the dead live to us, as well may the dead profit us, as the past return. *This*, then, is the cause of this national transport, this national cry, which encompasses us. The past *has* returned, the dead lives. Thrones are overturned, and are never restored; States live and die, and then are matter only for history. Babylon was great, and Tyre, and Egypt, and Nineve, and shall never be great again. The English Church was, and the English Church was not, and the English Church is once again. This is the portent, worthy of a cry. It is a coming in of a second Spring; it is a restoration in the moral world, such as that which yearly takes place in the physical.'

Newman went on to describe the sad state into which the Church had fallen, the plight of its existence even fifty years before—'No longer the Catholic Church in the country; nay, no longer, I may say, a Catholic community;—but a few adherents of the Old Religion, moving silently and sorrowfully about, as memorials of what has been.' How different that was from the old days of faith: 'A *great* change, an *awful* contrast, between the time-honoured

Church of St. Augustine and St. Thomas, and the poor remnant of their children in the beginning of the nineteenth century! It was a miracle, I might say, to have pulled down that lordly power; but there was a greater and a truer one in store. No one could have prophesied its fall, but still less would any one have ventured to prophesy its rise again.' Then, in a moving passage, he described the fulfilment of just such a prophecy. 'A second temple rises on the ruins of the old. Canterbury has gone its way, and York is gone, and Durham is gone, and Winchester is gone. It was sore to part with them. We clung to the vision of past greatness, and would not believe it could come to nought; but the Church in England has died, and the Church lives again. Westminster and Nottingham, Beverley and Hexham, Northampton and Shrewsbury, if the world lasts, shall be names as musical to the ear, as stirring to the heart, as the glories we have lost; and Saints shall rise out of them, if God so will, and Doctors once again shall give the law to Israel, and Preachers call to penance and justice, as at the beginning.'

It was an age in which men were not ashamed to give vent to their emotions; by the time the sermon was ended there was hardly a person present who was not in tears. For Wiseman, seated on his throne and surrounded by his bishops and clergy, to hear the labour of his lifetime and the crowning of his ambitions for the English Church thus eloquently extolled in the words of the man whose conversion to the Faith was so much the result of his own work and prayers, was an experience beyond the power of his generous heart to control. 'All were weeping,' declared one eye-witness,[1] 'most of us silently, but some audibly; as to the big-hearted Cardinal, he fairly gave up the effort at dignity and self-control, and sobbed like a child.' This moment, indeed, may well be looked upon as the greatest in Cardinal Wiseman's life. His whole ambition was to fuse into one the various strands which made up the Catholic community; the old Catholics with their traditions going back to penal times, the monastic orders whose introduction into England he had so greatly favoured, and above all the converts, with whom he stood in so special and intimate a relationship. At this moment, as the greatest of the converts preached to this assembly in which all these different traditions were represented, united in

[1] Canon Crookall. Quoted by Butler, *Life of Ullathorne*, Vol. I, p. 197.

their purpose, it seemed that Wiseman's most cherished ambition had reached fulfilment. This, alas, was not so. Many disillusionments, many disappointments, even bitternesses, were to lie ahead. Old loyalties and ancient traditions were to prove at times too strong to accommodate themselves to new requirements, and there was to be much unhappiness. But for a moment the clouds had rolled back and disclosed the shining vision. The clouds would gather again, but the vision would not be forgotten. If Wiseman was not to see such unity again in the flock over which he ruled, he must have known that eventually it would return, even if he himself had by then passed from the scene. His great share in bringing to fruition this 'second Spring' was acknowledged on all sides. 'The conducting of this Synod was the masterpiece of Cardinal Wiseman,' Bishop Ullathorne later wrote.[1] 'He it was who drew up the decrees, excepting the constitutions of the Cathedral Chapters, which were committed to Bishop Grant and myself. The unity and harmony which pervaded that Synod is one of the most delightful reminiscences of my episcopal life. Certainly no one but Cardinal Wiseman, who concentrated his whole capacious mind upon it in one of his happiest moods, could have brought it to so successful an issue, or have given it so great an amount of ecclesiastical splendour.'

Such was the generous testimony of one who was present. To those on the look-out for trouble, however, for the heresy-hunters and the discontented, another picture was presented. For all the appearance of unity the germs of future discord were discernible for those who looked for them. The secular priests of the older generation were far from reconciled to the new monastic orders, which they considered both un-English and unnecessary. The bishops were discontented about the arrangements for the control of the four seminaries, which now had to be shared between thirteen dioceses. The mission priests were disappointed that the parochial system had not been introduced with the new hierarchy; and the old Catholics considered that the Cardinal showed too marked a preference for the converts, whose schemes he favoured at the expense, so it seemed, of those who had borne the heat and burden of the day. To Monsignor Talbot, viewing the scene from the distance of the Vatican and ever ready to find trouble-makers,

[1] Ullathorne: *Autobiography*, p. 258.

discover plots, and expose traitors, the picture presented by the Synod was not quite such a peaceful one as Bishop Ullathorne, for all that he was present at it, would suppose. Talbot's misgivings were expressed in a letter, written to Wiseman's secretary, Monsignor Searle, on 10th September 1852.

'I have several times intended to write to you,' Talbot's letter began, 'to thank you for your kind letter in which you give me so interesting an account of the Oscott Synod, which I am delighted to hear has gone off so well. I hope it will have happy results, and indeed I have no doubts of it, because I feel that when the Holy See has authorized the bishops of a Province to meet in Synod, and when it will have confirmed the decrees, the blessing of God is upon the act, and it must in due time bring forth good fruit. I say this, because there is a party in England which takes a very different view of the matter. There is a party which sets its face against everything the Bishops do, even criticizes the acts of the Holy See, and whose voice has been heard even here, and who gives a most deplorable account of the state of the Catholic Church in England. As for myself I look upon them as Puseyites half converted. In fact I have seen a letter which says that the Hierarchy, the Synod, and everything the Bishops do, does, and is likely to do more harm than good. It says that conversions are falling off exceedingly, and that apostasies are increasing. That nothing is done at all for the poor of London, and that they are in an infinitely worse state than they were before. The leading men in this party of critics are Lewis, Ward, McMillan etc. They have, as few Puseyite converts have, no respect whatever for Episcopal Authority, and very little even for that of the Holy See which sanctions and confirms the actions of the Bishops.'[1]

That there was a growing opposition to Wiseman would soon become apparent, but Talbot was quite wrong in thinking it would come from the converts (least of all from the ultramontane Ward who, layman and convert that he was, Wiseman had just appointed Professor of Theology at St. Edmund's College) or that it would imply disloyalty to the Holy See. It was an unfortunate characteristic of this busy Monsignor that he identified opposition to his own ideas, or the ideas of others whose champion he considered himself to be, with disloyalty to the Sovereign Pontiff. This

[1] Southwark Archives.

was to cause endless trouble in future, and was to mean that many of the genuine grievances of the English bishops, when reported to the Vatican through the agency of Talbot, were to be strangely distorted. Dr. Grant, the Bishop of Southwark and a former Rector of the English College at Rome, was a particular victim of Talbot's misguided suspicions. One would gather from Talbot's correspondence that this bishop was wholly given over to the principles of Gallicanism whereas, in fact, his devotion to the Holy See was never in question and was to be vindicated at the time of the Vatican Council (had it, in fact, ever been in doubt) though by then his one-time accuser had been two years confined in a mental home.

It was, in fact, from the bishops, and from the Bishop of Southwark especially, that opposition did come. The special circumstances of Wiseman's appointment to the See of Westminster and the fact that some of the new bishops were his former pupils at the English College, tended to make him somewhat overbearing in his relations with the rest of the hierarchy. It must be remembered that all bishops, under the Pope, have equal authority and jurisdiction in their own dioceses, and that the primacy of the Metropolitan See did not extend to the internal and domestic problems of the other bishoprics, though it was natural that they should act in concert whenever possible and that it rested with the Archbishop to convene meetings and preside at any such gatherings, while the scarlet of the Sacred College gave him an added primacy of honour. But it was felt by some bishops that Wiseman overstepped the limits imposed by tact as well as by tradition in the exercise of his metropolitan duties and that he enjoyed an all too autocratic sway over the Province. To this problem another was added, for the ill-feeling which still prevailed in official circles as a result of the 'Flaminian Gate' Pastoral had embarrassed the Cardinal's relationship with the Government so that it was necessary for the bishops to look to someone else as their representative in this respect. The natural choice was Dr. Grant, both on account of his own abilities and of the fact that his diocese of Southwark placed him in close proximity to the seat of government. But in arranging this delicate matter the feelings of the Cardinal were deeply hurt. He felt that the matter had been settled behind his back, though if this was indeed the case it was probably done only to spare him embarrassment.

Whatever the cause, it appears that Dr. Grant came in for the Cardinal's censure and wrote, no doubt, to explain his case. In a reply, written in April, 1853, Wiseman poured out a long list of his complaints, which is a sad commentary on the deterioration of affairs since the Synod had met at Oscott only nine months before. 'I never have objected, nor could object,' the Cardinal wrote, 'to each bishop acting for himself, as he thinks right. And any grievances your Lordship finds in your Diocese you have a right to get redressed as *you* think right. And if your cases lead to the application of a general remedy, every one will accept it with gratitude.

'I have said to several persons, that if the Bishops had expressed an opinion (as has often been done at our meetings) that one should be deputed to arrange any given affair, I never should have thought of objecting; for I am glad to get anything put upon another. And if your Lordship had been delegated to undertake army and navy grievances I should have consented without difficulty. But I do object to anything like an arrangement being made partially, by private consultation at a meeting called by me, with express exclusion of me, from the determinations taken and delegation being made to anyone (in an affair where I have an equal interest) with an understanding that I was not to know it, but was to be left to find it out, and acquiesce tacitly. Confidence will be lost among us, if this new way of transacting business is to be carried on: and I find *several* bishops look upon this result as risked by what has happened.

'As to my being personally obnoxious to Government or to the Queen, I think that would be quite a good reason for me voluntarily to enter into an arrangement among ourselves to prevent my misfortune becoming an obstacle to any good being done: but not a ground for others to push me aside, or take measures over my head, because of my unpopularity. Suppose it had been known to Government that your Lordship had my full consent and understanding in acting, and that I had made no difficulty in keeping back, both out of self-respect and from having no wish to embarrass them, surely this would have pleased you and me and all other parties in a higher and better, and freer position, than if it should be seen and known (as I believe it is) that in condescension to *their* prejudices, your Lordship and some other bishop had thought it better to shove me aside, and not even consult me, but to act directly with them?'[1]

If, indeed, such negotiations had been going on behind the Cardinal's back, he had every reason to be displeased, for all that the motive for doing it may simply have been to spare him pain, for there is no doubt that he took his estrangement from Government and official circles very much to heart. Something of his previous mood of depression and feeling of isolation appears in the final paragraph of his letter, where he speaks of attempts to have him removed from his post. 'I must add in all confidence,' the letter ends, 'what you perhaps are not aware of, that the present Secretary of State is employing (I know not for what) the same instrument employed by Lord Malmesbury, to negotiate at Rome preliminary steps to get me away. But I must say, that the surest way to effect this, would be to divide us one from another: for were I ever to see that the Bishops thought they could get on better without my being in the way, than with me, I should be the first to apply to the Holy See to recall me from a position which of late has been more painful, more distasteful, and more burthensome to body and soul than it ever was during the worst storm of the *Aggression* tumult.'

Wiseman was already at cross-purposes with Dr. Grant over the division of the revenues of the former London District from which the two dioceses of Westminster and Southwark had been formed. The loss of St. George's Church, which had been the largest in the old District, and was now the Cathedral of Southwark, had been a blow to Wiseman, and now further difficulties arose over the division of other properties and funds. Wiseman could not claim a strong sense of business among his many other accomplishments and the matter dragged on in an unsatisfactory manner until eventually Dr. Grant took the case to Rome. The negotiations were long drawn out and acrimonious, and in the end the Bishop of Southwark was proved to be in the right, but when he first decided to refer the matter to Rome the Cardinal was vociferous in his indignation. 'Here is a sad business about to happen . . .' he wrote off in exasperation to Monsignor Talbot: 'The very idea of a suffragan[2] of the new Hierarchy, almost within a year, going off to Rome to carry thither

[1] Southwark Archives.

[2] Suffragan here denotes a bishop of a Province other than the Archbishop. It does not denote an auxiliary bishop to a diocesan in the sense in which the term Suffragan Bishop is used in the Anglican Church.

a case against his Metropolitan, and that one should be Dr. Grant, *homo pacis meae*, put at Southwark because he was my friend, is fraught with scandal.'[1]

It was thus in a portentous mood that Wiseman set out for Rome in the October of 1853. He was received with the usual cordiality and saw the Pope the day after his arrival, dining with him the next day in the company of the Grand Duke of Tuscany. He preached in English at the Church of St. Andrea delle Fratte, noticing in the congregation both Thackeray and Lockhart, the biographer of Walter Scott. He attended the Consistory at which the Archbishop of Perugia was nominated to the Sacred College, and attended his reception in the evening. It was this same Cardinal Pecci who would one day, as Leo XIII, place a red hat on the head of John Henry Newman. The familiar sights of Rome, and a visit to his beloved Monte Porzio, soon restored the Cardinal's spirits. 'I hope that my coming to Rome will prove to be of great use to me in many things which are not matters for letters,' he wrote in November to his old friend Henry Bagshawe; 'Personally I have already received benefit in health and spirits, for I was losing both fast before I left England. But how different I find things here, and how truly I am at once at home among those who can understand my conduct and know my principles and motives, and do not by rule misjudge me!'[2] Chief among those with whom he found himself so much at home were Talbot and Manning, the latter of whom was still pursuing his theological studies at the *Accademia dei Nobili Ecclesiastici*. Wiseman sought an audience with the Pope to ask that Manning should return at once to work in London, but Pius IX decided to keep him in Rome for another year. He was, however, able to secure the degree of Doctor in Philosophy for W. G. Ward, to whose appointment as professor at St. Edmund's the Pope had raised no objections; indeed, when a prelate had objected to a married man teaching in a theological seminary Pius had answered: 'It is a novel objection to the fitness of a man to do God's work that he has received a sacrament of Holy Church which neither you nor I have received.'[3]

Wiseman's chief purpose in visiting Rome was to get the decrees of the Oscott Synod ratified by the Holy See, and to discuss some of

[1] Butler: *Life of Ullathorne*, Vol. I, p. 203.　　[2] Ward, Vol. II, p. 71.
[3] Ibid., p. 74.

the complaints that were beginning to reach Rome about the conduct of affairs in England, such as the problems already mentioned which had arisen between himself and Dr. Grant. In such matters it is not the custom of the Court of Rome to come to hurried decisions and the points at issue were not decided for some years. For the moment the Cardinal had every reason to be satisfied with the results of his visit to the Eternal City. Dr. Grant, however, need not have feared that he was unappreciated by the inmost circles in Rome, as transpired in an interview given by the Cardinal Secretary of State to Lord Lyons, then British diplomatic representative at Rome. 'Cardinal Wiseman has announced his intention of leaving Rome this week for England,' Lyons reported on 28th March 1854. 'On my alluding to the circumstances in conversing this morning with Cardinal Antonelli, his Eminence, after a moment's reflection, told me, confidentially, that he hoped Cardinal Wiseman would be careful not to give offence in England by an unnecessary display, and that he would discharge his religious functions there in a quiet and unostentatious manner. Cardinal Antonelli said that he had himself urged the importance of this upon Cardinal Wiseman, and had pointed out to him the necessity in a country like England, to shun as much as possible irritating public opinion. Cardinal Antonelli mentioned with approbation the conduct of Dr. Grant (titular Roman Catholic Bishop of Southwark) who, he said, applied himself to his spiritual duties with unremitting zeal, but at the same time avoided obtruding himself unnecessarily on public notice.'[1]

The rumour, to which Wiseman himself had referred in his letter to Bishop Grant, that there was a movement against his returning to England, was mentioned by Lord Lyons at the conclusion of his report, though he dismisses such an eventuality as being, at the most, unlikely. 'The prolongation of Cardinal Wiseman's visit to Rome gave rise to many rumours that he was not to return to England, or at all events not to remain there long. It was said that his brother Cardinals considered the unrecognized and insignificant position he occupies there, as derogatory to the dignity of the Roman purple; and a general feeling (rather, however, implied than expressed) appears to exist here, that his conduct in England had not been judicious and that the erection of the hierarchy, and especially

---

[1] Public Record Office, FO 43/58.

the manner in which it was announced and carried out, were mistakes in religious policy. The prevailing report was that the Pope was likely to place Cardinal Wiseman at the head of the Propaganda, in the room of Cardinal Fransoni; whose age and infirmities render him unequal to the post, and throw a great amount of business on the Secretary, Monsignor Barnabò, than he is well able to perform. The tone of Cardinal Antonelli's conversation with me, so far as it could be said to give any indication one way or the other, rather implied that Cardinal Wiseman was likely to remain in England; and so, I understood, did expressions made use of by Cardinal Wiseman himself, in a sermon delivered by him last Sunday.'

Cardinal Wiseman certainly had no intention of resigning from his position as Archbishop of Westminster, though it is very likely that it was during this visit to Rome that he first put forward the suggestion that he should share the burdens of government with an assistant or coadjutor. There were various reasons why he should wish this. His health, never perfect, had been showing signs of deterioration in the past year, and he had been in the hands of surgeons. In addition to this there was an increasing demand from both Catholics and Protestants to hear him as a lecturer, an art in which he excelled by the geniality of his manner and the breadth of his erudition, making him a compelling and informative discourser on a wide variety of topics. Despite the fatigue involved by these occasions Wiseman felt that they were important in bringing himself before a large public and thus, perhaps, helping to dispel something of the lingering prejudice in which Catholics and Catholicism were held. To this it must be added that Wiseman was not over-efficient in the routine administration of diocesan affairs, preferring to leave to others the day-to-day *minutiae* of business and organization, leaving himself free for more general schemes and projects.

That Wiseman first broached the subject of a coadjutor either while he was in Rome in the autumn and winter of 1853, or soon after his return to England in April 1854, is suggested by a letter from Monsignor Talbot to the Cardinal's secretary, Monsignor Searle, dated from the Vatican, 24th September 1854. After a paragraph devoted to the Cardinal's recurrent ill-health, and the possible danger to his life, Talbot continues: 'But for the Glory of God, the advancement of the Church, and the salvation of souls, something must be done to prolong the life of the Cardinal. You say well, that he has three distinct characters in England. He is *quasi* Primate—he is the leader of the Catholic *litterateurs*—and he is a Bishop, with all the routine work of the Archdiocese of Westminster. The first two positions no one can occupy but himself, and as you say, his lectures are invaluable, which I believe from what I can hear of their effect on the English public. As for the third position, he might have someone to take a great deal of the work off his own shoulders.

'I have, therefore, after receiving your letter spoken to the Holy Father and suggested to him the possibility of Cardinal Wiseman applying for an auxiliary. An auxiliary I said, not a coadjutor which would be a much more serious matter of consideration. An auxiliary bishop can be removed at pleasure, so that the Cardinal would not feel himself too tied to him if he did not like him.'[1]

Whether the suggestion originated with Searle, with Talbot, or with Wiseman himself, it is difficult to say, but for once, when the decision was finally taken a year later, it was unfortunate that Talbot's advice was not taken and an auxiliary appointed. In the event a coadjutor was appointed with the right of succession to the See of Westminster, thus involving Wiseman in one of the most distressing episodes of the close of his career. Talbot's letter to Searle ended with an assessment of Manning's suitability for the position of auxiliary which shows the extent to which this convert of three years standing had already impressed himself upon the Pope's confidential adviser. 'As for Dr. Manning,' Talbot concludes, 'the great objection felt to him, is that he is yet a neophyte, but still it is a difficulty which I think might be got over if the Cardinal wished to have him as an Auxiliary. He certainly would be useful as a means of gaining converts, who are growing in number and power every day. The only objection I have heard made to him is that he retains a good deal of the Oxford and Puseyite way of viewing things, and that some people do not think he is yet heart and soul a Catholic, but I think this is more manner than else, and that he will get over it in the course of time.'

Few people, in fact, could have been more heart and soul a Catholic than the former Archdeacon of Chichester, but his hour

[1] Southwark Archives.

was not yet come. His appointment would have been utterly unacceptable to the old Catholics with their deep-seated distrust of converts. They had already objected at the haste with which Manning had been rushed to the priesthood, and any further preferment would have been strongly resented. But that Manning's name should have come forward for consideration at all at this early date is a tribute to the power and forcefulness of his personality, an indication of the strength upon which the increasingly invalid Cardinal would soon come to rely so much.

Wiseman performed one further act before he left Rome for England in the spring of 1854. In 1851 Newman had gone over to Ireland at the invitation of Dr. Cullen, then Archbishop of Armagh and later of Dublin, to lecture on education and to give advice on the formation of a Catholic University. In November of that year he had been appointed Rector of the embryonic University and was to spend the next seven years labouring against overwhelming odds to see the institution firmly established. From the beginning he had found the work frustrating and disheartening. In order to give him encouragement in this work and to strengthen his position with regard to the Irish hierarchy, Wiseman now persuaded the Pope to confer the dignity of a titular bishopric upon Newman. The Pope was delighted to honour so distinguished a convert and Wiseman was glad to make public reparation for his negligence in the matter of the Achilli trial. Newman welcomed this mark of confidence in his work with touching gratitude. 'My dear Lord Cardinal,' he wrote in answer to Wiseman's letter telling him of the nomination, 'Your Eminence's letter arrived yesterday evening, the very *anniversary* of the day of my having to appear in court, and of the sentence from Coleridge. And to-morrow, the Purification, is the sixth anniversary of the establishment of our Congregation, and completes the fifth year of our settlement in Birmingham. As to the Holy Father's most gracious and condescending purpose about me, I should say much of the extreme tenderness towards me shown in it, did not a higher thought occupy me, for it is the act of the Vicar of Christ, and I accept it most humbly as the will and determination of Him whose I am, and who may do with me what he will.'[1]

The news of the appointment soon became public and congratu-

[1] Ward, Vol. II, p. 74.

lations poured in. The Duke of Norfolk sent the bishop-designate a gold chain and other gifts reached the Oratorian. But a sad fate seemed to have fallen on the relations between Newman and Wiseman. Weeks passed and no news came of the consecration, which the Cardinal had said he wished to perform himself. The weeks stretched into months and there was still no word either from Westminster or Rome. It was like the Achilli case all over again. At length it became clear that no consecration would take place. Wiseman, in his impulsive generosity, had acted without properly consulting the Irish episcopate, and Archbishop Cullen, who wished to keep the ultimate control of the new University in his own hands, had no desire to see Newman's position so publicly consolidated. Strong pressure was brought to bear at the Vatican and the question of Newman's bishopric was allowed quietly to be dropped. But to so sensitive a nature as Newman's it was a bitter blow, and it was in no way softened by an embarrassed silence from the Cardinal-Archbishop of Westminster. 'The Cardinal never wrote to me a single word,' Newman later complained, 'or sent any sort of message to me, in explanation of the change of intention about me, till the day of his death.'[1] Thus Wiseman's endeavour to repair the damage to their friendship, springing from the best intentions and kindest motives, only resulted in a further unhappy estrangement.

[1] Newman: *Autobiographical Writings*, p. 318.

XVI

O n his return journey from Rome to London Cardinal
Wiseman spent a few days in Paris. He was at this time an
admirer of the Emperor Napoleon III whom he looked upon
as the man who had saved France from anarchy and revolution, and
who was prepared to defend the temporal power of the Pope. He
had shown his partiality for the Imperial cause in London when he
visited the French chapel there which was served almost exclusively
by royalist priests, who were wont to pray for the king rather than
for the emperor in the prayers for the head of the state after Mass.
The Cardinal showed his disapproval of this custom by chanting
'*Domine salvum fac Imperatorem nostrum*' in a very loud voice, to the
confusion of the priests who had been used to substitute the words
'*Regem nostrum*' at this point in the service. It was thus a matter of
considerable pleasure for him when, upon reaching Paris, the
Papal Nuncio to the French court arranged for him to be received by
the Imperial couple. 'I received a message that (the Emperor)
would give me an audience next day after Mass,' Wiseman wrote to
his sister on April 29th. 'On that day (the letter continues) he and
the Empress were to hear Mass at 12 below in the Chapel, and hear
the last Lent sermon. Three *priedieus* and *fauteuils* gilt and velvet
were placed before the Altar, for them and the Grand Duchess
Stephanie of Baden. It is customary for Cardinals to assist in full
costume on such occasions, so I went of course in best rochet, etc.
My place was opposite the pulpit at the side of the royal party, just
behind them. As they entered and went to take their places, each
gave me a most gracious bow. After the gospel their chairs were
turned round so as to face the pulpit, so that they would have their

backs to me. But the Empress turned her chair to one side and sat sideways, though they say in Spanish *"Las Senoras no tienen espaldas."* She was in mantilla, the Emperor in a plain suit, with one star. After Mass we followed the royal party upstairs, accompanied by the Duke of Bassano. The state apartments of the Tuileries are far more magnificent than they have ever been, as Louis Napoleon has spent an immense sum on decorating them. We were met by a Chamberlain, who told me that H. M. would receive me in the Empress's apartments, the Pavillion that looks over the *quai*. After passing through an anteroom full of the Court, I entered alone into a beautifully furnished room. The Emperor, Empress and Duchess were standing in the middle, and received me very condescendingly.

'After a few minutes general conversation, opened by the Emperor saying (and the Empress repeating) that he had long wished to know me, etc., and had hoped to make my acquaintance at Amiens[1] and continued about the Pope and Rome, etc., he asked me to sit down, and directed me to the *fauteuil* by the fireplace; next sat the Empress, then the Duchess, and he took a seat on the ottoman opposite. The conversation was most familiar and friendly, they asked me all sorts of questions about England, conversions, Puseyites, Lord Shrewsbury, the Duke of Norfolk, etc. The Empress is one of the sweetest, most amiable persons I ever saw. She asked me if I was not Spanish and had not been a few years ago in Spain. But upon our rising and introducing Mgr. Searle, Dr. Miley, and another who formed my *cortège*, the Empress opened in Spanish and we had quite a private chat about Spain, Seville, etc. I was really quite charmed . . .'

Wiseman closed his letter with the warning: 'Take care not to let anything of this audience get out, where there would be a chance of its getting into a newspaper.'[2]

This was the period when leaders of Catholic opinion in France still looked upon Napoleon III as a second Charlemagne, though at least one prelate[3] had been cynical enough of the emperor's intentions to express the hope that he would not ask for a *Te Deum* every time a conspiracy succeeded. It was not long before the more

---

[1] Wiseman had preached at Amiens on his way out to Rome when the relics of St. Theodosia were received in the Cathedral. Between twenty-five and thirty Cardinals, Archbishops and Bishops were present on this occasion.

[2] Rome, English College. The Fano Papers.   [3] Cardinal Pie.

liberal Catholics, the followers of Lacordaire and Montalembert, realized that Louis Napoleon's championship of the Church sprang from opportunist rather than religious motives and that he would have supported Mahommedanism with equal tolerance had it been the religion of the majority of Frenchmen. Wiseman himself came to see that the enthusiasm he had felt for the French emperor was misplaced. Had the Cardinal's life been prolonged by another five years he would have shared with Napoleon III, as he had already done with King Louis-Philippe, the experience of ministering to him in exile.

From the agreeable associations of Rome and the sumptuous hospitality of the Tuileries Wiseman returned to find himself involved in an unpleasant situation as soon as he set foot once more upon English soil. He was sued for libel by one of his own priests. The originator of this action was a certain Mr. Boyle, one of the dwindling minority of priests who still held strongly Gallican views. Boyle had been the assistant priest at a church in Islington which had come under the reforming hand of Wiseman when he was first appointed Vicar Apostolic of the London District. The church was failing to meet the needs of the area it served and the Bishop decided that a complete change of staff was necessary. The priest in charge of the Mission agreed to leave, but Boyle declared that Wiseman had no right to dismiss him, especially as he had spent a large amount of his own money on building the mission house. Eventually, after much persuasion, he was prevailed upon to leave, but only after he had demanded and received compensation for his financial losses. Both Wiseman and the Vicar Apostolic of the Western District offered him other employment, but this Mr. Boyle ostentatiously refused to accept, taking instead a situation as clerk in a business house. This was how things stood when the hierarchy was restored in 1850. Early in 1854 some articles appeared in the French journal *Ami de la Religion*, an organ of Gallican opinion, which roundly attacked the religious policy of the Church in England and in particular criticized the establishment of the hierarchy, suggesting that Wiseman had encouraged the measure from motives of personal ambition.

To those familiar with his personality it was clear that the mind of Boyle was behind these articles, which must have been based upon information supplied by him to the author, the Abbé Cognat.

Wiseman's friends in France came to his support in a series of articles which appeared in the Ultramontane journal *Univers* in the months of April and May. On May 15th the Cardinal addressed a long letter to the editor of the *Univers* thanking him for his support and depicting, in no uncertain terms, the disagreeable character of the priest upon whose testimony the other articles had been founded. The *Ami de la Religion* had described, in pitying terms, the spectacle of this priest 'pious and zealous, who had grown grey in the service of the altars, who perhaps had laid the first foundation stone of his church, receiving all at once a notice, conveyed in a simple note, that he had ceased to be Pastor of his flock . . . and at the same time condemned, in his declining years, to languish in the depths of distress'. This clear, but incomplete, picture quite failed to note that Boyle was only the assistant priest, that he was removed because the church was empty and his work inefficient, and that he had been offered, but declined, two other appointments. All this, and much more, Wiseman pointed out in this letter. If Boyle's career lacked the sensational highlights which had characterized that of Dr. Achilli, his story was none the less unedifying, displaying a temperament unsuited to the office of the priesthood and a career of continual obstruction to canonical obedience.

Wiseman's letter was written in English. He began his denunciation of Boyle (whom he never actually named) by revealing that once he had been a member of a religious order from which he had subsequently been removed. Here the Cardinal had indicated the use of the French word *renvoyé* to make his meaning clear, but the translator had instead employed the stronger expression *expulsé*. Wiseman's letter to the *Univers* was reproduced in full in a subsequent issue of the *Tablet*, but instead of obtaining the original English version from the Cardinal, that journal (assuming, perhaps, that Wiseman had written in French in the first place, as he might well have done) simply issued a re-translation of the French text. In this form the passage which was to form the basis of the action for libel read as follows: 'Let us suppose that we look at the information thus given, and that its outcome is that the Priest who presents himself or who is presented to the public as the victim of Episcopal tyranny and oppression, was formerly a member of a religious society from which he was expelled; that he was kindly given occupation in a diocese, but that he was never incorporated in it; that instead of having grown grey in the service of the altars, and of having founded a church, he was only employed for some years, and that it was in the quality of Curate or assistant Priest.'[1] Boyle had indeed been a member of the Society of Jesus, but he was not 'expelled'; he had left the Society because he had felt himself unequal to accepting the vows which the Society expects its members to take.

Cardinal Wiseman was to face three trials as a result of this unfortunate mistranslation. The case was first heard at Guildford on 18th August 1854, before the Lord Chief Baron. The Judge, who treated the Cardinal with marked courtesy, was not persuaded that the translation containing the objectionable word 'expelled' was published on the Cardinal's responsibility, and Boyle was accordingly nonsuited. An appeal was made against this verdict, however, and at the second trial damages amounting to a thousand pounds were awarded to Boyle, both judge and jury showing strong feeling against the Cardinal. But in a final act to the drama the Court of Exchequer set aside this verdict on the ground of 'excessive damages and improper reception of evidence'[2] and yet another trial was ordered for the summer of 1855. But by this time Mr. Boyle had become weary of the law's delay or did not dare risk the chance of another favourable verdict and proposed a compromise which was eventually negotiated without further litigation. At the beginning of the hearings the press had once again raised the old cry of 'No Popery' and the Cardinal was subjected to its now familiar onslaught, but as in the Achilli case there was a reaction in his favour after the second trial when some indignation was shown at what was clearly felt to be an unduly heavy assessment of damage.

Wiseman found distraction from the cares of office and the irritations of litigation by completing a work of fiction which he had started on his journey to Rome in the autumn of 1853. He finished this work while staying at the seaside town of Filey, where he had gone for a brief rest after the first trial. The book was ready in September 1854 and was published under the name of *Fabiola*. How this book came to be written he describes in the Preface. 'When the plan of the *Popular Catholic Library* was formed, the

[1] Ward, Vol. II, p. 89.　　　　　　　　　　　　　[2] Ibid., p. 95.

author . . . was consulted upon it. He not only approved of the design, but ventured to suggest, among others, a series of tales illustrative of the condition of the Church in different periods of her past existence. One, for instance, might be called "The Church of the Catacombs"; a second, "The Church of the Basilicas"—each comprising three hundred years; . . . In proposing this sketch, he added—perhaps the reader will find indiscreetly—that he felt half inclined to undertake the first, by way of illustrating the proposed plan. He was taken at his word, and urged strongly to begin the work.'

Fabiola, he tells us, had been 'written at all sorts of times and in all sorts of places; early and late, when no duty urged, in scraps and fragments of time, when the body was too fatigued or the mind too worn for heavier occupation; in the roadside inn, in the halt of travel, in strange houses, in every variety of situation and circumstances—sometimes trying ones. It has thus been composed bit by bit, in portions varying from ten lines to half-a-dozen pages at most, and generally with few books or resources at hand. But once begun, it has proved what it was taken for,—a recreation, and often a solace and a sedative; from the memories it has revived, the associations it has renewed, the scattered and broken remnants of old studies and early readings which it has combined, and by the familiarity which it has cherished with better times and better things than surround us in our age.' The idea of a Cardinal writing a work of fiction was sufficiently unusual for it to cause some consternation among the author's fellow Princes of the Church when news of it reached Rome, but the high tone of the narrative, its skilful presentation of Christian principles against the background of a Pagan world, and the instant and wide success which it enjoyed, soon reconciled even the most conservative of them to so unconventional an event. It was described by the Archbishop of Milan as 'the first good book which has had the success of a bad one'.[1]

In a century so prolific of great novels as the nineteenth, *Fabiola* cannot be said to hold a very high place, and to the modern reader this story of persecution and martyrdom in early fourth-century Rome is interesting more for the wealth of antiquarian scholarship displayed by the author than for its qualities as a work of fiction.

[1] Edward Hulton, 'Catholic English Literature' in *The English Catholics 1850–1950*.

The narrative is not lacking in exciting episodes but the characters rarely come to life, and the reader soon wearies of the lengthy theological disquisitions with which the Christian characters in the story improve every occasion—even the slaves, one feels, would have qualified, in a more peaceful age, for at least a Bachelor's degree in Divinity. It is, indeed, altogether too much of a study in black and white; the pagan characters, except for a heroine obviously destined for conversion, lacking almost any qualities other than the most villainous or craven. But one cannot read it without being aware of the sincerity of the author, who was avowedly writing a work of propaganda. If one can no longer agree with the verdict of the Archbishop of Milan and still regard it as a good book which has, or deserves, the success of a bad one, it cannot be denied that it is obviously the work of a good man. Despite the weight of scholarship which belies the modest disclaimer of the Preface, and despite the rather fustian phraseology which indulges in such expressions as: 'Haughty Roman dame! thou shalt bitterly rue this day and hour. Thou shalt know and feel how Asia can revenge,'—one is left at the end with a strong impression of the deep and simple conviction of the mind which inspires the narrative.

These are the reactions of a modern reader. At the time of its publication *Fabiola* had an instantaneous and even spectacular success, and in a short time had been translated into Italian, French, Spanish, Portuguese, Hungarian, German, Danish, Polish, Slavonian and Dutch, an achievement which even the most ambitious author could view with some complacency; and at the present day, as a recent writer[1] has recorded, it 'has become as national to Italian life as olive oil and pasta'. The success of his book certainly gave Wiseman great pleasure. 'You would be amused if I were to tell you half the things I hear from the Continent about *Fabiola*,' he wrote to his friend Canon Walker. 'The King of Prussia's reading it is like Assuerus's tale. He could not sleep one night, and he sent for it, and read it through at once. He spoke to the Archbishop of Cologne about it, and he told me—not with those details, however. One German Benedictine Abbot sent me a splendid ring as a token. But the most curious of all is Rome. When it was first announced that I had written "a romance" there was terrible commotion among

[1] Bernard Wall: *Report on the Vatican*, p. 175.

my cardinalitial brethren. Now, however, from the Pope down-wards I have nothing but thanks and compliments, and all Rome is placarded with it, my name in large type. I consider this a perfect revolution, a great triumph of the "spirit of the age" or "progress" over forms and etiquettes.'[1]

Despite the harassing business of the Boyle trial and the cares of administering the archdiocese, the period just before the appoint-ment of Dr. Errington as coadjutor was upon the whole a happy one for the Cardinal, and found him upon occasions in excellent high spirits. This pleasant mood is seen in his correspondence with Bishop Patterson, who at this time was the Cardinal's Master of Ceremonies. In Patterson's presence the Cardinal could unbend in a way he was never able to do in front of strangers, who often found him remote and formal, and in writing to him showed a lighter side that children could always bring out in him but those who knew him only in his official capacity would not have thought existed. Thus when the Bishop of Amiens visited Wiseman, and brought with him a musician of unusual stoutness, the Cardinal informed his Master of Ceremonies: 'There is come with the Bp. of Amiens (not of his suite) a priest with a 20 serpent, 5 double bass, and 10 trombone power combined, who sings a solo in plain chant *à merveille*. They are anxious that he should break all the windows for us tomorrow . . . by the detonation of his intonation. He would sing, if there be room for it, an *O Salutaris* after the Elevation or the Gradual. Ask Mr. McQuoin if he can give him an opportunity of exploding. It is considered the best voice in France, and the instru-ment is in proportion to the sound, being of 5 canon dimensions. If the music be Gregorian in any part, he can act as a pedalpipe to it.'[2]

The visit of another French prelate, the Bishop of Bayeux, gave Wiseman an opportunity to indulge in a volley of puns, a form of humour more beloved by the nineteenth than the twentieth century. 'There will be a sweet variety of costumes in the choir,' he wrote to Mgr. Patterson, 'the Bishop having requested that Canons should appear in *habits de choeur*, upon which I placed my hand on my *coeur*, or the habits over it, and bowed over the same with my ear to the shoulder, which was meant for a gracious assent thereto.'[3]

[1] Quoted by Ward, Vol. II, pp. 100–1. [2] Ibid., Vol. II, p. 195.
[3] Ibid., p. 196.

The readiness of Wiseman's humour could sometimes save him from embarrassing situations. This happened upon the occasion of a Corpus Christi procession when the Master of Ceremonies was a man of more eccentric potentialities than Mgr. Patterson, for he suddenly halted the procession, announcing that he had been told by special revelation to stop. The Cardinal took the situation quite calmly; he paused a few moments, and then quietly told the Master of Ceremonies: 'You may let the procession go on. I have obtained permission, by special revelation, to proceed with it.' This explanation appeared thoroughly satisfactory to the other, and the ceremony was resumed.

It was at this time[1] that Robert Browning's poem *Bishop Blougram's Apology* was published, and was generally taken to represent Browning's opinion of Cardinal Wiseman. That the poet did indeed have the Cardinal in mind when he wrote *Blougram* he later on admitted in a letter to Dr. Furnivall written after Wiseman's death: 'The most curious notice I ever had was from Cardinal Wiseman on *Blougram*—i.e. himself. It was in the *Rambler*, a Catholic Journal of those days, and certified to be his by Father Prout, who said nobody else would have dared put it in.'[2] Browning, of course, never knew Wiseman. His poem simply gives us an idea of the impression Wiseman might have made upon someone who knew very little about him except what could be observed from the outside—a prelate of considerable bulk who appeared to enjoy the pleasures of the table, the *amateur* of music, poetry and art, the accomplished writer and lecturer, urbane and polished if a little sceptical on the finer points of belief. As a picture of the real Wiseman it bore no relation to the truth but no doubt represented the sort of impression made by this figure upon whom 'all eyes turn with interest' when the eye rested only upon the external and did not care to discover what lay beneath the genial, slightly pompous, prelatical figure in scarlet robes.[3] The review to which Browning referred in his letter does not give the reader any reason to suppose

---

[1] 1855. [2] *Letters by Robert Browning*, collected by Thomas V. Wise, p. 195.
[3] Mr. Algernon Cecil, in *Queen Victoria and Her Prime Ministers*, (p. 214) suggests Wiseman as a possible original for the Cardinal in Disraeli's novel *Lothair*, though the description of this character's appearance and the fact that the book was published five years after Wiseman's death, would point to Manning as a more likely candidate; though in making him a Cardinal in 1870 Disraeli anticipated Pius IX by five years.

that its author had a very high opinion of the character represented by Bishop Blougram, but it ends on a characteristically optimistic note which might well have come from the pen of Wiseman: 'If Mr. Browning is a man of will and action, and not a mere dreamer and talker, we should never feel surprised at his conversion.'[1]

As tempers cooled after the 'aggression' hysteria had died down, Wiseman began to be accepted as a part of the London scene, a notable and, indeed, distinguished figure now that he was no longer regarded as an agent of the Inquisition wholly devoted to the enslavement of Englishmen to a foreign usurpation; and the Cardinal himself became a little less ostentatious in his public appearances. He used a less splendid carriage and no longer expected to be met by torchbearers when he dined out. He adopted a less conspicuous style of dress than the cardinalitial scarlet for purely lay occasions, though he can hardly have passed without notice at the private views of the Royal Academy where his simple clerical habit was set off by scarlet gloves and skull-cap. He made himself very accessible to visitors who came to him with problems or questions even when these were not directly related to ecclesiastical affairs. When Charles Kean, the actor, was to appear in the *rôle* of Cardinal Wolsey in Shakespeare's *Henry VIII* he sought Wiseman's advice about his costume. The Cardinal asked the actor to call on him, and then had all his robes brought and vested himself in them, describing each article as he put it on, giving a brief sketch of its history and origin. Kean proposed having a box at the theatre draped so that the Cardinal could sit there unobserved to watch his performance.

It was primarily as a lecturer that Cardinal Wiseman came into contact with those outside his own flock, and was able to establish contact with a larger world, which had previously known of him only as the 'aggressive Popish Cardinal'. In this world still spared the horrors of modern mass entertainment, the lecture was a popular form of relaxation, combining recreation with information, and it was a form in which Wiseman excelled. 'To the London world,' *The Times* wrote at his death, 'and to the public at large, Cardinal Wiseman's name was rendered most familiar by his frequent appearance on the platform as a public lecturer upon a wide range of subjects connected with education, history, art, and science; and in

[1] *Rambler*, January 1856.

that capacity his Eminence always found an attentive and eager audience, even among those who are most conscientiously opposed to his spiritual claims and pretensions.' Someone who heard Wiseman lecture has left us an impression of the occasion, contrasting his manner with that of his successor, Cardinal Manning. 'Cardinal Wiseman's public speaking had two special characteristics; he appeared full of his subject, and he was in close sympathy with his audience, and had the art of winning their sympathy. Both his voice and his manner were sympathetic. His presence was extremely impressive, but very different from the no less impressive presence of his successor, Cardinal Manning. I should say that Manning suggested the ascetic Apostle, whose words and thoughts were in a region above the hearer; while Wiseman's presence was that of the great prelate or Prince of the Church and his discourse though less highly finished than Manning's, showed greater eagerness on his part to enter into the minds and tastes of his hearers and persuade them. A certain *bonhomie* accompanied the dignity of his manner, which was absent in Cardinal Manning's case. His discourses were remarkable for the abundance of poetic imagery. At his best he was very fluent and brilliant.'[1]

In discussing Wiseman's lectures mention might here be made of his *Recollections of the Last Four Popes and of Rome in their Times*, for though this was not published in book form until 1858 it was based on a popular series of lectures, and remains to this day probably the most readable of the Cardinal's published works, and the most interesting to the modern student of his times. The book presents a lively picture of Rome in the last decades of the papal monarchy, and though the scene is peaceful enough the rumble of revolution can be heard off-stage. It is a personal rather than a political record, for Wiseman had little sympathy with the *Risorgimento* and was a firm supporter of the temporal power of the Pope. Written at a difficult and troublous period of his life he looks back with a certain nostalgia to the days when he was a young student, and the criticism that he viewed the scene through rose-coloured spectacles carries a certain amount of conviction.[2] The age which

[1] Quoted by Reynolds: *Three Cardinals*, p. 117.
[2] *Vide* Frederik Nielsen: *The History of the Papacy in the XIXth Century*, Vol. I, p. 207.

immediately preceded the reign of Pius IX was not the most glorious in the history of the Catholic Church, but Wiseman's concern in these pages is more with the ordinary life of a young ecclesiastic placed in an advantageous position to view the personal qualities of the various Pontiffs, than of one qualified to criticize them in their political acts. He came into close personal contact with both Leo XII and Gregory XVI, and was a witness of the all too brief pontificate of Pius VIII, and the picture he gives us of these Popes in their more private moments or in the exercise of their purely pastoral duties is not without significance in an age which now only remembers them for the unfortunate character of their public administration as the last representatives of the *ancien régime*. He is always conscious of the intellectual life of the times, for this was his own *métier*, and any reader familiar with the author's temperament would not be surprised that he should be more interested in literature, science and art, than in secret societies, revolutionary intrigues or the inability of the administration to come to terms with the rising tide of political liberalism.

This did not prevent his book from being the subject of a bitter attack by a former priest, an Italian patriot then living in exile in London. In the same year that the Cardinal's book was published there appeared *My Recollections of the Last Four Popes, an Answer to Dr. Wiseman*, by Alessandro Gavazzi. This work took the form of a vicious and vituperative attack upon Wiseman and upon the Popes whose reigns he had chronicled, and was also made the occasion for an equally abusive onslaught upon Pius IX, then reigning, though this Pope was not one of the subjects of Wiseman's study. The writer, however, had no control over the flow of his invective, and what might have been a legitimate criticism of Wiseman's omissions is rendered ridiculous by its absurdly intemperate style. Thus, in discussing, or rather dismissing, the Venerable English College, he writes: 'Even the mouse recalls with pleasure the trap from which he escaped, after having devoured the bacon and cheese it contained. We shall the more willingly permit Wiseman to indulge in this grateful recollection of his college, as it was there that he was transformed from a humble Tipperary worm into a splendid gay butterfly.'[1] His comment on Gregory's reaction to the first

[1] Gavazzi: *My Recollections*, etc., p. 171.

hints of revolution is in more questionable taste. 'The revolution did, in truth, irritate his mind more than the cancer[1] irritated his nose, whatever Wiseman may write to the contrary. It is certainly wretchedly illogical of our Melipotamus to try to persuade us that "the Pope displayed the utmost calm", when he himself exhibits so much acrimony and ill-concealed spite in giving his reminiscences of him after a lapse of twenty-seven years. Wiseman, Wiseman! beware, lest you betray your race in your anxiety to defend it. When you would deceive, be cautious not to laugh; your laugh being forced, displays the sharp teeth of the ravenous and insatiable beast of prey, still red with the blood of its victim.'[2] Such extraordinary flights of fancy destroy the force of any legitimate criticism the author might wish to make, but credulity reaches its limit in his picture of the venerable Pope Gregory XVI given over entirely to the pursuit of Venus and Bacchus.[3] The renegade Father Alessandro Gavazzi was a critic whom Wiseman could well afford to ignore.

The Cardinal visited Rome again in 1854 for the ceremonies concerned with the definition of the dogma of the Immaculate Conception of the Blessed Virgin Mary. This was the culmination of the movement which Pius IX had set on foot during his exile at Gaeta in 1849, when he had asked for the opinion of the worldwide Catholic episcopate. Of the six hundred and ten replies received all had expressed belief in the doctrine, four only opposed its definition, while fifty-two expressed a doubt as to the opportuneness of the time. Over the next years petitions reached the Holy See from all quarters asking for the definition, until nine volumes were filled with these requests. The dogma was finally proclaimed on 8th December 1854, Wiseman being one among fifty-one Cardinals and one hundred and fifty-two Archbishops and bishops who surrounded the Pope in the great Basilica of St. Peter's. The decree defining the doctrine was read by the Pope from the apostolic throne. 'He had not, however, proceeded far,' Wiseman wrote after the ceremony, 'before tears and sobs interrupted his speech, and it was only by an effort . . . that he could make his words struggle through the tide of his emotions.'[4] When the Pope had finished reading and the Cardinal Dean had returned thanks on behalf of

---

[1] Gregory XVI suffered from a facial cancer of the skin.   [2] Ibid., p. 183.
[3] Ibid., p. 277.   [4] Ward, Vol. II, p. 110.

the assembled episcopacy and faithful the whole assembly joined in singing the *Te Deum*.

Two days after this moving ceremony Wiseman assisted the Pope in another duty which must have brought back vivid memories of his student days in Rome thirty-one years before. With five other Cardinal Archbishops he helped the Pope consecrate the newly-built Basilica of St. Paul's whose destruction by fire he had witnessed in August 1823 as the aged Pius VII lay dying; a scene which he would describe in his *Recollections of the Last Four Popes*. The great church had now been rebuilt, a replica of the one which had stood there before, as much material as could be saved from the old building being incorporated in the new. To a man of Wiseman's imagination and historical sense it must indeed have been a proud moment to assist at this consecration.

The Cardinal returned to England at the end of January 1855. His visit had not escaped the notice of Lord Lyons. In a letter to the Marquess of Normanby written on the 21st he repeated the old rumours that the Court of Rome wished to remove Wiseman from England, adding as an additional cause 'the certainly not very dignified figure he has presented before an English Court of Justice in the Libel Case, in which he has been recently concerned'. The report that Wiseman wished to have an auxiliary or coadjutor appointed was now common knowledge, but Lord Lyons interpreted this in a way which would probably have caused the Cardinal considerable surprise had his eye fallen upon the letter. 'It is said that it will now be easy for Cardinal Wiseman to fix his presence at Rome, and without abandoning the title which he arrogates to himself of Archbishop of Westminster,' Lyons continued, 'to leave the administration of affairs in England in the hands of the coadjutor about to be appointed, and it seems to be thought that the Court of Rome may recommend him to adopt this course, in order to remove him, in fact, from England without making so open an avowal of his appointment having been an error in policy, as would be implied by his formally resigning the so-called Archbishopric.'[1]

In actual fact, of course, the idea of appointing a coadjutor was not to make it easy for Wiseman to retire to Rome still clothed in the dignities of his office, but to free him from routine work so that he

[1] Public Record Office, FO 43/60.

could participate more fully in the life of the Catholic Church in England. It is only fair to Lord Lyons to add a further sentence from his letter in which he admits that, while the view stated was very commonly entertained at Rome, he could not undertake to say confidently 'whether or no they predominate in the high and influential quarters'. He was, however, correctly informed upon one point, and with this he ends his letter. 'It is generally believed that Dr. Errington of Plymouth will be the Bishop elected as Coadjutor by the Pope, and that he will be nominated with right of succession, on the next vacancy, to the so-called Archbishopric of Westminster.'

XVII

The appointment of Dr. George Errington as coadjutor was viewed with some misgivings both by himself and by many others over whom he would rule in the Archdiocese of Westminster. He had the reputation for being a stern disciplinarian who stood for the letter rather than the spirit of the law, but he had the great merit, in the eyes of some, of not being a convert. Errington himself had no wish to leave Plymouth, where he had been bishop since 1851, and had written to Talbot, while Wiseman was still in Rome, putting forward his objections, and adding, in support, that the work could be done just as well by Vicars-General and that 'Coadjutors never got on well here',[1] an observation that was soon to be proved sadly true. His objections, however, were brushed aside, and in April 1855, he was transferred from Plymouth to his new post as coadjutor, being created Archbishop of Trebizond *in partibus infidelium*, and given the right of succession to the See of Westminster.

Wiseman and Errington had been friends since they first met as schoolboys in 1814. From Ushaw they had gone together to the Venerable English College in Rome, and when Wiseman became Rector he appointed George Errington as Vice-Rector. Later on, when the former was made Bishop and President of Oscott, Errington was made Prefect of Studies and took over much of the administration so as to free the Bishop for his work outside the College. But despite this long friendship and association, the characters of the two men were very different, representing, indeed, almost opposite extremes. Dr. Errington did not share Wiseman's

---

[1] Rome, English College. The Talbot Papers.

enthusiasm for the Oxford Movement nor did he feel any particular sympathy with the converts who joined the Roman Church as a result of it. He had none of the Cardinal's exuberance, but viewed life bleakly from behind his dark blue spectacles. He was suspicious of the Italian devotions which Wiseman and Faber were so eager to introduce, remarking, upon the subject of meditation, that 'the best form of meditation is to look at a dead body; and it is a very old form'.[1] He was an authority upon canon law and believed in its rigid enforcement. He made such strict regulations on the subject of the visits of priests to the dying that some complained that if they followed them to the letter the sick would die without the Sacraments, but the only reply this drew from the bishop was that if the dead were deprived of the Sacraments according to canon law, then the law was to blame and not him. One is hardly surprised at the verdict of Mother Mary Hallahan: 'You were hewn out of rock, Dr. Errington,' said this redoubtable Dominican nun; 'and I am sure you never had a mother.'[2] To this rather grim picture must be added the opinion of Canon Morris, the friend both of Wiseman and Errington, that 'in private life Archbishop Errington was gentle and affectionate, and his friends were warmly attached to him; but in his official relations he was stern and inflexible'.

Wiseman was neither the one nor the other. For him justice was always tempered with mercy and his flexible intellect would turn in any direction that truth would allow to further the cause which he espoused or assist the friends who appealed for his help. Generosity and open-handedness were to him almost a fault, and it was indeed this fault, if one may call it so, that was responsible for this ill-advised appointment. To many observers who knew the Cardinal and the Archbishop of Trebizond it was clear that they could never work happily together, but Wiseman refused to be guided by their advice. Errington was his friend and he was sure that he and 'old George' would get on. As the appointment was to be made *cum jure successionis*, and Errington would therefore in all probability succeed to the Metropolitan See, his name, with two others, was formally brought before the Westminster Chapter for submission to the Holy See. The Canons, knowing his reputation for stern authoritarianism, had no very great desire to request his removal to

[1] Ward, Vol. II, p. 265. [2] Ibid., p. 259.

London from the safe distance of Plymouth, and only did so because of the Cardinal's known wish to have Dr. Errington by his side. The newly appointed Archbishop, himself remembering former difficulties, consented to the appointment on the understanding that he should have absolute control over diocesan administration, freeing Wiseman for his wider activities, being insistent that there should be no appeals from his decisions. To this Wiseman agreed.

Trouble began within six months of Dr. Errington's appointment. Wiseman requested him to undertake a visitation of the diocese, which meant making a detailed investigation of every mission and parish as well as inspecting all diocesan institutions which came under the bishop's jurisdiction. Before he began the visitation the Archbishop of Trebizond repeated his request that there should be no appeal from his decisions, but when some of the priests objected to his stern interpretation of canon law and rushed to the Cardinal with their complaints, Wiseman's kind heart got the better of him, and he reversed the Archbishop's decrees. This naturally incensed Errington, who in such cases brought all the papers concerned in the matter and placed them on the Cardinal's desk declaring that Wiseman must finish the visitation of that place himself as he had promised not to interfere but had done so in spite of his promise.[1] It was an embarrassing situation made none the easier by the fact that the Cardinal and the Archbishop were living in the same house at York Place which had been scarcely big enough for Wiseman and his staff when he was on his own.

The crisis came to a head when the Archbishop paid a visit to St. Edmund's College, where Dr. W. G. Ward was Professor of Dogmatic Theology, an appointment he owed to the Cardinal. It had already been noted that Archbishop Errington had no especial liking for converts as such, sharing the view which had previously been held by Bishop Griffiths, and which was still the opinion of a great number of the old Catholics. To him the idea of a layman and a convert teaching theology to young men training for the priesthood was utterly abhorrent, nor was it likely that he would alter this idea when Dr. Ward made no attempt to hide the contempt he felt for the system of instruction then practised by most of the staff at St. Edmund's, nor failed to expatiate upon what he chose to consider

[1] *Vide* Ward, Vol. II, p. 258.

the ignorance of many of the old Catholics. Dr. Errington, himself a member of an old Yorkshire Catholic family, can hardly have been amused by these sallies of the Professor, nor be won over to his point of view about the proper running of an ecclesiastical seminary. It is, therefore, not surprising that the Archbishop's report contained many unfavourable passages about the organization of the College; and the presence of Dr. Ward there, as well as the principles he represented, came in for a major part of the criticism. He imposed such restrictions on Ward that the latter immediately resigned, but not before he had written at length to the Cardinal putting forward his own justification, which necessarily implied criticism of the Archbishop.

Wiseman accepted the resignation with evident reluctance. He had himself appointed Ward to St. Edmund's, he greatly admired his character and abilities, and had, as has been seen, secured for him recognition in the form of a papal degree as Doctor in Philosophy. He was uneasy about the whole business and was obviously open to persuasion as became clear when Ward's letter was followed by Ward in person. He had a long interview with the Cardinal whose sympathy he already possessed and who needed little encouragement to reverse, once again, the decision of the Archbishop of Trebizond. If Wiseman required any further inducement Ward was able to provide it in the plea of his President, who was unwilling that his students should be deprived of Dr. Ward's unusual talents. It was, therefore, agreed that Ward should return to St. Edmund's, but Wiseman, who stood in some awe of his coadjutor, could not bring himself to tell the grim Archbishop such unwelcome news. He put off the embarrassing revelation from day to day until the time came when Errington was due to visit St. Edmund's once again. The Cardinal accompanied him to the station. When the Archbishop was at the window of his compartment and the train had already started, so that a reply was impossible, Wiseman blurted out the remark: 'Dr. Ward will continue to lecture in theology at the college,'[1] and left the Archbishop to pursue his own thoughts for the rest of the journey.

[1] *Vide* Dr. Rymer's account in Butler's: *Life of Bishop Ullathorne*, Vol. I, p. 286. Dr. Rymer was, in Abbot Butler's words, one who had 'been through the whole affair and knew the personages involved'.

For Errington it was not simply a question of whether or not Dr. Ward was a fit person to lecture to 'divines' on dogmatic theology, it was a question of whether the new ideas, the 'Roman spirit' as Wiseman liked to call it, was to prevail over the old-fashioned spirituality which had characterized the days of the Vicars Apostolic. To Ward and his supporters the ideas of the Archbishop of Trebizond represented a generation that was rapidly passing, and they believed that the new age which had been ushered in with the hierarchy called for new methods, and that those who opposed this new spirit, if they had their way, would hold up for many years the work of the Church for the conversion of England. They looked upon Wiseman as their champion and they could only be dismayed at the thought of the leadership of the hierarchy passing to one whom they regarded as the personification of reaction. To Errington it was equally alarming to think of the Church handed over to the charge of converts whose enthusiasm was untempered by experience, who were foreign to the traditions of Bishop Challoner and the old penal days, whose ancestors had not shed their blood for the sake of the Old Religion.

He saw quite clearly that it was impossible for there to be any harmony between himself and the Cardinal; that they represented wholly incompatible points of view, and that no good purpose could be served by their continuing in an association which was so manifestly lacking in any sort of mutual confidence. These ideas he expressed, shortly afterwards, in a long letter to Monsignor Talbot. 'I am satisfied that I do not possess that influence with the Cardinal, nor his confidence to that degree which would be necessary for effectual working under him in my position,' the Archbishop wrote with clear insight. 'The Ward affair was in reality, as the public I find has considered it, a trial of strength between my influence and one opposed to it, and in the contest that influence prevailed . . .' and he went on to describe the difficulties he had to contend with over the visitation and the misunderstandings and jealousies it had occasioned. He could see little profit in his continuing with the Cardinal: 'Altogether I do not think that we can now get into satisfactory working relations, and hence I see more chance of my interfering with the great good in so many respects he could and would do by himself, than of my doing good; on the other hand, the report of our being at variance having become common from Ward's affairs, will certainly lead to a great scandal, and there will be always plenty of persons ready to increase and make use of the division.' This was a moderate and charitable estimate of the difference, and from it Dr. Errington drew what to him was the only sensible conclusion: 'Hence I have serious thoughts of begging the Holy See to remove me from my present position to any occupation, place, or country the Holy Father may think fit, where I might do good instead of harm . . .' As an interim measure he suggested that he might be given temporary charge of the diocese of Clifton which had just become vacant through the death of the bishop.[1]

On receiving this letter Monsignor Talbot wrote at once to Cardinal Wiseman urging him to make a determined effort to reach some sort of *modus vivendi* with his coadjutor. He wrote in plain and strong terms, at the risk of offending the Cardinal, and offered advice which he must have known would be unwelcome to the recipient. It was a balanced and sensible letter, and one can only regret that the Monsignor did not retain this detached attitude in the later stages of this unhappy dispute when a new element was introduced into it after Manning's establishment in London.

Talbot's letter was dated from the Vatican, 4th September 1855: 'I have just received a most painful letter from the Archbishop of Trebizond,' he began, 'from which it appears that he is greatly hurt by the want of confidence which you manifest towards him, and which has determined him to renounce his office of your coadjutor. It is hardly necessary for me to say that this would cause a great scandal and be the source of great displeasure to the Holy Father himself, as well as to all those who have had to act in his name.

'The object of the nomination of Dr. Errington was that he might take upon himself all the odium of the administration of your diocese, whilst your Eminence would have the direction of the more general and important affairs of the Church in England. This was done in order to relieve you from all the details of government, which were a constant source of annoyance to you, and from the neglect of which constant complaints were being made to the Holy See. Now I hold it for certain that if a rupture were to take place between you and the Archbishop, it would cause a great scandal,

[1] *Vide* Ward, Vol. II, pp. 261-2.

and it would be openly proclaimed in Rome that it is impossible to satisfy you. Already it is thought a pity that Dr. Grant of Southwark should have been your nominee, and I know not what will be said if the Archbishop of Trebizond cannot agree with you.

'Already I understand a party has been formed in London against Dr. Errington, which has placed him in an unpleasant position. He can do nothing towards organizing the work of the diocese or to making his visitation, without having to bear all the odium of being a reformer. If I were your Eminence I would cast upon him all the responsibility, all the labour, and all the odium of the visitation and not mix myself up with it in any way whatever; otherwise I am sure he will not undertake it, and he will be quite in the right.

'Excuse me, dear Cardinal Wiseman, if I have spoken on this subject with too great warmth, but really I have done it out of love for you, for I fear the consequences to you of a rupture with Dr. Errington.'[1]

As a result of this exchange of letters between the Cardinal, the Archbishop, and Monsignor Talbot, it was agreed that Dr. Errington should remain at his post but that for the time being he should take charge, as he had himself suggested, of the diocese of Clifton until the Holy See nominated a successor to that bishopric. As things were to turn out it was a pity that Talbot did not agree to the Archbishop's request that his resignation be accepted and he be appointed to some other post, for the time would come when both Talbot and the Pope would beg him to do this very thing. The fact that he would then not do so was very largely Talbot's fault, and if his resignation at this point seemed likely to cause scandal, it was nothing in comparison to what was to come, though no one, least of all Monsignor Talbot, could foresee this at the time.

During Errington's absence at Clifton Manning's position in the diocese of Westminster was finally settled by the establishment of the Oblates of St. Charles, an institute or congregation of secular priests which he had founded at Cardinal Wiseman's request. The Cardinal had, for many years, wished to have in the diocese a group of priests entirely at the disposal of the bishop who would be able to take up work on his behalf at any place where their presence was required. He had turned to the various existing Orders for help

[1] *Vide* Butler, *Life of Ullathorne*, Vol. I, pp. 280–1.

in this respect, but almost always the provisions of the Rule under which they lived had prevented their being able to place themselves at his disposal for work of this sort. This he had found a matter of great frustration, as he had expressed in 1852 in a long letter on the subject to Father Faber. 'Now look at the position in which I am,' he had written. 'Having believed, having preached, having assured Bishops and clergy, that in no great city could the salvation of multitudes be carried out by the limited parochial clergy, but that religious communities alone can, and will, undertake the huge work of converting and preserving the corrupted masses, I have acted on this conviction, I have introduced or greatly encouraged, the establishment of *five* religious congregations in my diocese; and I am just (for the great work) where I first began! Not one of them *can* (for it cannot be want of will) undertake it. It comes within the purpose of none of them to try. Souls are perishing round them, but they are prevented by the rules, given by Saints, from helping to save them—at least in any but a particular and definite way! But what makes it to me more bitter still, from *them* comes often the cry that in London nothing is being done for the poor!'[1]

In his dilemma the Cardinal had turned to Manning when the new convert was still undecided as to what form his work in the Church should take, and suggested that he undertook the establishment in England of a community on the lines of the Oblates of St. Charles, an order of secular priests founded in the sixteenth century by St. Charles Borromeo for work in Milan on the very lines which Wiseman had looked for in vain among the religious communities established in nineteenth-century London. The object of this community was, as their name implied, that they should offer themselves entirely to the service of the bishop. Manning undertook the work after some hesitation 'not from unwillingness or disobedience', as he later wrote,[2] 'but from doubt of myself', and went to Italy to study the work and rule of the Congregation in Milan itself. The chief characteristics of the order he outlined in a letter to Wiseman: '1. That they should be closely united to the bishop, and be as it were his *familia*. 2. That they should have just so much internal constitution as to raise and preserve their spirit and theological standard, and consolidate both. 3. That they should be completely

[1] Ward, Vol. II, pp. 117–18.   [2] *Manning: Anglican and Catholic*, p. 44.

mixed among the clergy of the diocese.'[1] This was exactly what Wiseman required. Manning drew up his first outline of the Rule in 1856 and this was accepted by the Cardinal, who sent Manning to Rome where the Rule was approved by the Cardinal-Prefect of Propaganda and by the Pope. The community met for the first time on Whit Sunday, 1857, in the church at Bayswater which the Cardinal had made over to them.

While Manning was in Rome it so happened that the Archbishop of Trebizond was there also. Realizing that sooner or later his new Community was likely to come under the direct rule of the Archbishop, as Wiseman's successor, Manning sought him out, explained his whole object in detail, and asked for Errington's co-operation. This the Archbishop declined to give. Despite the fact that the Oblates were to work for the bishop it seemed to Errington that Manning was keeping a firm control over them himself and the fact that three of the new Oblates were on the staff of St. Edmund's College, the scene of his dispute with Ward, increased the Archbishop's alarm. He was soon to have another reason for dismay at the turn of events in the diocese he would one day be called upon to govern.

Early in 1857 Dr. Whitty, the Provost of the Metropolitan Chapter of Westminster, decided to enter the Society of Jesus. This meant that his office, and also his stall as canon, became vacant, and Wiseman hoped that the latter, at least, should be filled by the Superior of the Oblates. 'I particularly entreat that should the Holy Father name you Canon you will not decline,' he wrote to Manning, who was still in Rome. 'There are many reasons for it. It will be the first time the Holy Father will have exercised the prerogative of nomination and I wish the precedent to be given. It will be most gratifying to the Chapter. It will be acceptable to every class of Catholics. It will prove that the Oblates are not a distinct Order, but true secular priests. It will give at once a high position to the Institute in the diocese, and stamp it with the strongest seal of approbation both from Rome and here. For everybody will and shall know that I have most fully concurred in the nomination.'[2] This letter shows that Wiseman had already sensed the feeling of

---

[1] Purcell: *Life of Manning*, Vol. II, p. 67.
[2] *Manning: Anglican and Catholic*, p. 45.

237

opposition which some Catholics felt for the new Institute, else he would not have considered that it required so marked a sign of papal and archiepiscopal approval. His desire to protect the new foundation resulted in his adopting an altogether too sanguine view of the prevailing sentiment towards Manning and his Oblates among the senior clergy of his diocese. It was by no means certain that such an appointment would be most gratifying to the Chapter, and even less certain that it would be acceptable to every class of Catholics. To at least one class, the old Catholics who looked upon Dr. Errington as their leader, the appointment would have been most unacceptable indeed.

But Wiseman need not have worried lest the Pope refuse to favour Manning with a sign of papal approbation. Pius IX did not, indeed, name Manning a Canon; he named him Provost of the Chapter. He did this without any reference to Cardinal Wiseman, who had intended to nominate his Vicar-General, Dr. Maguire, but there can be no doubt that the appointment received the Cardinal's enthusiastic approval. To Manning the nomination came as a complete surprise: 'I cannot but believe that there has been some departure from your intention in this; remembering our conversation about Dr. Maguire, to whom I shall rejoice to transfer what I think must have been intended for him,'[1] Manning wrote to the Cardinal on receiving the Rescript of his appointment. But there was no question of transferring the Provostship. If the Cardinal felt that he could not himself have suggested Manning for the post over the heads of many others with prior claims of service (for Manning had been scarcely six years a Catholic) there can be little doubt that he rejoiced that the matter had been taken out of his hands and the appointment made, in a manner so congenial to his desires, by supreme authority.

Thus when the Archbishop of Trebizond handed over his charge at Clifton and returned to London to resume his duties as Wiseman's coadjutor, he discovered that far from having secured the arch-diocese from the influence of converts and the infiltration of novel ideas, the most influential of the converts was installed as Provost of the Metropolitan Chapter and was at the same time in charge of the Oblates of St. Charles, whose avowed purpose was to spread the

[1] Purcell: *Life of Manning*, Vol. II, p. 75.

'Roman spirit' throughout the diocese; that three members of this order, owing allegiance to Provost Manning, were already at work on the staff of St. Edmund's College; and that one of them, Father Herbert Vaughan,[1] occupied the position of Vice-President in the place of a man who had been Dr. Errington's chief supporter and a strong opponent of the new system.

It should be pointed out that up to the time of his appointment as Provost, Manning was little known to the Catholic clergy of England. His conversion had, of course, caused a considerable stir, and the somewhat critical comment occasioned by his rapid ordination has already been noted, but from that time he had lived for the most part in Rome, only paying periodical visits to England, so that when he returned as Provost he was known only for his reputation as a close friend of the Cardinal, a man who was clearly a favourite in the highest circles in Rome, and one who was almost wholly a stranger to the traditions of the Church in England prior to the re-establishment of the hierachy. His very rapid advancement to high preferment also suggest that he was ambitious to exercise power and not over-scrupulous as to how he attained it, though those who hinted such things were either unaware that his appointment to the Provostship had come unsought or that he had previously been offered, but had declined, the position of Chamberlain to Pius IX, a post which would have made him, with his abilities and the favour he enjoyed, a formidable influence at the Papal Court. He had refused this office, which carried the rank of prelate, because he wished to return to work in England, though when the offer was made he had no notion that his work there would fall in any more exalted sphere than that of an ordinary parish priest. His claim, made later in life, that 'all that has come upon me has come without any seeking' could not be denied by those who knew the truth.

To the old Catholics and to the Archbishop of Trebizond in particular, Manning represented, in a single person, all that they most feared from the influence of converts, and because of his long residence in Rome since almost the moment of his conversion, he appeared now as the very embodiment of that 'Roman spirit' or 'new system' which they feared, not because it was Roman or because they held any disloyal feelings towards the Holy See, but

---

[1] Afterwards Cardinal and third Archbishop of Westminster.

because they felt it represented a rejection of the old traditions of Catholic piety, perilously guarded in penal times and hallowed with the blood of martyrs. Wiseman was himself by birth an old Catholic and he was known to revere all that was most sacred in the old traditions; he was also known for his fearless support of the converts and his tireless advocacy of the 'Roman spirit'; but because Manning was wholly identified with this spirit the opponents of the new ideas came to regard Wiseman as being completely under the Provost's influence in so far as the 'Romanizing' movement was concerned. An additional emphasis was given to this wholly inaccurate estimate of the situation by the fact that Wiseman's health was in a state of gradual decline, which often made him subject to periods of lassitude and exhaustion, in marked contrast to the vigorous and energetic Provost. They thought that Wiseman need only have his eyes opened to the dangers of the situation and the day of the Romanized convert would be over. Wiseman appeared to the Archbishop and his supporters like an old lion that lay asleep. 'In order to awaken him,' Dr. Errington declared, 'it is necessary to bring every form of external pressure to bear upon him. One day he will awake, he will put out his paw and then he will drive them all away.'[1] But it was not to be the Provost who would be driven away when the old lion was stirred into action.

Certainly to the Archbishop of Trebizond everything that he stood opposed to seemed to be concentrated in the person of Dr. Manning whose influence now looked like becoming paramount in the affairs of the diocese. Manning, therefore, became the main object of attack in his campaign to bring 'every form of external pressure' to the task of waking the old lion. Even before leaving Rome, when Manning had discussed the plan for forming the Institution of the Oblates with him, Errington had expressed the opinion that Manning was not carrying out the Cardinal's wishes but was instead keeping the chief control of the Congregation in his own hands, and he repeated this accusation to the Cardinal-Prefect of Propaganda, to the Rector of the English College, and to Monsignor Talbot. When he returned to London he elaborated this charge more exactly. He secured a copy of the Rule and subjected it to a hawk-like scrutiny, comparing it in every detail with the

[1] *Manning: Anglican and Catholic*, p. 48.

Rule of the original foundation in Milan. He at once noticed a discrepancy which struck him as having a marked and sinister significance. In Manning's Rule the Superior was empowered to recall any Oblate from the work he was doing to live in community, and also reserved the right of the Superior to determine, in association with the bishop, the locality in the diocese where the Oblates should be sent to serve. These prerogatives, which gave the Superior an authority which could technically be used, in the case of recalling Oblates to live in community, against the desires of the bishop, were unknown to the Milanese Rule, a fact which Errington lost no time in pointing out to Cardinal Wiseman.

The Archbishop brought his complaint to the Cardinal at the beginning of 1858. Wiseman considered that Dr. Errington's fears were based largely on prejudice, but he could not deny the discrepancy in the rules. He pointed out that the Rule had only been approved on the condition that it should be revised later should this appear to be necessary after a trial period, but the Archbishop was not satisfied. Accordingly in May the Cardinal authorized a modification of the Rule which deprived the Superior of his right of recall, and ensured that all Oblates who had taken the missionary oath should be subject to the bishop alone like any other secular priest. Manning accepted this limitation of his authority with edifying obedience and an equanimity that hardly suggested a voracious appetite for power.

Dr. Errington, whose obsession with the question of the Oblates was out of all proportion to the dangers he sensed in their activities, now sought a new line of attack. At all points in this distressing business no one ever doubted or called in question the essential goodness of the Archbishop of Trebizond, who was a man of great ability and who lived, despite his exalted rank, in conditions of apostolic poverty. It has to be remembered that the motives which inspired his onslaught on the Oblates were as important to him, and as disinterested, as any that inspired those who were devoted heart and soul to the new ideas. It must also be borne in mind, as will be shown, that at this period of his life Dr. Errington was in very poor health, suffering from a form of nervous exhaustion, and this physical condition may well have affected his sense of proportion in a matter of such urgency to him. In attempting to understand and assess his line of action these points must not be overlooked; and the aphorism must be recollected that the conflict between good and evil is rarely so tragic as the conflict between two forms of good.

The Church of St. Mary of the Angels, the unfinished church building in Bayswater which the Cardinal had made over to the Oblates, was the next point of contention between the Cardinal and the coadjutor. The ground on which this building stood was bought from endowments left by a certain lady for the benefit of the secular clergy, and it had been the original intention to call it St. Helen's as the benefactress had borne the name of this saint. The property had been vested in trustees chosen from among the secular clergy, but Wiseman requested them to resign their trust to four new trustees who were all members of the new Community (though technically secular priests) and the church was newly dedicated as Mother House of the Oblates. Dr. Errington strongly opposed this action on the part of the Cardinal, claiming that it was an infringement of the rights of the diocesan clergy and a grave injustice. Wiseman sought legal opinion with the result that he was shown to be fully within his legal rights in making the transfer, but the matter did not make for any return of good feeling between the two men who found it increasingly difficult to work together.

Up to this moment the dispute had been confined to the Cardinal and his coadjutor, involving Manning only when he had to defend his conduct as Superior of the Oblates of St. Charles or answer the Archbishop's inquiries as to the purpose and interpretation of his Rule. By the summer of 1858, however, the dissensions had spread to the Chapter, over which Manning presided, where the Archbishop of Trebizond had two staunch allies in Dr. Maguire, the Vicar-General, and Monsignor Searle, the Cardinal's secretary. In taking the side of Errington, Monsignor Searle brought the dispute into the very household of the Cardinal, a fact which only added to Wiseman's distress. Personal antipathy to Manning certainly played a part in dictating Searle's line of action. Having occupied for many years a position involving him in intimate day-to-day contact with the Cardinal, between whom and himself there had existed a long-standing friendship, there can be no doubt that he felt jealous of the influence exercised by the Provost. Searle, who had great skill in managing the business affairs of the Cardinal, was not a man of intellectual tastes or of any great learning, and in the questions which now divided the Chapter he showed himself to be entirely on the side of the old Catholics. His defection caused the Cardinal a pang of grief. 'Searle is no longer *my* secretary,' he complained in a letter to Patterson later that year, 'for he seems the secretary of the Chapter; and instead of that confidence which has existed between us for twenty years, he has his own secrets and I mine, and we hardly speak.'[1]

It was the question of the diocesan seminary which now divided the Chapter and brought the quarrel between Wiseman and Errington into a wider field. It will be recalled that three members of the staff of St. Edmund's College had become Oblates and that one of them, Father Herbert Vaughan, was Vice-President. As Oblates they were the spiritual subjects of their Superior, Provost Manning, which suggested to the Chapter that they were no longer at the free disposal of the Archbishop of the diocese. They further believed that their object in being there was to introduce the customs of Italian seminaries, which to them meant a system of espionage, tale-bearing, and unwholesome devotions, into the College, practices which ran contrary to all the traditions of St. Edmund's. In short, they feared that the whole college was in danger of being handed over to Dr. Manning. After discussing the matter at one of their meetings they called upon Manning to bring a copy of the Rule of the Oblates for their scrutiny at the next Chapter meeting.

Before taking any further action Manning went to the Cardinal and placed the matter before him. The Cardinal was most indignant at the demand of the Chapter, which he declared beyond their powers to make, and told Manning to refuse to submit the Rule for their inspection. The Chapter, however, were prepared for this, and produced diplomas given to them by Wiseman himself, in which he had appointed two of their body to be deputies, in accordance with the decrees of the Council of Trent, whose special duty was to look after the diocesan seminary. Wiseman had issued the diplomas at the time when the Chapter was created and had then forgotten all about them in a manner thoroughly characteristic of his unbusinesslike nature. He was, however, undaunted by this flourish of documents, for all that they were drawn up under his

[1] Ward, Vol. II, p. 327.

own hand. He replied that as St. Edmund's was a college for the mixed education of boys and clerics or 'divines', it was not a seminary in the sense in which the term was understood by the Council of Trent.

This game of ecclesiastical box and cox might have gone on for ever had not Manning agreed 'most willingly' to bring copies of his Rule for the Chapter to see, as long as it was understood that they should examine the Rule privately, and not during a capitular session. Copies were duly brought but the Chapter insisted on an official examination. Manning objected strongly but the Chapter had their way; and so, as the Provost later explained to the Pope, 'after a long resistance I entered a protest in the Capitular Book, and was silent'.

'The Chapter then proceeded to examine the Rule and Constitutions capitularly;' Manning's account continues,[1] 'and one of the Canons, Mgr. Searle, called on me to leave the hall of the Chapter, on the ground that the subject in discussion touched my *commodum*. I declined to do so. An adjournment having been carried, the whole Chapter withdrew, and in an hour returned with a petition to the Cardinal Archbishop, naming the Congregation of St. Charles by name, with a comparison of its Rule with that drawn up by St. Charles, and praying its exclusion from the College.' When the petition was brought before Cardinal Wiseman he again declared that the Chapter was acting outside its province, and after consulting various authorities, he annulled the proceedings.

Shortly after doing this the Cardinal wrote a long letter to Pope Pius IX,[2] in explanation of his dispute with the Chapter and in defence of the Provost. As the Archbishop of Trebizond had come out strongly in support of the Chapter the letter was also, by implication, a strong censure on the conduct of the coadjutor. 'Most Holy Father,' the Cardinal wrote, 'The deplorable differences which have arisen between myself and my Chapter have their origin in matters relating to the Institute of the Oblates of St. Charles in this city. Your Holiness is already well informed with regard to its foundation as it was in Rome, and almost at your

[1] *Vide* Ward, Vol. II, p. 275.
[2] The proceedings of the Chapter were annulled on December 1st. The letter to the Pope is dated 25th December 1858.

Holy Feet, that the first draft (of the Rule) was made, being afterwards completed with the help of wise and saintly persons dear to your Holiness. In fact, its founder, the Rev. Dr. Manning, gained your sovereign approbation for it as befitted a newly created Institute. Furthermore, in nominating him to the vacant Provostship of our Chapter, your Holiness condescendingly showed him signs of your great esteem, at the same time making clear that he continues to remain a member of the secular clergy of this metropolis.

'Now in the memorial presented to me by the Chapter, the source of my vexation, this body, after having discussed in various sittings the merits of the Institute, have taken the course of making known to me their unfavourable opinion of the said Corporation in relation to the diocesan Seminary, asking me not to allow them to exercise the slightest influence, but treat them like a regular body, extraneous to the secular clergy . . .' After declaring that Dr. Manning would be coming to defend the Oblates at Rome, the Cardinal continued to say that he himself wrote 'willingly, spontaneously, and respectfully this account to accompany him to your Holiness'. He then made the following points about Dr. Manning:

'1. I declare that whatever this ecclesiastic has done he has done with my knowledge and approval.

'2. That I consider the spirit which his Congregation tries to propagate to be of the utmost usefulness to the diocese—that is, the ecclesiastical spirit, Roman and generous in its ministry.

'3. That at the mission in Bayswater, headquarters of the Institute, despite the fact that there was no house, no school, a church as yet unfinished, in two years all was provided, and that for this reason I consider the Institute as having been especially useful to the Catholic Religion, (i) in a material interest, owing to the considerable sums there dedicated to the uses of the Church, (ii) in the ecclesiastical interest, owing to the numbers of workers who have been attracted, and (iii) in the spiritual interest shown by the numbers of conversions, by the excellent condition and conduct of devout Catholics who form our ever increasing congregation, and finally by the Protestant fury shown by the creation of a new anti-Catholic association on the same spot, the object of which would be to repress the progress of Catholicism.

'4. That at the seminary, the two or three Oblates that are there give particular edification by their piety and their observance of the rules, without trying to obtain admiration by exaggerated conduct or trying to distract others from the way of ordinary life of secular priests. Further, that even according to the opinions of persons prejudiced against them, it would be disastrous for the College to remove them from it.'

The Cardinal's last paragraph was a direct answer to one of the charges which Dr. Errington had made against both himself and the Oblates. Under his fifth heading he declares: 'That rumours having been started to the effect that in the instrument by which the title of the church and its buildings in Bayswater were made to the Congregation, there were certain conditions prejudicial to the Diocese and its rights, with insinuations almost of fraud or at least of not too correct dealings, I myself went through the document, banishing all which, in my opinion, could be said to the contrary, and I added my own written opinion, submitting it together with the instrument to the famous lawyers Bagshawe, father and son, so that they could consider it and inform me. I did this without Father Manning or his advisers knowing anything about it, and the copious answers I received from these two were most favourable on every point, so much so that they found nothing to alter or re-touch.' Having thus dealt with one of his coadjutor's most damaging accusations, the Cardinal finished by commending Manning to the Holy Father's care in the formal phraseology of the Papal Court. 'I place myself at the sacred feet of your Holiness, to whom I most warmly recommend both the person and the cause of the most worthy Provost, imploring for myself your Apostolic Benediction.'[1]

Between Wiseman's action in annulling the proceedings of the Chapter and writing to the Pope, the Archbishop of Trebizond had taken a direct hand in the affairs of the Chapter, thus showing himself openly opposed to the Provost and the Cardinal. The Canons determined to answer Wiseman by an appeal to Rome to decide whether or not they had a right to inquire into the affairs of the College by virtue of the decrees of the Council of Trent. Errington not only took the side of the Chapter, but being an expert canonist, he accepted their request to draft the appeal, an act of

---

[1] Rome, English College Archives. The Talbot Papers.

defiance against the Cardinal whose coadjutor he was supposed to be. 'My Coadjutor has been acting as solicitor against me in a law suit,'[1] was Wiseman's comment when he heard this piece of news; only Manning could see a possible good outcome from these sorry divisions. 'All my own affairs are of little importance to me compared to the trial in which your Eminence stands for a moment,' he wrote before the Chapter met to discuss their appeal to the Pope. 'I say for a moment, because I believe it to be a crisis permitted to put an end for ever to an unsound state, full of future dangers of a graver kind. The last three Masses I have said, I may say, for you. And I am as calmly and firmly convinced that all this is for the solid good of the Diocese and of the Seminary, for the final rooting of the Congregation (of the Oblates), and the ascendancy of a Roman over every other kind of spirit, as I can be of anything which rests on the acts of men. I go to this Chapter with a light heart and with a feeling that nothing can give me pain, for I have felt that all the pain has come upon your Eminence. I wish I knew how I could lighten it.'[2]

The Chapter duly met and the appeal to the Pope, which took the form of two petitions drawn up by Archbishop Errington, were placed before the Provost for his signature. These petitions Manning flatly refused to sign, saying that they were derogated by the Cardinal's act in cancelling the previous proceedings of the Chapter, when Wiseman had declared the question of the Seminary to be beyond the scope of their competency. He was then asked to leave the Chapter-room, but when he refused to do this also, the petitions were signed by the senior Canon with the words *renitente praeposito* added. In this form they were sent to Rome. Thus it was that the Pope found himself faced with the Cardinal's letter and the Chapter's appeal, both followed soon afterwards by Father Patterson representing the Cardinal, and Provost Manning himself, who came, not as the Cardinal's representative, but to defend his own conduct and that of the Congregation of which he was Superior. But the two clergymen might just as well have saved themselves the trouble of the journey, for the Pope, considering that the English Catholics must sort out their own problems, referred the whole matter back to a Synod of the English Province.

[1] Ward, Vol. II, p. 276.   [2] *Dublin Review*, January 1923, p. 110.

XVIII

At the height of the dispute with the Chapter Wiseman paid a visit to Ireland. For the first part of this visit he was accompanied by Monsignor Talbot, and there can be little doubt that the Cardinal took the opportunity to pour out all his complaints against his coadjutor and to express his indignation at the conduct of the Chapter for the benefit of the Papal Chamberlain, who returned to Rome fully convinced of the necessity for Dr. Errington's removal from his post. Talbot had previously occupied a neutral position, appealing to both the Cardinal and the Archbishop to make every effort to work in harmony, if only to avoid scandal. But in the latter stages of the dispute, especially after the case had been relegated to Rome, he appeared to be entirely on the side of the Cardinal and the Provost. He did not, unfortunately, confine himself to pleading the Cardinal's cause. He imputed wholly misleading motives to the other side; suggesting in influential quarters that the opposition was tainted with 'Gallican' sentiments (a favourite term of opprobrium in the mouth of the Monsignor) and that its distinguishing feature was disloyalty to the Holy See. By this irresponsible gossip Talbot was to add the final complication to the already sufficiently confused situation and was, indeed, to frustrate the last chance of a dignified and equitable solution to the problem of the coadjutorship.

The Cardinal's visit to Ireland proved to be a spectacular success. He went originally at the invitation of the Bishop of Clonfert who had asked him to preach at the consecration of a new church at Ballinasloe, but the enthusiasm of the Catholic Irish in welcoming to their land a member of the Sacred College of Cardinals who was himself of Irish ancestry turned the visit into a triumphant progress. People flocked in their thousands to hear him, and before he returned to England he was to deliver sermons, lectures, and addresses that filled a book of four hundred pages. In every town he was accorded a civic welcome and in Dublin the Lord Mayor gave a banquet in his honour. He visited Waterford, where he had spent his few years in Ireland as a child, and travelled to many other parts of the country receiving ovations on all occasions. People rushed to the railway stations to see his train and knelt to receive his blessing as it passed. He was invited to Trinity College, Dublin, the great stronghold of Protestantism, and the treasures of its famous library were opened for his inspection. It was typical of the versatility of his mind that while in the Irish capital he found time to lecture on the subject of 'Ornamental Glass found in the Catacombs'. Newman was in Ireland at the time and described the 'spirit and intellectual power' with which the Cardinal met the numerous calls on his talents as preacher, lecturer, after-dinner speaker, public figure and Prince of the Church. Of the volume of the addresses he delivered, Newman declared that 'though nothing remained of Cardinal Wiseman for the admiration of posterity of all that he has spoken and written but what is therein contained, there is enough to justify the estimation in which his contemporaries have held the talents and attainments of the first Archbishop of Westminster'.[1] When he returned to London the Metropolitan Chapter had two documents to present to him; one was their petition against the Oblates of St. Charles and the other a Congratulatory Address on the success of his tour in Ireland.

Wiseman had little reason to look forward to the forthcoming Synod with any feelings of complacency. The harmonious atmosphere which had prevailed at the first Synod had evaporated. The other bishops were mostly of a conservative turn of mind and considered that Wiseman was introducing new ideas at all too fast a pace, while they resented his desire to carry things by the weight of his own archiepiscopal authority rather than by discussion and vote. Quite apart from his dispute with the Chapter on the question of the desirability of the Oblates remaining at St. Edmund's, the Cardinal and the other bishops were still divided on the question

[1] Article in the *Rambler*, quoted by Ward, Vol. II, p. 291.

of the government of the Colleges. St. Edmund's, Oscott, and Ushaw, had now to serve for the education of priests from various dioceses, and all the bishops contributed to the expense of running the colleges and naturally claimed the right to have a share in their management. This was resented by the bishops in whose dioceses the Colleges stood; these wishing to retain for themselves individual control. On this issue Wiseman was supported by Dr. Ullathorne, the vigorous Bishop of Birmingham, but most of the others wished to see the colleges placed under the care of a committee of bishops with equal authority. The question of the registration of Catholic trusts was another bone of contention. Recent legislation had made the registration obligatory but Wiseman considered that the law, as it stood, was prejudicial to Catholic interests and wished the bishops to ignore it, while they, having no desire to be embroiled in further controversy with the government, pressed for the right to decide the matter according to their own individual interpretation of the issue as it affected their particular dioceses. To Wiseman, with his high notions of his position as Cardinal-Archbishop, such an independent line, for all its obvious reasonableness, savoured of disloyalty. The knowledge that upon almost all these points Dr. Errington was in full agreement with the other bishops only added to the Cardinal's melancholy forebodings.

His own health was far from good, a fact which caused considerable alarm to Manning, Talbot, Faber, and the Cardinal's other supporters, for they feared that his death might occur at any moment, as a result of which Dr. Errington would immediately become Archbishop of Westminster by virtue of his right of succession. But Dr. Errington was also in poor health, a fact which the Cardinal discovered early in 1859. It seemed to him that this fact might induce the Archbishop to resign his post on grounds which had no connection with their own unhappy disagreements, and wrote at once to Monsignor Talbot to suggest that another post be offered 'elsewhere and more proportionate to his strength', expressing at the same time his alarm at the prospect of an open clash between himself and his coadjutor at the Synod.

The Cardinal began his letter, which was dated 8th March 1859, by saying that he had had a long talk with Archbishop Errington which caused him great distress 'because he declared himself all in favour with the conduct of the Chapter, even to the point of being their supporter in all that they had done. He has studied, and is studying for them, and is preparing to defend them at the next Synod. I made him realize the scandal that would arise out of the fact that we had not only differing ideas, but that we were leaders, so to speak, of utterly opposing sentiments, because he evidently proposes to make himself head of the bishops, who otherwise would not allow themselves to be beguiled in that manner. I was compelled to tell him in clear terms that it was impossible to have a common government of a diocese where the coadjutor supported a system which was antagonistic to the bishop; and where the latter could not put his faith in the former.'

Wiseman then passed on to the question of Dr. Errington's health. The letter was written in Italian, and though the Cardinal and Talbot seemed to correspond indiscriminately in both English and Italian, it is very probable that Wiseman wrote in Italian on this occasion because he intended the letter as much for the eye of Cardinal Barnabò, the Prefect of Propaganda, and possibly also for the Pope's, as for the eager eye of Monsignor Talbot. For the Cardinal-Prefect, who took a dispassionate view of English affairs, could not necessarily be relied upon to support his fellow Cardinal in England with the same unquestioning devotion which Wiseman could rely upon in George Talbot. 'All this,' the Cardinal concluded of his talk with the Archbishop of Trebizond, 'I repeated to him in round and clear terms. I did not, however, push it any further than that for the following reasons:

'Some days before, on finding myself alone with Dr. Hawkins, a man who has my complete trust, he began to tell me that Mgr. Errington had been to consult him about his health. I *had* actually heard that he had consulted him some time before Christmas but neither the one nor the other had mentioned the fact up to now. I only noticed that he had changed his diet and asked Searle if he knew the reason, but he in turn could not enlighten me. So Hawkins told me then, that before Christmas Mgr. Errington had consulted him complaining of brain fatigue, that he was finding it difficult to concentrate or apply himself, that he (Hawkins) had advised him to get away from his work for a period of time, that he left for Ireland where he spent a month, but that although he then felt better for a few weeks his old symptoms had now returned, that is, after two and a half hours work he would become all confused, could hardly see for dizziness and that going out of doors would hesitate and could hardly walk. . . .

'The Archbishop told me nothing about all this and I began to feel within me a grave responsibility. For that reason I asked Searle, with whom I am on confidential terms, if he knew that the Coadjutor had consulted a doctor (many had already noticed the change in him). He replied that he had seen Hawkins and that he was deliberating on what to do. He did not say more but went to Hawkins and asked him if there was really anything serious the matter. Hawkins answered yes, and said that it was absolutely necessary that the Archbishop went away now and for not less than six months: but then he added, 'I must inform you that even this will not be enough. *He will never be able to put up with the strain of London*; his brain has suffered, *and it will be impossible for him to bear the mental work* and the application necessary for the administration of this Diocese.'. . .

'This then is how the matter stands. Would it not be better to make known to him that the doctor, without being prompted, has considered it his duty to relate to me all these facts about his health, affirming that it is impossible for him to continue in the strain of this coadjutorship, and that it would be better and in his own interest if he assumed Archiepiscopal charges elsewhere and more proportionate to his strength? I could write a letter to Cardinal Barnabò giving the formal opinion of the doctor, in case His Holiness decides to adopt this device which seems to have been ordained by Providence, and so avoid the scandal which might otherwise arise.'[1]

Whether the Archbishop's ailment had some psychosomatic cause, due to the stress to which he was subjected as a result of his differences with the Cardinal and his frenzied hostility to the Provost and the Congregation of the Oblates, it is difficult to say, but it seems to have had no permanent effect upon him. He was to outlive Cardinal Wiseman by twenty-one years; indeed he was destined to die in the same year as Monsignor Talbot, the only distinguishing characteristic of his demise, in comparison with the other's, being

[1] Rome, English College Archives. The Talbot Papers.

that he departed this life in full possession of his mental faculties. He may, therefore, have been in sounder health than either of these opponents, but that he was seriously ill at this period (as he admitted himself in a letter to Cardinal Barnabò) cannot be doubted and may explain, to some extent, his fanatical line of conduct.

But if ill-health contributed to the Archbishop's conduct of his case there was nothing in Talbot's handling of the affair that was likely to soothe or encourage him to fall in with the wishes of either Wiseman or the Pope. Talbot blundered from the very beginning. He made no effort to disguise the nature of his feelings for Errington, whom he considered bent on undoing all the work Cardinal Wiseman had done in the Archdiocese, writing to tell Manning that 'the worst thing I have done (with regard to Errington) has been to tell Mgr. Searle in a private letter that my opinion is that he is radically anti-Roman and retrograde in his policy.'[1] Knowing the friendship that existed between Searle and the Archbishop, was Talbot really so simple as to imagine that this information would not be passed on? Of course it soon reached the ears of the Archbishop of Trebizond who was justifiably indignant. 'These most grave accusations,' he wrote to Talbot in some heat, 'calumnies if they are false, are contradicted by the tendencies of my education, by the practical testimony of my life, and by my express declaration of their falsity.'[2] Talbot was apparently unmoved by this dignified denial of his ill-considered charges; he continued to make similar accusations so that when he wrote, on behalf of Cardinal Barnabò, to offer Dr. Errington another post, the Archbishop felt that an acceptance would amount to an admission of the truth of Talbot's unfounded insinuations. Indeed, Talbot's letter, in which the Archbishopric of Port of Spain in Trinidad was offered to Dr. Errington, was such a model of tactlessness that its very phraseology made acceptance almost impossible. 'The Holy Father,' Talbot concluded, 'who has full confidence in your goodness and ecclesiastical spirit, desires to arrange this affair as quietly as possible, and to prevent the scandal of having recourse to more vigorous measures.'[3]

Nobody realized more clearly than Dr. Errington the difficulties involved in any further attempt to try to work in harmony with the

---

[1] Purcell: *Life of Manning*, Vol. II, p. 100.   [2] Ward, Vol. II, p. 332.
[3] Ibid., p. 333.

Cardinal. It could no longer be achieved. He had never desired the office he now filled; he had already begged to be relieved from it and transferred to some other position; but the terms of Talbot's letter, with its dark hints at 'recourse to more vigorous measures' made him feel that he could never resign his present post until he had vindicated himself from the charge of being anti-Roman or of conduct that merited the displeasure of the Holy See. He refused to answer Talbot's letter, which he had every right to consider insolent, but wrote directly to the Cardinal-Prefect of Propaganda. His letter was of considerable length, and set out to justify his motives for declining the offer of Port of Spain, making it quite clear that Talbot's campaign of calumny and gossip was responsible for his decision: 'But now, as I have been accused by Monsig. Talbot (and others, who think as he does, repeat it here) of anti-Romanism, Anglo-Gallicanism and other failings, which, if they really existed, would be incompatible with the faithful fulfilment of the episcopal duties, and as these accusations are given as reasons why I should not remain here, it does not seem to me that I can of myself take any step for my own removal, since such a step would confirm these erroneous assertions and accusations, and hence would bring much damage not only on myself and my future work, if God gives me grace to continue it, but also on the credit of those (not a few) who are said expressly, or supposed by the same accusers, to think as I think, instead of viewing our affairs with the same eyes with which Monsig. Talbot and others see them.'[1] He refused to accept any other post, save by the express command of the Pope, until he had had the chance to defend himself in Rome.

After writing this letter the Archbishop retired to the country to rest, on his doctor's advice, and also to prepare for the Synod, which was due to meet in two months time.[2] Wiseman had sufficient misgivings about the behaviour to be expected from his coadjutor that he wrote to him just before the Synod opened to remind him that a coadjutor was supposed to be the *alter ego* of his bishop. To this piece of advice the Archbishop replied somewhat cryptically that he was studying his rights, a rejoinder which the Cardinal took

[1] Ibid., p. 335.
[2] Errington's letter to Cardinal Barnabò is dated 7th May 1859. The Synod met in July.

to mean that he must fear the worst. His fears were to be fulfilled in every detail. When the Synod met Wiseman had to face opposition from his coadjutor on almost every point that came up for discussion, and was further disgruntled to see the decision on the question of the government of the Colleges go against him. To a man of Wiseman's temperament such a defeat appeared as a personal humiliation; the fact that the bishops should differ in view from him he looked upon as disloyalty to himself rather than mere divergence of opinion. But on the question of the Chapter's appeal, which Rome had referred to the Synod, the Cardinal's view triumphed despite the open support which Dr. Errington gave to the canons, declaring that he did so in his capacity as an independent Bishop and not as a coadjutor, a piece of casuistry which did little good to his cause. The Cardinal's view that the Colleges were not Seminaries and that the provisions of the Council of Trent did not apply to them was maintained by the Synod, and no sooner was this declared than the Chapter, in the person of Dr. Maguire, made prompt and edifying submission. This was followed by a formal apology which was immediately endorsed by the rest of the Chapter.

If the inability of the Cardinal and the Archbishop to reach a settlement of their difficulties had to some extent mystified, up to this moment, the authorities in Rome, where, in the words of Manning's biographer, 'supple and compliant Italian cardinals, unaccustomed to the sturdiness of the English character, were amazed and even somewhat amused at two obstinate and pugnacious but honest Englishmen ready, rather than yield a point or budge an inch, to fight their battle out to the bitter end,'[1] the action of Dr. Errington at the Synod in publicly placing himself in open opposition to his coadjuted Cardinal-Archbishop made them realize that such a situation could not be allowed to continue. To Talbot, of course, the Archbishop's unbecoming conduct had its good side. The tragedy of the situation was lost on him; he could only see it as a move in the game, a false move by the opposing faction. 'I think, as matters have turned out,' he told Patterson, 'that it was very fortunate that Dr. Errington went to the Synod, as whilst he was there it appears that he acted in such a factious manner that he set against him some Bishops who before were inclined to support

[1] Purcell: *Life of Manning*, Vol. II, p. 94.

him, and besides he incurred a serious canonical irregularity in opposing his "Coadjuted", even after the Cardinal had read the letter from Cardinal Barnabò, and the opinion given by Mgr. Tommasseti, one of the best canonists in Rome, which declared that he could not vote or speak against his Coadjuted Archbishop. . . .'[1] Certainly only one result could come from the unhappy scenes of this third Synod; the question of Wiseman and his coadjutor would now have to be settled in Rome.

And so the protagonists took themselves, at the end of 1859, to the Eternal City. Both were sick men, and the Cardinal was deeply wounded in his pride by the turn of events. That he, the architect of the restored hierachy, who had once left Rome in such triumph from out of the Flaminian Gate, should now be dragged back there to defend his conduct against complaints from his suffragans and disagreements with his coadjutor when the new hierachy was barely ten years old, was a situation fraught with bitterness. A serious illness had delayed his departure for Rome, but the tonic atmosphere of that city which never failed to do him good, soon saw him rally in both health and spirits. Optimism took the place of gloom. The law knows many delays and endless formalities dragged out the proceedings between the two contestants who spent weeks in drawing up detailed statements of their cases in long *scritture* of many pages to be submitted to the Commission of Cardinals appointed to hear the question and report to the Pope; but Wiseman's delight at being back in Rome mitigated against the melancholy reasons for his being there, and resulted in even further procrastination. 'The chief cause of delay,' Talbot wrote with some irritation, 'is Cardinal Wiseman himself. He is writing a most voluminous *scrittura*, and he is like a child. Every amusement interferes with it.'[2]

But if Wiseman was responsible for the delays it was Talbot who was responsible for the real trouble, for it was his rash accusations of 'Anti-Romanism and Anglo-Gallicanism' that now stood in the way of an amicable solution. The dispute dragged on into the new year without a solution. The Pope received the Archbishop of Trebizond in audience and entreated him to resign, again offering him the archiepiscopal see of Trinidad. Errington declared that he would not resign of his own free will but would obey the Pope's

[1] Ward, Vol. II, p. 340.   [2] Ibid., p. 347.

command if ordered to vacate his post. When Pius begged him more vehemently to reconsider his decision Errington took out his pocket-book and began to take down the Pope's words, to the considerable annoyance of the Holy Father, who had never met with such treatment before. The Pope made no effort to conceal his anger. Startled guards and prelates of the court who stood in the antechamber were amazed and alarmed to hear the voices of the Sovereign Pontiff and the Archbishop raised in clamorous argument. Dr. Errington was obdurate; he would not resign while the accusations which Talbot had made remained unanswered, despite the fact that no formal charges had been brought against him. He was like Luther at the Diet of Worms—'Here I stand, I can do no more'—differing only from the stubborn heresiarch in that he would submit to a direct command of the Pope, but to nothing else.

The three Cardinals who the Pope had ordered to examine the case were delayed by further illness on the part of Cardinal Wiseman, who had suffered a mild heart attack, and it was not until June 1860 that they were able to reach a decision. They were unanimous in their verdict that Dr. Errington should be liberated from the office of coadjutor and deprived of his right of succession. There was no mention of any canonical offence on the part of the coadjutor; the reason given was simply and solely that it was impossible for Dr. Errington and the Cardinal to work in harmony and that their continued association might prove harmful to the Church in England. At the suggestion of Cardinal Barnabò, and in order to make the decision easier for the Archbishop of Trebizond to accept, it was suggested that he should first be offered another post, and then required to resign from his coadjutorship after a short interval of time. Dr. Errington considered the proposal for three days before once again refusing to resign of his own free will. He then left Rome with dramatic suddenness and with the words: *'Vim patior, patior injustitiam'*—'I suffer violence, I suffer injustice.'[1]

It now only remained for the Pope to remove Dr. Errington from his coadjutorship and to deprive him from his right of succession to the See of Westminster by an act of his supreme pontifical authority. There can be no doubt that Pius IX was most unwilling to do this. He had tried every other way to induce the Archbishop

[1] *Vide* Ward, Vol. II, p. 378, and Butler, *Life of Ullathorne*, Vol. I, p. 216.

to resign, even going to the extent of begging the Archbishop to do it as a personal favour to himself. On every occasion he had met with a stubborn refusal. The offer of the Archbishopric of Port of Spain should have been enough to convince Dr. Errington of the Pope's confidence in his personal character and a sufficient indication that Talbot's malicious suggestions were not entertained by the Pope or held against him, but the Archbishop refused to see it in that light. He left the Pope with no alternative, and accordingly on 22nd July 1860, he was formally deprived of his rights and appointments as coadjutor *cum jure successionis* to the archbishopric of Westminster by a supreme act, which even Pius IX himself found unique enough to call '*Il colpo di stato di Dominiddio*'—'a *coup d'état* of the Lord God'—and another has described as 'an exercise of his supreme authority and an exertion of power altogether unwonted and perhaps unprecedented'.[1] Dr. Errington accepted the papal decree without a murmur, submitting with absolute obedience to the voice of the Vicar of Christ.[2]

Manning was only indirectly involved in the removal of Dr. Errington from his coadjutorship. As the question of the work of the Oblates of St. Charles had been one of the principal points at issue Manning was called upon to defend them, and also to speak on his own behalf as Provost of the Chapter, but at no point in the dispute was he called upon to make any direct move against the coadjutor. This was the business of Cardinal Wiseman alone, and though Manning supported him fully and went so far as to express his belief that the triumph of Archbishop Errington would set back the work of the Church in England for a generation and 'would undo the whole onward movement of the Church in and upon England',[3] the final removal of Dr. Errington from Westminster was in no sense his doing.[4] At the most he may be said to have strengthened the Cardinal's resolve when it seemed to waver, or to have pointed out how all Wiseman's own work would be endangered if Errington succeeded him in the Metropolitan See. But

---

[1] Dr. Frederick Rymer, quoted by Butler: *Life of Ullathorne*, Vol. I, p. 302.

[2] Dr. Errington was twice offered preferment in later years, but on both occasions refused. He worked for some years as an ordinary parish priest and ended his life teaching theology at Prior Park.

[3] Purcell: *Life of Manning*, Vol. II, p. 133.

[4] As it is suggested by Purcell and Lytton Strachey.

to hint that Manning engineered the removal of Errington as an obstacle in the path of his own ambition is a grotesque misinterpretation of the facts. It is true, however, that Manning welcomed the removal of the coadjutor, not because he stood in the way of his own promotion but because he stood in the way of the new spirit which Cardinal Wiseman represented. Indeed, so much did he believe this spirit to be identified with the Cardinal that even with Errington's influence removed he feared for its survival in the event of Wiseman's death. 'So long as the Cardinal lives I do not anticipate any great attempt to make a reaction,' he wrote to Talbot two months after Errington's dismissal, 'but if he were taken away, I think you and I, and those who have stood together in this contest, will have to look about us. It is of the first importance that we should be foresighted, and that we should keep the Propaganda fully informed of everything.'[1]

Wiseman himself took occasion while he was in Rome to write a long defence of the Provost against the criticism levelled against him by Dr. Errington. It was similar to the letter he had already addressed to the Pope on the same subject but on this occasion was directed to Cardinal Barnabò, and was very much longer and more detailed. After enumerating all the good works which Manning had done for the diocese, and the list was impressive, he rebutted his coadjutor's verdict on the Provost in the form of a simple question: 'I think I may now ask your Eminence, who has such experience of men, if a man, I will not say who has worked, but whom God has made use of in order to effect so many and such great things for His glory, is to be despised, and treated as a man merely ambitious, cunning, dishonest, seeking nothing but his own interests and to gain influence?' Wiseman's own answer to this question has already been quoted: 'I do not hesitate to say that in all England there is not another priest who in double the time has done what Dr. Manning has for the advantage of the Catholic Church.'[2]

If Cardinal Wiseman had hoped that the removal of Dr. Errington would bring peace to the Church in England he was soon to discover his mistake. The various issues which had divided the

---

[1] Purcell: *Life of Manning*, Vol. II, p. 101.
[2] Wiseman's letter to Cardinal Barnabò is given in full in Ward, Vol. II, pp. 354-65.

bishops at the last Synod still remained, and the fact that Wiseman had tried, while in Rome, to get the Synodical decision on the question of the Colleges reversed, or its ratification at least postponed, did not help to restore confidence. Furthermore, the Cardinal's rapidly deteriorating health made it more and more difficult for him to reach decisions and attend to urgent business so that he came to rely upon Manning more than ever. He had been suffering from diabetes for some time and he was now to be subjected to continual heart attacks so that his life was often in danger and to those who relied upon his guidance seemed, at times, to hang by the merest thread. The ordeal of the past months had greatly affected his nerves so that shortly after his return to England his doctor informed one of the bishops that he was now 'incapable of looking all round a big question and obstinate in maintaining his own views'.[1]

He was, in fact, a broken man after his return from Rome. The distressing business of the Errington affair, and misunderstandings and disagreements which estranged him from some of his suffragans, bore heavily upon him, and his shattered health deprived him of the energy to face the situation with his old zeal and enthusiasm. From time to time he would rally, and the old fire would flash forth once more, but too often he would give way to moods of despondency and depression, or would allow business to pass unattended for days on end. Seeing him in this weakened state, with the vigilant Provost ever at his elbow, it was not unnatural that people should imagine him to be entirely in Manning's hands. But this was not so. Though without a doubt he relied greatly on the Provost's help it was still the Cardinal's own hand that guided his affairs, for all that the grasp was now weak. This is shown clearly enough by Manning's own fear that Monsignor Searle exploited the situation created by the Cardinal's ill-health to foster his own policy. 'It is my deliberate judgement,' Manning wrote to Talbot after a particularly disagreeable passage of arms with the Secretary, 'that Searle's rude and overbearing manners have intimidated the Cardinal; and that his state of nervous depression puts him more than ever in his power.'[2] In fact, the Cardinal was determined to be in no one's power but his

---

[1] Butler: *Life of Ullathorne*, Vol. I, p. 220.
[2] Purcell: *Life of Manning*, Vol. II, p. 104.

own for his few remaining years on this earth as was made quite clear by his determined resistance to any suggestion that he should have another coadjutor to lighten the burdens of his office.

The annual meeting of bishops in Low Week, 1861, emphasized the fact that the divisions disclosed at the Synod were still unhealed. On the question of the Trusts the bishops outvoted the Cardinal's point of view, but fearing to discuss their plans in his presence arranged to meet again when he was not there, a decision hurtful to Wiseman's pride though brought on entirely by his own dislike of deciding things by majority decisions, especially when the majority was not on his side. It became clear that there would be another appeal to Rome, and in November Bishops Ullathorne and Clifford left to present the case of the bishops while Manning went as the Cardinal's representative. Once again Pius IX and Cardinal Barnabò found themselves attempting to sort out the squabbles of disputatious English bishops and though the Pope remained serene, declaring to the bishops, 'There seems no difficulty here; at all events you shall have justice,' and of Wiseman, '*Il Cardinale è bene merito della Chiesa in Inghilterra*,'[1] there were moments when Barnabò seriously thought that the English Church was threatened with the possibility of schism.

Wiseman knew his bishops better than to entertain so alarming a fantasy, but it did not prevent him, in a moment of depression, from writing in terms more suitable to the indiscreet pen of Monsignor Talbot. 'I fancy the episcopate is roused to exhibition of its true colours,' he wrote to Manning on learning that Bishop Ullathorne had asked the Pope to accept his resignation and allow him to retire to his monastery: 'They have hauled down the Tiara and Keys and displayed their "Confederate" flag, the Gallic cock that crowed against St. Peter. However, I have given up troubling myself much on the matter, but calmly await the decision of the Holy See.'[2] The Pope received Ullathorne's request in a more tranquil spirit and saw no necessity to draw parallels with the civil war then raging in North America. In the middle of the celebrations in honour of the Feast of the Purification in St. Peter's the Pope suddenly called Ullathorne to the papal throne and said: 'Monsignor, in the name of St. Peter, I tell you from this holy chair of

[1] Butler: *Life of Ullathorne*, Vol. I, p. 230. [2] Ibid., p. 237.

truth that your resignation cannot be accepted. Stand to your place. Persevere until death. You have yet many things to do.' Ullathorne's request had probably sprung from a sudden weariness of controversy though Manning and Talbot could only interpret it as a subtle move of policy. The Pope's instinct had been right. Ullathorne fell to his knees. 'I kissed his ring,' he wrote afterwards, 'and returned to my place amidst the wonderment of all onlookers ... I withdrew to my place feeling completely calm and firm, as I have done ever since, having these words constantly before me.'[1]

Wiseman, waiting in London, felt isolated and alone. His solitary position was emphasized all the more when Ullathorne, returning from Rome, passed through London without calling on him, though he wrote his excuses afterwards from Birmingham pleading the lateness of the hour of his arrival. Wiseman had written a kindly letter to welcome him home despite their disagreements. A further slight awaited the Cardinal when the time for the next Low Week meeting came round. 'The following is the state of our prospects of a meeting,' he informed Provost Manning. 'Bishops Cornthwaite, Roskell, and Amherst have accepted the summons and come. Dr. Grant, supposing we should have no meeting, has undertaken a marriage at Plymouth, though it has always been supposed that every bishop kept Low Week free, so says *Rogo te habe me excusatum.* Dr. Turner is very busy preparing for his journey to Rome, so *rogo te*, etc. Dr. Clifford "in the present state of affairs avows that he looks forward to a meeting not without some degree of apprehension", but if I do not write to the contrary will come. A cross letter from Birmingham: We shall be "in a straitened position from having received no answer on the matter on which we are so anxious", did not expect a meeting, has been so long away and on the point of returning to Rome, that a day is valuable to him, and he cannot spare it, but if I permit will run up and go back on the first day. Summary, four have accepted, two declined, one will come for one day. Hexham prevented probably by health and absent; three ... have not answered.'[2]

To Cardinal Barnabò and the authorities in Rome it was more important that harmony should be re-established among the bishops than anything else. He realized that the bishops, many of whom had

---

[1] Ibid., pp. 233-6.
[2] *Dublin Review*, January 1923, p. 127.

been Wiseman's pupils, were often irked by the superiority of the Cardinal and that Wiseman himself did not perhaps defer to them as often as they might wish. The whole episcopacy were expected in Rome in May, 1862, for the canonization of the Japanese Martyrs and Barnabò seized on this opportunity as a chance to restore concord. Wiseman, he believed, should declare to the other bishops that he was indifferent as to the decision on the questions at dispute, that he wished to disclaim any intention to displease others, and that he should express his regret had he done so contrary to his intentions. Barnabò had suggested this sensible solution to Manning, who passed it on to Talbot with the comment: 'The *more generously* this is done, and the *sooner*, the better, before any communication is made by Propaganda or by the Holy Father, as its effect will depend upon its most perfect and evident *spontaneity*.'[1]

To what extent Wiseman accepted this advice of his brother Cardinal is not recorded. The fact that a better spirit did result from this visit of the English bishops to Rome was due primarily to the action of Pius IX. No better time could have been chosen than this when three hundred bishops from all parts of the world were gathered in Rome at the centre of Catholic unity. After the impressive ceremonies of Canonization were over the English bishops were called into the papal presence. After welcoming them to the Eternal City and complimenting them on the progress of religion in England, Pius went on to say (in Wiseman's description of the scene) that 'he was sorry there had been differences amongst us—no wonder, they existed between SS. Peter and Paul. As to these his wish was—and he added later this must be considered a command—that we should take the highest and largest mountain in the Alps and put it over all past questions and dissensions without any tunnel through to get to them. They were never to be referred to again or brought up under any circumstances.'[2] The Pope then told them that they must continue their annual meetings as before, and trusted them to deliberate '*con pace, concordia, e libertà*' (this, perhaps, a hint to Wiseman and the 'superiority' to which Cardinal Barnabò had already made reference). According to Wiseman's description the bishops went out 'blank and speechless'.

[1] Purcell: *Life of Manning*, Vol. II, pp. 117-18.
[2] *Dublin Review*, October 1921, p. 182.

To Monsignor Talbot this audience appeared as a complete triumph for the Cardinal. 'There is no doubt that we enabled Cardinal Wiseman to gain a great triumph in Rome,' he wrote to Manning, complacently apportioning the credit between them when one might have thought that some, at least, was due to the Sovereign Pontiff. 'I shall never forget the bishops' look after their last audience, in which the Pope gave them a severe lesson.'[1] Talbot was a little premature in his judgement, for the Pope's rebuke to the bishops must be taken in consideration with final findings by Propaganda on the points at issue, and these did not by any means go all in favour of the Cardinal, in fact, on the question of the Trusts and the government of the Colleges, which was to be by a Committee of bishops, the decisions went against him. Furthermore, the Cardinal was advised, in the interests of peace, to withdraw the Oblates from St. Edmund's College, a decision which must have made Dr. Errington wonder at his retreat on the Isle of Man.

It had been a hard time and, for the most part, a time of bitter experience for Wiseman, a period in which his strength and his patience had been put to a severe test while his health had slowly declined. At more than one moment the work of his lifetime had seemed to be at stake, and if a mountain was henceforth to cover the disputes which had clouded the last few years, the memory of them could not be so easily blotted out. He could no longer look to the future with the same confidence as of old when the conversion of England had seemed so promising a possibility. But he was not without friends, many more than he supposed, who shared in his unchanged and unchanging ideals, and of these, few had a better understanding of his deepest feelings than had Manning. This understanding sprang not so much from personal feelings of friendship as from a complete identity of outlook between the two men. But that friendship had its part is shown by this New Year letter which the Cardinal received from the Provost at the close of this sad episode in his life. 'I hope this new year will bring you many consolations and that you may see the end of the few troubles which remain,' Manning wrote. 'But perhaps this wouldn't be good for you, and happily Our Master takes better care of you than to give you your way in everything. If it be woe to us when all men

[1] Butler: *Life of Ullathorne*, Vol. I, p. 249.

264

speak well of us, it must be woe to us when all things go well with us. And as I have often said to you, your crosses are measured upon your works. And such a work as yours will not be let off with the crosses of common men and ordinary lives. I am afraid you have been eating your heart. And I think I could put down no small part of the things and thoughts which have vexed you. I wish I could talk them out with you for I believe two-thirds of them have no reality. And of what remains much might be easily remedied . . .'[1] Manning wrote these lines from Rome, which Wiseman would never see again. His visit at the time of the Canonization of the Japanese Martyrs was to be his last to this city which he loved so much.

[1] *Dublin Review*, January 1923, p. 129.

XIX

'I cannot but think that Cardinal Wiseman's coming to Rome for the Canonization of the Japanese Martyrs has been a most providential circumstance, as he has been completely restored to the position he held before the row,' Talbot wrote with characteristic optimism to Manning after the Cardinal's return. 'I am glad to hear he is so well in health,' the letter proceeds, 'and I hope he may continue to be so for many years longer. Certainly the position he occupied in Rome at the Canonization was one of the greatest events of his life.'[1] In fact, the Cardinal had less than three years of life ahead of him, but in comparison to the previous few years it was to be a time of relative peace. The quarrels and disputes which had darkened the past five years must be looked upon as the inevitable growing pains of the new hierarchy. If Wiseman's unique position in the new system made him at times a difficult man to work with it must be remembered that the vigorous life which the Catholic Church now enjoyed in England was due more to him than to any other single man, and the very fact that his conception of the future *rôle* of the Church in this country was on so much more ambitious a scale than was envisaged by his hard-working but less utopian suffragans was bound to result in impatience and irritation and in occasional conflict. It takes time for any new system to settle down and it is fortunate indeed if this process can be achieved without friction of some sort. It was unfortunate that at this critical phase the Cardinal's strength, both physical and intellectual, was undermined by the ill-health which greatly diminished his powers of decision and leadership. It may also be considered as unfortunate

[1] Purcell: *Life of Manning*, Vol. II, p. 149.

266

that in his two principal advisers, Manning and Talbot, he was served by men who, for all their great abilities, were not expert in the art of accommodation and who were always looking for a motive (and usually what they chose to regard as a sinister motive) in the opinions of others, especially when such opinions did not run parallel to their own. Talbot in particular seemed to imagine that anyone who expressed a difference of opinion from that of the Cardinal was guilty of a conspiracy, and it was in this light that he viewed the honest opposition of such men as Ullathorne and Grant, the Bishops of Birmingham and Southwark, both of whom had, in fact, a steadying and consolidating effect on the establishment of the 'new system' when it might have been upset by some of the Cardinal's more rhapsodic moods.

It was a happy circumstance that in these final years the Cardinal was to appear once again on the European stage in surroundings more in keeping with his earlier days as an intellectual leader in the world of Catholic scholarship and thought. This was when he attended the Congress at Malines in the summer of 1863. The Congress met to discuss the question of the relationship of the Catholic Faith with modern civilization, a question which had occupied Wiseman's mind so much in his student days, and which had resulted not only in his lectures on the connexion between science and revealed religion but in his lifelong awareness of all that went on in the world of science, art, and literature. Another factor linked this event with his own youth, for one of the principal speakers was to be the Count de Montalembert, a friend of his Roman days, whose participation in the Congress was viewed with some trepidation by the more conservative elements among those who attended it.

Herbert Vaughan accompanied the Cardinal on this journey and reported back to Monsignor Searle who was anxious that Wiseman should not overtax his strength: 'All goes well thus far. The Cardinal listened to speeches yesterday from three till a quarter past eight without fatigue. Indeed, he says he is much better than he was at Bruges.' Vaughan goes on to describe the work of the Congress. 'We are still at it disputing and settling the affairs of the world! Montalembert has just come—he is to speak twice. He is a demigod in the eyes of the *assemblée*. I shall be surprised if he does not put his foot into it when he speaks about liberty and liberty of conscience.' The Cardinal, Vaughan went on to say, had had a long interview with the King[1] 'who expressed himself much pleased with His Eminence, etc., before the interview took place. The Audience was very satisfactory'. Finally he gave his own opinion of the Congress, which hinted that perhaps the young priest was not so adept at listening to endless speeches without fatigue as was the elderly and ailing Cardinal: 'A great deal of excellent spirit has been shown, and though we have been preached to more than we should like, specially from laymen, yet the effect on the Catholic party must be very important.'[2]

The Cardinal himself wrote to Searle after both he and Montalembert had addressed the Congress. 'After attending the public meetings each afternoon,' he wrote, 'my turn came on, on Friday, or the last afternoon, after a long course of most eloquent discourses by professional orators, some of which were very superior, especially Montalembert, whose doctrines, however, made terrible, though silent confusion. However, I had to speak two hours and a half earlier than I expected. Still, I addressed over three thousand people for two and a half hours without sitting down, or feeling at the end any fatigue—none in the chest. Next day I spoke again at the banquet, but, of course, more briefly. All seems to have gone off well as far as I am concerned, and I am, as usual, most hospitably treated.' Of his audience with King Leopold he noted in the same letter that 'he said to me that he had long wished to make my acquaintance, to thank me for my kindness to his mother-in-law, Queen Marie Amelie, who often mentioned me in her letters'.[3]

Wiseman's address was on the state of Catholicism in England, delivered, as Vaughan later told Wilfrid Ward, 'fluently in French, though the accent was somewhat English',[4] and at the end of it he was enthusiastically applauded. His topic was neither controversial nor spectacular but was in the nature of a justification of the decision he had himself made many years before when he had decided to abandon an academic career in Rome and devote his talents exclusively to the conversion of England. He could now show how, in comparison with the state of affairs in the first year of Catholic

---

[1] Leopold I, King of the Belgians, Queen Victoria's uncle.
[2] Southwark Archives. Letter undated.   [3] Southwark Archives. Letter undated.
[4] Ward, Vol. II, p. 458.

emancipation, the numbers of priests had risen from under five hundred to over one thousand and two hundred; how in that year there had been but sixteen converts, while in 1863 there had been one hundred and sixty-two; how in that year there had been no monasteries or religious houses for men, while in 1863 there were over fifty. Of the persecution that was still remembered and the disabilities that still remained he spoke in terms generous to the spirit of his Protestant fellow countrymen: 'We have unbounded confidence in the fairness of our compatriots, and are certain that they will in the end give us justice.'[1]

Montalembert's discourse, on the other hand, had not avoided controversy. Its very title, 'A Free Church in a Free State' could hardly have been better calculated to alarm the conservatives, as it was a phrase employed originally by Count Cavour, the invader and desecrator of the Papal States, and arch-enemy of the Ultramontanes. For all its misuse in the hands of the enemies of the Church, Montalembert maintained that this remained the principal ideal of liberal Catholicism, and he attacked the old attachment of religion to the state by pointing out how disastrous this had been for the Church, contrasting conditions under Charles X of France with those prevailing after the Revolution of 1848: 'In 1830 all the priests, the abbé Lacordaire amongst others, were reduced to not going out into the street except in the disguise of a layman. . . . In 1848 that same Lacordaire appeared in a Dominican habit in the Assembly.' Democracy also came in for a bitter attack when it was not permeated with the spirit of Christianity. 'The more one is a democrat the more it is necessary to be Christian,' he told the assembly, 'because the fervent and practical cult of God made man is the indispensable counter-weight of that perpetual tendency of democracy to establish the cult of man believing himself God.'[2] Despite these inherent dangers he remained the passionate advocate of democracy and ended his speech with an appeal for the liberty of education, of association, and of the press. For all the 'terrible, though silent confusion' which Wiseman considered these ideas to spread, the speech was greeted with the greatest enthusiasm.

It is not very surprising that after the Congress had dispersed Montalembert was told that his opinions had been denounced at

[1] Ibid., p. 459. [2] Vide E. E. Y. Hales: *Pio Nono*, p. 267.

Rome; but what added to his distress on hearing this news was the tale that it was his old friend Cardinal Wiseman who had denounced him. It was, in fact, true that both Ward and Manning had been active in expressing their strong dislike for Montalembert's opinions, though Ward's attack, which was originally intended for the *Dublin Review*, was not published in that journal but printed for private circulation. When Montalembert made inquiries at Rome after an attempt had been made to have his addresses to the Congress condemned by the Congregation of the Index, rumour there linked Wiseman's name with Ward's and Manning's as being among his accusers. Montalembert's immediate response on hearing this was to write to Phillipps de Lisle, a mutual friend, expressing his regret that so old a friend should take such hostile action against him, and de Lisle passed the letter on to Wiseman in the assurance that nothing could have been further from his mind than any wish to render impossible an attempt at reconciliation between the Church and the nineteenth century.

Wiseman had, at this time, little sympathy with the ideas of the Count, as his letter to Searle showed clearly enough. His experiences under the government of Lord John Russell had conditioned his feelings towards political liberalism in much the same way that Pius IX's liberalism had been conditioned after his period of reflection in exile at Gaeta. In both cases it may be said that experience of liberalism in action had turned them into conservatives. But these facts did not destroy the Cardinal's belief in the right of others to express their own opinions, or of Catholics to hold any political view that did not contradict the Church's teachings on faith or morals. As to Ward's attack, he was ignorant of its very existence.

Despite an inflammation of the eyes which made writing painful to him he at once dispatched a letter to de Lisle which denied in the strongest terms that he had taken any action, at Rome or elsewhere, against the Count. 'I do not know to what Count de Montalembert alludes,' he wrote in obvious perplexity. 'I have never seen any pamphlet of Mr. Ward's about his Malines address, nor am I aware of his having published one. As to myself, I have never written a word to Rome, nor given any authority to anyone to speak unfavourably on the Count's eloquent speech. Still less has it ever entered into my mind to denounce it to the Index, or ask to have it even reproved, still less condemned. Though I did not and do not agree in its political principles and tendencies, there was no error in it against faith or morals, which could have authorized anyone to denounce it, especially a stranger in the presence of the Metropolitan. You may assure the Count of this, and of my undiminished respect and affection for him.'[1] So the matter closed and a friendship dating back to his early years was preserved. The proclamation of the celebrated Syllabus of Errors the following year (8th December 1864) was to hold up the development of such ideas as Montalembert represented until the next pontifical reign, but with this Wiseman had little concern, for in less than three months after its promulgation the Cardinal was no more.

Wiseman now spent a great deal of his time in the country, leaving much of the routine work of the diocese to his Vicar-General, a suggestion, had he but known it, which Archbishop Errington had made long ago to Talbot, when wishing to decline the offered post of coadjutor. It was while in the country that he wrote to Searle a letter of reconciliation on hearing that the other, just returned from Rome, had complained of the Cardinal's continued coldness to him. The letter is a melancholy comment on the sadness which still so often oppressed the Cardinal's spirit, and the feeling of solitariness and isolation which he was never entirely able to cast off in his latter years. 'Last evening,' the letter begins, 'I received a letter from Dr. Hearn, which does not allow me to let a post pass without writing to you, to remove as completely as possible, a painful impression which he tells me has been produced on you, by my deportment towards you. He tells me that you have been made miserable by my coldness, since your return, that it freezes you, etc., etc. I can assure you, that if my manner has produced these painful impressions, it has not for a moment been intended or conscious. Restrained I have certainly felt, by finding (though probably I was wrong) that you seemed glad to get away from my society, avoiding almost every meal, when conversation could have passed between us, and showing indifference to my trying to preserve it. But I do not say this in any set-off against what you have felt or observed, I merely mention it to explain (or

[1] Ward, Vol. II, p. 462.

at least state how I explain) what I thought your wish not to be oppressed by my presence or conversation, as some of your best friends, and indeed yourself, told me had been so much the case before you went abroad, as to have been the cause of your illness.

'I believe some of them thought that you were afraid of the repetition of the same cause, and of its effects, and therefore wished to keep your movements, engagements, etc., independent of mine. Now, *nobody* knows how acutely I have felt the constant solitude and isolation in which I have lived of late, but I have felt embarrassed and unhappy at the idea that your return would be no remedy, but leave me to my solitary meals, drives, and writing, day after day. *Restrained*, therefore, I *did* feel, not knowing your intentions, or feelings; though this very feeling on my part proves that I was not, and am not, cold.

'When a man comes to the last possible decade of his life, and looks back to see how short the prevíous one, though entire, has been, he cannot wish to spend the poor remnant of his life without peace, or to make others, long close to him unhappy. . . . If anything that I have said or done has inflicted pain on you, I regret it most sincerely, and beg you to forgive it. But I can say from my heart, that it was totally unintentional; and as, I feel sure, must have been anything that has led to erroneous impressions in me, respecting you. I trust, therefore, that in future there will be no more room for misunderstanding: but you must not forget that the infirmities of age have come thick upon me, and that one of the merits of the young and strong and more perfect consists in bearing with the weakness for which in their turn they may have to entreat compassion. God bless you.'[1]

There were, of course, brighter moments in this life of semi-retirement and solitude. One such occasion was when he visited Canterbury in October 1863, and was able to visit the Cathedral without being recognized. 'Yesterday I made a pilgrimage to Canterbury Cathedral, where St. Augustine, St. Wilbrid, St. Anselm yet repose, and St. Thomas once received the worship of thousands,' he wrote to Herbert Vaughan. 'But scarcely less interesting to me was to rest against Cardinal Pole's tomb, the first Cardinal that ever entered that splendid Cathedral, since he was in it, alive

[1] Letter dated 3rd May 1863, Southwark Archives.

272

and dead! And no Protestant archbishop has ever been buried in it.'[1]

Another matter which caused him great pleasure in this same year he described in a letter to Manning: 'The Queen has expressed herself greatly pleased "and seemed deeply touched" by the manner in which I had spoken of the Prince Consort in my lecture. I have this on two certain authorities, one of her physicians and her librarian, who mentioned it to her, having been present at its delivery. You who know how the struggle for the Hierarchy and the personal jealousies and antipathies erected at Court by it will understand how important and gratifying it is to have slowly and effectually worked back over the ground and, without yielding an inch, overcome prejudices and malicious influences.'[2] Wiseman was most jealous of his character as a loyal Englishman, and indeed always described himself as such, though he might with equal accuracy have called himself Irish,[3] and he had resented the accusations of disloyalty and even of treason which had been flung at him by the more frenzied partisans of Protestantism at the time of the 'Papal aggression' disturbances and since. He had thus every reason himself to be pleased and touched when he learnt that his tribute to the Prince Consort had not passed unnoticed by the Court which had never granted any official or even unofficial recognition of his position as ecclesiastical head of Her Majesty's Roman Catholic subjects and which chose, when it had to deal with matters concerning the Catholic Church, to treat with some other prelate than the author of the Pastoral from out of the Flaminian Gate. This thaw in the frigid attitude of the Court was slight indeed, but it was welcomed with sincere gratitude.

Though Wiseman was only in his early sixties it was clear to those who surrounded him that his life could not be prolonged much longer. In addition to the chronic diabetic condition he was subjected to increasingly frequent heart attacks any of which might prove fatal. But the old lion (to use Archbishop Errington's metaphor) could still lash out with his paw when stung to action. When Garibaldi visited England in 1864 Cardinal Wiseman was deeply distressed to see the Pope's most formidable enemy fêted on all

[1] Letter in the possession of Mr. Joseph H. Vaughan.

[2] *Dublin Review*, October 1921, p. 188.

[3] The Wiseman family, though resident for some generations in Ireland, claimed descent from the Essex family of that name.

sides and received with rapture by grave politicians and equally rapturous, if possibly less grave, society ladies. It was, however, no particular concern of his what went on in Downing Street or in ducal drawing-rooms, but his disgust became vocal when the Italian revolutionary and avowed atheist was made the recipient of flattering attentions from the bishops of the Anglican Church, who thus gave the impression that militant atheism was a small price to pay for anti-Papalism.

The Cardinal was determined that his own flock, at least, should be left in no doubt as to the religious opinions of the guest whose company the Anglican hierarchy seemed to find so agreeable. To illustrate this he quoted a passage from Garibaldi's letter in which the one-time tribune of the Roman Republic had referred in contemptuous terms to the action of Napoleon III in sending his troops to protect the Pope. In this Garibaldi had praised France for the fact that in 1789 she had 'in that solemn moment' given to the world the Goddess Reason, while now 'she is reduced to combat the liberty of nations, to protect tyranny, and to direct her only efforts to steady on the ruins of the Temple of Reason that hideous and immoral monstrosity the Papacy,'[1] This was the man who Anglican bishops came forward to meet and to whom (it was said) English ladies knelt. 'Oh, pity, pity,' the Cardinal commented, 'at least, if not worse, that such a spectacle should have been exhibited to England at the time, the moment, when every energy on every hand should be put forth, not to dally with, but to crush the spirit . . . of infidelity as well as disloyalty.'[2]

The Times, that old enemy of the Cardinal, took him up on his quotation and accused him of tampering with the evidence to help his case: 'he inserts a word or two to make it suit his purpose, and then feigns a transport of pious horror at our impiety in doing honour to such a reprobate'.[3] But for once Wiseman could catch *The Times* in its own net, and must surely have felt a little mild satisfaction when he was able to point out to 'the thunderer', whose thunderbolts had so often been aimed at his own head, that the quotation from Garibaldi whose accuracy it questioned was, in fact, taken *verbatim* from its own translation of the letter. In their issue of May 31st *The Times* was compelled to withdraw its charge, which

[1] *Vide* Ward, Vol. II, p. 468.   [2] Ibid., p. 469.   [3] *The Times*, 25th May 1864.

was done handsomely enough, though no one can really have been expected to believe the comment which accompanied the apology, that 'we can hardly doubt that the General himself, if he could now revise this strange rhapsody, would withdraw the offensive contrast between the idolatry of Reason and the Papacy, as freely as we do the imputation on the Cardinal's good faith'. There was, in fact, no doubt at all that the General's opinion of the papacy remained unchanged, and it was not for nothing that when the Italian nation came to erect a statue to him in the Pope's former capital it was so constructed that its back was turned on the Vatican, while that of his wife was made to point a pistol at the dome of St. Peter's. But Wiseman had at least succeeded in making the Anglican bishops look foolish and *The Times* eat its words, some small compensation, had he been of a vindictive nature, for the insults which both had flung at him in the stormy days of 1850.

Wiseman's rapidly deteriorating health and the evident approach of death raised once more the problem of his successor. To the Cardinal himself, weary of controversy and wishing only to be left in peace, the subject was both distasteful and distressing, but Manning and Talbot, ever fearful lest the old Catholic interest should yet triumph, could not let the matter rest. It was suggested in Rome that Errington believed that his right of succession had merely lapsed and that it would revive on the Cardinal's death, a point of view which certainly caused a good deal of alarm to Cardinal Barnabò, drawing from him the remark that a man who could take down the Pope's words in a private conversation in his own presence was no doubt capable of doing many strange things;[1] but the story was in fact without any foundation and was strongly denied by Dr. Errington himself, who wrote to say that after what had happened he had never entertained the notion that he could again claim the succession. It was clear, however, that he considered himself as being still eligible for the post if nominated by the Chapter when the vacancy should occur. The danger of this happening so terrified Monsignor Talbot that he lost all restraint and such sense of proportion as he still retained. 'I feel convinced that all the bishops in England would unite to recommend Dr. Errington for Westminster,' he wrote to Manning, 'not from liking the man, but from an English

[1] *Vide* Butler: *Life of Ullathorne*, Vol. I, p. 259.

feeling of triumphing over Cardinal Wiseman and gaining a victory over the Holy See.'[1]

If one had only Talbot's unbalanced correspondence for guidance one would begin to wonder why the English Church had not fallen into schism long ago; Manning, who was on the spot, was not so alarmist, though he still dreaded the influence which Searle might bring to bear on the ailing Cardinal. 'The "old priests" are reduced to a handful,' he wrote back reassuringly to Talbot, 'but being encouraged by the hope of Dr. Errington's return, may give trouble. I think the Cardinal is hardly aware how few they are, and how little weight they have in the diocese. A new race has grown up, and the Orders and Congregations have overpowered them. The public feeling of the diocese is against the old spirit, which is dying out. But some who are near the Cardinal, I suspect, intimidate him. And Searle is Searle . . .'[2] In fact, Manning very much exaggerated the influence of the Cardinal's secretary upon whom Wiseman relied for the management of his business affairs and the organization of his establishment, but for little else.

The Cardinal, however, was quite determined not to repeat the experience which had already cost him so much trouble and anguish. 'My past experience,' he told Talbot in a letter of 26th June 1863, 'where friendship from early life had made me acquainted with character has perfectly spoilt me for [choosing another coadjutor]. I shrink sensitively and irrepressibly from having any one again in my home. I feel that if Searle, to whom I am so accustomed, but is very poorly, were to leave me (as he did for some months in the winter) I should almost be obliged to live alone. . . . I know *no one* who would suit me as a *companion*.' He went on to declare that he did not need a coadjutor as the routine work of the diocese could be carried on just as well by the Vicar-General, while appointing a coadjutor raised special problems which he wished very much to avoid. 'My obtaining a Coadjutor is not like another bishop's doing so. I give by it a superior not only to my diocese but to the whole episcopate; in my present relations with many of the bishops, this is a very grave matter, and heavy responsibility—in fact, a ground for a new quarrel. You know that Cardinal Barnabò has been always inclined to take the side of the suffragans, and count

[1] Purcell: *Life of Manning*, Vol. II, p. 175.　　　　[2] Ibid., p. 175.

up the numbers of those against me, and complain that I did not make enough of their numbers, etc. Now that we have a lull—not a peace—why should I take upon myself a responsibility not belonging to me (for after death I have none) to bring on myself new differences and recourses to Rome, when I want peace above all things. . . .'[1]

The Cardinal's request would have seemed reasonable enough to anyone but Talbot, who was obsessed with the idea that Gallicanism and anti-Romanism would break out like a plague if the succession to the see of Westminster was not made secure before the Cardinal died. He now suggested the appointment of Dr. Ullathorne. To avoid any possible friction it was his idea that Dr. Ullathorne should remain as Bishop of Birmingham until Wiseman's death, when he should succeed to Westminster, and that Manning should be made a bishop *in partibus* to help Wiseman in London, and then he should succeed Ullathorne at Birmingham. Wiseman, however, was determined to be left alone. He felt that every one was scheming and plotting all round him while all he wanted was to be left in peace and leave the whole question of his successor to the Holy See. He was furious with Manning for trying to impose Ullathorne on him, and told him frankly that he felt as if his last friend had left him.[2] He wrote to Rome begging to be allowed to end his days in peace and his request was eventually granted. At the end of February Manning, who had been in Rome, wrote to tell him that: 'On the subject of the coadjutor you may consider the matter as in your own hands. Cardinal Barnabò read to me your letter, and said that the Holy Father had no intention of pressing anything; and that he should answer, leaving it to you.'[3] For the remaining year of life left to the Cardinal nothing more was heard on the question of his successor.

[1] Rome, English College Archives. The Talbot Papers.
[2] Purcell: *Life of Manning*, Vol. II, p. 183.   [3] Ibid., p. 188.

XX

Ever since the time of his serious illness in 1860 Cardinal Wiseman had realized that his days were numbered. In that year he had composed his own epitaph, leaving only a space for the actual date of death. After he returned from the Malines Congress in 1864 his life was almost completely that of an invalid, though he was able to preside over a meeting of the bishops in December. On 15th January 1865, he was taken seriously ill, and it became clear that the end was near. In the remaining month left to him he drifted gradually from life, enduring his illness with exemplary patience while consciousness lasted. Monsignor Searle and Canon Morris, both lifelong friends, attended him in his last hours.

During his last days on earth his memory often returned to the time when he had lived in Rome, and he especially liked to recall the summer retreat at Monte Porzio where the English College used to retire during the hottest months of the year. Once when Canon Morris visited him he said: 'I am sure it would do me more good to have a long talk about Monte Porzio than to be kept so much alone.' The Canon encouraged him to talk, and the dying Cardinal dwelt on the beloved place which had been the scene of the earliest triumphs of his career, when youth and enthusiasm had yet to learn the disappointments and frustrations which came with the passing years. He recalled with wonderful clarity the beauty and peace of this village in the hills beyond Rome: 'I can see the colour of the chestnut trees, and Camaldoli, and the top of Tusculum. What a beautiful view it is from our Refectory window! A newcomer does not value Monte Porzio properly. It takes a year's work in Rome to enable you to appreciate it. I loved it dearly . . .' He went on to recall the great occasion when the Pope had come to visit the English students. 'They have kept the Rector's chair in the place where I used to sit. I got that gold chair for Pope Leo's reception, and I always used it afterwards. I used to sit there writing for hours after everyone was in bed, and then I would refresh myself by a look out of the open window into the moonlight night.'

Wiseman was in no doubt that there would be no recovery; that this was his last illness. He called for his Master of Ceremonies and gave detailed instructions for his funeral and requiem with complete calmness, adding characteristically: 'See that everything is done quite right. Do not let a rubric be broken.' Later he told Morris: 'I want to have everything the Church gives me, down to the Holy Water. Do not leave out anything. I want everything.' Despite these instructions, and the solemn request for all the rites wherewith Holy Church comforts the dying, the Cardinal's sense of humour did not desert him in his final hours. When he appeared to be almost unconscious Canon Morris had to give him a mixture that must have been very disagreeable, 'a concoction of strong beef tea and brandy'. Morris was sure that the Cardinal was unable to distinguish one thing from another, but to his surprise and amusement the dying man opened his eyes and announced: 'That is what I call dull—beef and brandy!'[1]

News that the Cardinal was sinking soon spread among his friends. Monsignor Talbot heard the news in Rome and wrote to Phillipps de Lisle a letter in which genuine grief, anxiety for the future, and a slightly unnecessary comment on the Cardinal's orthodoxy, were all curiously mixed: 'What a loss the death of the Cardinal will be to the Church in general and to England! A crisis awaits the Church in England. He it was that gave such a helping hand to the movement which has brought so many Anglicans into the Church, and he has always been so orthodox in the midst of it all. His value will only be appreciated when he is gone. I have known him intimately for nearly twenty-one years. I have not heart to say anything more on this sad topic.'[2] Manning was also in Rome when news reached him that the Cardinal was *in extremis*. He returned

[1] Ward, Vol. II, pp. 511-15. Here Ward records Canon Morris's memories of Wiseman's last hours, from which the above quotations are taken.
[2] Purcell: *Life of Phillipps de Lisle*, Vol. I, p. 405.

home at once, bringing with him the Pope's special blessing. It is doubtful whether Wiseman recognized the Provost when he approached his bed, but on being told of the Pope's blessing he murmured 'I thank him' several times.

To Morris he spoke of his love for the Church and the great ceremonies of the Catholic liturgy. It was not among the least of his achievements that he had restored a proper attention to liturgical worship in the English Church, where such things had been sadly neglected during penal times; and his request that his funeral should be properly ordered was a final testimony to his love for the richness and beauty of Catholic ritual. 'I have never cared for anything but the Church,' he said, 'my sole delight has been in everything connected with her.' And in a characteristic phrase already noted he added: 'As people in the world would go to a ball for their recreation, so have I enjoyed a great function.'[1] He was told that some of the French bishops had ignored Napoleon III's decree which forbade them read the Syllabus of Errors in public. 'I am glad the French bishops are standing out so bravely for the liberties of the Church,' was his comment; 'That will console the Holy Father very much.' But he was saddened by his own inability to speak on this subject which was causing so much controversy: 'The French Bishops have spoken, but as yet I've said nothing.'[2] It was his last flicker of interest in the temporal affairs of the Church. Soon afterwards he sank into unconsciousness, and though from time to time he spoke it was only occasionally that those around him could catch the meaning of the words. Once Canon Morris thought he heard some murmured expression like 'rush through the angels into God', and again, 'I never heard of anyone being tired of the stars.'[3] These are the last words recorded of him save for his whispered thanks on hearing of the Papal blessing.

Cardinal Wiseman died at eight o'clock on the morning of Wednesday, 15th February 1865, in the sixty-third year of his age. He had been moved previously, at his own request, into the drawing-room of his house in York Place, and he lay there, according to the tradition for a Prince of the Church, vested in his robes with the sapphire ring on his finger, the symbol of cardinalitial authority. At the foot of the bed stood the Archiepiscopal Cross

[1] Ward, Vol. II, p. 510. [2] Ibid., pp. 511–12. [3] Ibid., p. 515.

which in former days had been carried before him in processions. Some days previously the Canons of the Metropolitan Chapter had heard him make his final profession of Faith and watched while the Sacrament of Extreme Unction was administered by the Senior Canon. His last words to them had reference to the quarrels which had clouded their relationship in the past few years. 'I have one word to say,' he told them, 'and it is to beg you to cherish peace, and charity, and unity, even though it may be at the price of our occasionally having to give up our own individual opinions for the sake of peace. And if in the past there has been anything that has made against charity and unity, in God's name let it pass into oblivion; let us put aside all jealousies, and let us forgive one another and love one another.'[1]

One further incident of the Cardinal's last days must be noted, for it formed a quaint link with his earliest days as a bishop in England. At that time when his hopes for a general conversion resulting from the Oxford Movement were at their most sanguine he had suffered a humiliating blow as a result of Mr. Sibthorpe's rapid submission to the Roman Church and almost equally rapid return to the bosom of Anglicanism. The name of Sibthorpe had become a byword among Wiseman's critics, and the shock of his defection had driven the bishop to his bed. For twenty years the wayward Sibthorpe had followed his curious career in the paths of Protestantism while in Catholic circles his name was only uttered by those who wished to illustrate the dangers of too rapid conversions or evoke a warning against the results likely to follow from too friendly a feeling towards the Establishment. Now, as Wiseman lay on his deathbed, he was told that Sibthorpe had returned to the Roman Catholic Church. The prodigal had come back, and the old humiliation of twenty years ago was wiped out. Wiseman insisted that Sibthorpe's first Mass after his reconciliation should be said in his own private chapel.[2]

The Requiem Mass for the repose of the Cardinal's soul was sung in the pro-Cathedral of St. Mary's, Moorfields, on February 23rd. At the Cardinal's own request the sermon was preached by Provost

[1] Ibid., p. 515.
[2] Sibthorpe remained a Catholic for the remainder of his life though some confusion was caused at the time of his death when he was discovered to have passed away clutching a copy of the Anglican prayer book.

Manning. To the twelve bishops of the Province, the assembled clergy, and a vast gathering of people he spoke movingly of the friend and father they had lost, sketching in the peroration an eloquent summary of the career that was now ended. 'He is gone; but he has left behind him in our memories a long line of historical pictures, traced in the light of other days upon a field which will retain its colours fresh and vivid for ever. Some of you remember him, as the companion of your boyhood, upon the bare hills of Durham; some, in the early morning of his life, in the sanctuaries of Rome; some see before them now his slender stooping form, on a bright winter's day, walking to the Festival of St. Agnes out of the walls; some again, drawn up to the full stature of his manhood, rising above the storm, and contending with the calm, commanding voice of reason against the momentary unreason of the people of England; some, again, can see him vested and arrayed as a Prince of the Church, with the twelve suffragans of England, closing the long procession which, after the silence of three hundred years, opened the first Provincial Synod of Westminster. Some will picture him in the great hall of a Roman palace, surrounded by half the bishops of the world, of every language and of every land, chosen by them as their chief to fashion their words in declaring to the Sovereign Pontiff their filial obedience to the spiritual and temporal power with which God has invested the Vicar of His Son. Some will see him feeble in death, but strong in faith, arrayed as a Pontiff, surrounded by the Chapter of the Church, by word and deed verifying the Apostle's testimony, "I have fought a good fight, I have finished my course, I have kept the faith." And some will cherish, above all these visions of greatness and of glory, the calm and sweet countenance of their best and fastest friend and father, lying in the dim light of his chamber—not of death, but of transit to his crown. These things are visions; but they are substance. "*Transit gloria mundi*", as the flax burns in fire. But these things shall not pass away.'[1]

The funeral procession from Moorfields to the burial ground at Kensal Green, a distance of seven miles, was marked by a show of quite extraordinary respect and sympathy. There was a long file of carriages following the hearse, in the first of which a Chamberlain

[1] Ward, Vol. II, pp. 530–1.

from the Vatican carried the scarlet Cardinal's hat and the insignia of Wiseman's orders of knighthood, the Grand Crosses of Malta, of Charles III of Spain, and of St. Januarius of the Kingdom of Naples. All along the route great crowds of people stood in silence to see the procession pass. 'Every part was thronged with spectators,' *The Times* reported, 'every window was crammed, every balcony, housetop, and even the roofs of churches were occupied. Those thousands, and even hundreds of thousands, waited patiently throughout the day.'[1] It was astounding to think of this respect shown to the man who only fifteen years before had been pelted by the mob. 'Not since the State funeral of the Duke of Wellington,' *The Times* report continued, 'has the same interest been evinced to behold what it was thought would be the superb religious pageant of yesterday. . . . Everywhere, however, the cortège was received with marks of profound respect. At least three-fourths of the shops along the line of route were closed—the streets were lined with spectators, and every window and balcony was thronged. Altogether the feeling among the public seemed deeper than one of mere curiosity—a wish, perhaps, to forget old differences with the Cardinal, and render respect to his memory as an eminent Englishman and one of the most learned men of his time.'

The sympathetic note struck by *The Times* was echoed in other newspapers in much the same way that they had once followed the lead of the same journal in execrating Wiseman's name at the time of the famous Pastoral Letter. Now all joined in praising him as the great Cardinal, though not all went so far as the *Hull Advertiser* which declared roundly that 'the greatest among the present generation of England's great men has ceased to be numbered with the living'. The *Daily Telegraph* drew a picture of Wiseman which must have made readers who were able to recall that paper's opinion of him in 1850 wonder that they were reading about the same man: 'His portly figure, his pleasant smile, and jovial, good-humoured face, accorded ill with the popular delusion which represents all the priests of the Church of Rome as ascetic fanatics or Machiavellian intriguers. Emphatically a man of the world, he knew how to hold his place, without arrogant pretension or any loss of real dignity, in a society which did not recognize his rank.' The *Sun*

[1] *The Times*, 24th February 1865.

283

also praised him in extravagant terms. 'He was a man of genius,' it declared, but concluded its appreciation of his life on a note that would have accorded Wiseman more pleasure than any belated tributes to his intellectual powers: 'Among his co-religionists he was beloved and revered. But, apart from them, in the midst of the general public, in assemblages of Protestants and Dissenters, the deceased Cardinal was always of late years received with the respect due alike to his learning and his virtues.'

Cardinal Wiseman's place in the ranks of the eminent Victorians has always been overshadowed by those two other Cardinals, Newman and Manning, both of whom owed their conversions to the Roman Catholic Faith so much to his influence and inspiration. Wiseman, as we have seen, foresaw this and welcomed it, but whether the final verdict of history will leave him in the third place after the two great converts remains to be seen. It is perhaps invidious to make such distinctions at all; Newman's transcendent qualities are hardly likely to be called in question, he is one of the unassailably great and unique figures of the Nineteenth Century; but there is much in the life of Wiseman—so short in comparison with the other two who both achieved patriarchal age—to encourage a favourable comparison with his immediate successor, despite the neglect from which the study of his life and work has suffered; for the curious investigator of the shelves of most libraries will find a whole section devoted to Newman, four or five shelves to Manning, but only a few individual works on Wiseman. Manning had all the qualities to make him a successful figure in the world; singleness of purpose, iron determination, immense strength of will, and the positive conviction that right was on his side. But in the world of ideas he had little to say. People are not interested much in what Manning thought, they are interested in what Manning did, and the intellectual notions which inspired his actions as a Catholic he derived as much from Wiseman as from any other of his contemporaries. It was not from motives of personal ambition that Manning accepted the papal nomination to the see of Westminster on Wiseman's death, but to ensure that Wiseman's work should be continued, and to frustrate the re-emergence of those influences which had worked against the Cardinal during his lifetime.

He saw himself as completing the work of Cardinal Wiseman to whom, as he himself confessed, he owed all that had befallen him in his life as a Catholic.

Despite the faults of character which he himself would have been the last to deny, Wiseman stood head and shoulders above his contemporaries in the Catholic Church at the time when her forces in England were augmented by the great converts from the Established Church, most of whom were men of singular, if not formidable, ability. Among these Wiseman could more than hold his own. He differed from those among his co-religionists who had been brought up in the last years of penal times by the vast range of his culture and the comprehensive view with which he regarded the Church. There was nothing insular about his religion; it was truly Roman. For him the Catholic Religion was not only the way of faith and the gateway to salvation; it was the religion which had been the inspiration of the great masters of sacred art; of the music which the greatest geniuses had offered to adorn the services of the Church; it was the voice of civilization down the ages. Born two years before the first Napoleon assumed the imperial crown, and living in his maturity through the revolutions which overthrew the monarchies of Charles X and Louis-Philippe, and which shook the very throne of St. Peter, he realized the danger to human civilization which was involved in the revolutionary attacks on the Church. This was an experience which his English Catholic contemporaries, sheltered by the channel from the turmoil of European affairs, did not share and the significance of which they failed to grasp. It was this which made so many of them unable to understand him when he returned to England after twenty years residence abroad.

It was this background which gave him so lively an interest in such a variety of topics which later he could turn to good account on the public platform as a lecturer. Some idea of the range and versatility of his mind, beyond his theological and linguistic studies, can be gathered from the following subjects taken from among the sixty-three titles listed after his name in the *Bibliographical Dictionary of English Catholics*: University Education; Highways of Peaceful Commerce; The Home Education of the Poor; The Stewardship of the English Nation; A Few Flowers from the

Roman Campagna; Points of Contact between Science and Art; Self Culture; Judging from Past and Present, what are the Prospects of Good Architecture in London; The Social and Intellectual State of England; to which can be added the lecture on William Shakespeare upon which he was labouring at the time of his death. It was this reputation for brilliant versatility, especially in conversation, that gave rise to *Bishop Blougram's Apology*, but despite the range of subject Wiseman could bring an informed mind to all of them. Ruskin read Wiseman on Chartres Cathedral and found him 'very wonderful and delightful'.[1]

Wiseman perhaps showed least perception as a judge of men. His dislike of denying favours and his charitable view of people made him often a poor judge of character. Bishop Patterson wrote of the Cardinal that 'speaking of a great disappointment and sorrow which had befallen him by the misconduct of another, who had deceived him, he said he would rather go on to the end believing in men and being often deceived, than lose all trust in everyone, for he thought next to losing confidence in God the greatest misery was to lose all confidence in man'.[2] This is the expression of a truly human and charitable sentiment, but the cynical might well remark that it is no principle on which to run a diocese. Some of the people in whom Wiseman placed his trust were ill-fitted to bear the confidence he placed in them. It was Wiseman who placed Talbot in his responsible place at the Vatican, but there can be little doubt that he was wholly unsuited to the position. Even Manning was later to describe Talbot as one of the most indiscreet people he had ever known. Wiseman's choice of Dr. Errington as coadjutor is even more difficult to understand or explain, for he had already had had plenty of opportunity to form a judgement of the Archbishop's character and was fully aware that their opinions differed on many points. Both Talbot and Errington had wished to decline the appointments; on both occasions Wiseman insisted (against all advice in the latter case) that they should accept.

His failure to appreciate the proper worth of some of his fellow bishops was another unhappy feature of Wiseman's character. Both Ullathorne and Grant were men of outstanding character but they were often at cross-purposes with him, and as often as not it

[1] Diaries of John Ruskin, Vol. III, p. 986.   [2] Ward, Vol. II, p. 177.

was the Cardinal's fault. But most unfortunate of all was the sadly awkward relationship which developed between Wiseman and Newman. Wiseman had striven so hard and so long for the other's conversion; it was in reading Wiseman that Newman felt his first real doubts about his position as an Anglican and became aware of that voice which told him, almost inaudibly at first, that Rome would always be found right in the end. But from the moment that he was received into the Church a malignant fate seemed to hang over their relationship. It was to have a distressing effect upon both of them but the reason for it is difficult, if not impossible, to discover.

On one occasion when someone had spoken critically of Newman's opinions at Rome it happened that Wiseman had been staying at the English College. A friend had gone to see the Cardinal and begged him to put in a good word for Newman at the Congregation of Propaganda. Wiseman burst into tears and said he would do anything he could for Dr. Newman. From what source did these tears flow? Were they tears of regret at the invisible barrier which seemed to have grown up between the two men? Newman was perhaps a saint—the Church may yet raise him to the Altars—and though the saints are the glory and triumph of the Church and her tireless advocates in heaven, they are not always the easiest people to get along with on earth. He was also notoriously touchy and, it may be said, both he and Wiseman were occasionally guilty of self-pity and a certain propensity to feel themselves the victims of other people's slights or ill-usage; to the great surprise, generally, of the people in question. They certainly reacted upon each other in this way, and evidently Newman came to feel that the Cardinal was one of those who had used him unjustly. There was no real reason for him to feel this, but the idea was possibly encouraged by the fact that two of the people most closely associated with the Cardinal in London, Manning and Faber, were both men with whom Newman had had considerable differences of opinion, while W. G. Ward, Newman's friend and disciple of Anglican days was, as a Catholic, to be one of his most severe critics, and was known to be on the most cordial of terms with Wiseman, his champion and protector. Whatever the reason may be one can only record with regret that the two men drew apart. Both were conscious that this had happened, and both felt guilty about it, but they seemed unable

287

to help it. One of the Cardinal's very last acts was to give his approval to Manning's scheme for preventing Catholics from entering the Universities of Oxford and Cambridge. Shortly before Newman had planned to open an Oratory at Oxford and had actually bought the land. With his last breath, almost, the Cardinal seemed once more to be frustrating the other's plans. 'The Cardinal has done a great work,' Newman wrote to a friend on hearing of his death: 'Alas! I wish he had not done his last act. He lived just long enough to put an extinguisher on the Oxford scheme—quite inconsistently too with what he had wished and said in former years.'[1] On this unhappy note their relationship ended.

One of Cardinal Wiseman's most providential gifts at this particular period in the religious history of his country and Church was the peculiar sympathy and understanding he had for the Established Church of England. This was unique in a Catholic of his generation, for either they were quite ignorant of the state of affairs within the body of that Church, or else they were bitterly opposed to it as the usurper of the heritage of the Catholic past. Wiseman was able to view the Anglican Church without any bitterness; he rejected as uncharitable the charge of insincerity which some Catholics levelled against the Tractarians, but rather encouraged them in their leanings in the hope that it would bring them, as in so many cases it did, into the bosom of the Roman Catholic fold. The more fanciful belief of Ambrose Phillipps de Lisle, that the Oxford Movement foreshadowed a general conversion of England, which had held Wiseman in fascination while he was in Rome, he soon abandoned after a few years of episcopal experience in England, especially after the rejection by the Established Church of the tenets of Tract XC. As a result of this he returned to the policy of making individual conversions, but he remained hopeful that the Anglican Church, for all that he saw it as 'the Divided House', might move yet nearer to Catholic Unity. In this sense he pioneered the more cordial Church relations of the present day.

Wiseman presented to the world a complex character in which many childlike qualities were mixed with the highest intellectual gifts and a deep underlying piety. He took an innocent pleasure in the pomp of his position as a Prince of the Church, would delight

[1] Ibid., p. 477.

in composing plays for children to act or in giving children's parties at his house in York Place, sending out secret orders for ice cream behind the back of his secretary who had to keep a rigid eye on the finances. On the intellectual side he may be accounted as among the first oriental scholars of his day, but in retrospect one must consider his theological and controversial writings as having had the most far-reaching effect, though these consisted mostly of pamphlets and articles for the *Dublin Review*, rather than books.

His articles, and the lectures he gave in the Church in Lincoln's Inn Fields, and later at St. Mary's, Moorfields, were to change the whole character of Catholicism in England. They gave confidence and a new sense of vocation to the recently emancipated Catholics; they opened the eyes of Protestants to the great mysteries of the Catholic Religion which had been a closed book to them for three hundred years. The importance of this aspect of Wiseman's work cannot be emphasized enough. The ignorance of the educated English public about the Catholic Church was unbelievably profound when Wiseman began his first lecture in London. They believed that from an intellectual point of view the Catholics had no case to present at all, and it was because of this that many Whig Protestants supported Catholic emancipation, for they could see no point in continuing to proscribe a cause that was so obviously finished. This was the line taken by Sidney Smith, the celebrated wit, who declared that 'there is no Court of Rome, and no Pope. There is a waxwork Pope, and a waxwork Court of Rome. But Popes of flesh and blood have long since disappeared, and in the same way those giants of the City exist no more; but their truculent images are at Guildhall. We doubt if there is in the treasury of the Pope change for a guinea; we are sure there is not in his armoury one gun which will go off . . . As for the enormous wax candles and superstitious mummeries, and painted jackets of the Catholic priests, I fear them not.' After Wiseman's lectures had opened the eyes and the minds of the people they could never talk in such terms again, whatever they might have thought about the substance of his talks. It was this work of his that prepared the way for the Tractarian leaders to enter the Church. Would they have looked towards Rome had they only known it as it had existed in England before Wiseman came to rekindle the sinking flame? As it was, Wiseman had to fight apathy and discouragement of the men of an older generation. Bishop Bramston's Pastoral after Emancipation indicates how easily the timid, cautious attitude might have continued until the Catholic community had dwindled into complete obscurity. Wiseman thrust aside this shy, apologetic attitude, and boldly proclaimed Catholic truth. It changed the entire Catholic community in England. 'He found them a persecuted sect,' wrote Wilfrid Ward, 'he left them a Church.'

The Lectures in 1835 were the first of the three major achievements of his life. The second was his Appeal to the English People which followed the unfortunate Pastoral from out of the Flaminian Gate of Rome. By then the great work which his Lectures had started had reached fulfilment. The small persecuted sect had become a recognized religious power in the country, there had been a great harvest of conversions, the ancient hierarchy of Catholic bishops, banished at the Reformation, had been restored by the Pope. But the reaction of the Protestant majority had been hostile and violent in the presence of this accomplished fact, and Wiseman's Pastoral had done nothing to calm its fears or abate its fury. The Appeal showed him at the height of his powers; fearless in defence of his rights, coherent and persuasive in presenting his argument, reasonable and urbane in refuting his critics, stern in admonishing wrong. It was a masterly achievement; and its influence was widespread in obtaining for Catholics a recognition of their rights, for if some blame must attach to Wiseman because of the tactlessness of his Flaminian Gate Pastoral, Catholics owe it to him that their right to the free exercise of their religion has not been questioned in England since.

The last of his three major works was the first Provincial Synod at Oscott in which was prefigured the lasting harmony which would ultimately be achieved among the various elements in English Catholic life, deriving from differing sources but progressing to the same end and eventually to be fused into a powerful whole. That this final unity would not be fulfilled again in the Cardinal's lifetime could not then be foreseen, but memories of the unity that did emerge there for a time were to show that it was not impossible of realization again in the future.

The years that followed were sad ones for Wiseman. There were moments when all his friends seem to have turned against him or had neglected him to quarrel amongst themselves. His health was broken and his spirits were often low. But to the ordinary people in the streets, and to the poor whose plight he never forgot, he remained that strange, splendid and mysterious figure, a Cardinal of the Holy Roman Church. England had not known a Cardinal in its midst for three hundred years, and no one could have filled such an image in the public eye more fittingly than Nicholas Wiseman with his large figure and genial manner, his wide learning and ready wit; and if the public figure disguised or hid much of the real man —the humble piety, the sadness of heart and isolation of spirit that were equally and perhaps more essentially a part of him—it explained, none the less, why the ordinary people turned out in such great numbers to watch his last journey to the grave. It was because they knew that a great man had passed out of life into the world beyond; that he had that quality of greatness which only the few possess and which cannot be assumed by the would-be great or the merely self-important, because it springs from an indifference to the good opinion of others and an unconcern with the verdict of the world. It is the unselfconscious greatness which comes from true simplicity of heart.

APPENDIX A

Record of Baptism of Cardinal Wiseman in the Church of
Santa Cruz in Seville

'On Wednesday, fourth of August of the year eighteen hundred and two, I, Friar Bonaventure of Ireland, Priest of the Order of Capuchins, of this Province of Andalusia, with the permission of Don Felix Joseph Reynoso, Parish Priest of the Parochial Church of Santa Cruz of Seville, did therein solemnly baptise Nicholas, Patrick, Stephen, who was born on the third of the said month, the legitimate son of Don James Wiseman and of Dona Francisca Xaviera Strange, natives of Ireland. His Godfather was Don Nicholas Power of this city, at present resident in the City of Waterford in Ireland; by powers given to Don Patrick Wiseman, who in his name took him from the baptismal Font, and was advised of his spiritual parenthood and its obligations.'

APPENDIX B

Cardinal Wiseman's Pastoral announcing the Hierarchy,
'Out of the Flaminian Gate of Rome'

NICHOLAS, by the Divine mercy, of the Holy Roman Church by
the title of St. Pudentiana Cardinal Priest, Archbishop of Westminster, and Administrator Apostolic of the Diocese of Southwark:
To our dearly beloved in Christ, the Clergy secular and regular,
and the Faithful of the said Archdiocese and Diocese:
Health and benediction in the Lord!
If this day we greet you under a new title, it is not, dearly
beloved, with an altered affection. If in words we seem to divide
those who till now have formed, under our rule, a single flock, our
heart is as undivided as ever in your regard. For now truly do we
feel closely bound to you by new and stronger ties of charity; now
do we embrace you in our Lord Jesus Christ with more tender
emotions of paternal love; now doth our soul yearn, and our mouth
is open to you, though words must fail to express what we feel on
being once again permitted to address you. For if our parting was
in sorrow, and we durst not hope that we should again face to face
behold you, our beloved flock, so much the greater is now our
consolation and our joy, when we find ourselves not so much
permitted as commissioned to return to you by the supreme ruler
of the Church of Christ.

But how can we for one moment indulge in selfish feelings, when,
through that loving Father's generous and wise counsels, the
greatest of blessings has just been bestowed upon our country, by
the restoration of its true Catholic hierarchical government, in
communion with the see of Peter?

For on the twenty-ninth day of last month, on the Feast of the
Archangel Saint Michael, prince of the heavenly host, his Holiness

Pope Pius IX was graciously pleased to issue his Letters Apostolic, under the Fisherman's Ring, conceived in terms of great weight and dignity, wherein he substituted for the eight Apostolic Vicariates heretofore existing, one archiepiscopal or metropolitan and twelve episcopal sees; repealing at the same time, and annulling, all dispositions and enactments made for England by the Holy See with reference to its late form of ecclesiastical government.

And by a brief dated the same day his Holiness was further pleased to appoint us, though most unworthy, to the archiepiscopal see of Westminster, established by the above mentioned Letters Apostolic, giving us at the same time the administration of the episcopal see of Southwark. So that at present, and till such time as the Holy See shall think fit otherwise to provide, we govern, and shall continue to govern, the counties of Middlesex, Hertford, and Essex as ordinary thereof, and those of Surrey, Sussex, Kent, Berkshire, and Hampshire, with the islands annexed, as administrator with ordinary jurisdiction.

Further, we have to announce to you, dearly beloved in Christ, that, as if still further to add solemnity and honour before the Church to this noble act of Apostolic authority, and to give an additional mark of paternal benevolence towards the Catholics of England, his Holiness was pleased to raise us, in the private consistory of Monday, the 30th of September, to the rank of Cardinal Priest of the Holy Roman Church. And on the Thursday next ensuing, being the third day of this month of October, in public consistory, he delivered to us the insignia of this dignity, the cardinalitial hat; assigning us afterwards for our title in the private consistory which we attended, the Church of St. Pudentiana, in which St. Peter is groundedly believed to have enjoyed the hospitality of the noble and partly British family of the Senator Pudens.

In that same consistory we were enabled ourselves to ask for the archiepiscopal Pallium for our new see of Westminster; and this day we have been invested, by the hands of the Supreme Pastor and Pontiff himself, with this badge of metropolitan jurisdiction.

The great work, then, is complete; what you have long desired and prayed for is granted. Your beloved country has received a place among the fair Churches, which, normally constituted, form the splendid aggregate of Catholic Communion; Catholic England has been restored to its orbit in the ecclesiastical firmament, from which its light had long vanished, and begins now anew its course of regularly adjusted action round the centre of unity, the source of jurisdiction, of light, and of vigour. How wonderfully all this has been brought about, how clearly the hand of God has been shown in every step, we have not now leisure to relate, but we may hope soon to recount to you by word of mouth. In the meantime we will content ourselves with assuring you, that, if the concordant voice of those venerable and most eminent counsellors to whom the Holy See commits the regulation of ecclesiastical affairs in missionary countries, of the overruling of every variety of interests and designs, to the rendering of this measure almost necessary; if the earnest prayers of our holy Pontiff and his most sacred obligation of the divine sacrifice, added to his own deep and earnest reflection, can form to the Catholic heart an earnest of heavenly direction, an assurance that the Spirit of truth, who guides the Church, has here inspired its Supreme Head, we cannot desire stronger or more consoling evidence that this most important measure is from God, has His sanction and blessing, and will consequently prosper.

Then truly is this day to us a day of joy and exaltation of spirit, the crowning day of long hopes, and the opening day of bright prospects. How must the Saints of our country, whether Roman or British, Saxon or Norman, look down from their seats of bliss, with beaming glance, upon this new evidence of the faith and Church which led them to glory, sympathising with those who have faithfully adhered to them through centuries of ill-repute for the truth's sake, and now reap the fruit of their patience and long-suffering. And all those blessed martyrs of these latter ages, who have fought the battles of the faith under such discouragement, who mourned, more than over their own fetters or their own pain, over the desolate ways of their own Sion, and the departure of England's religious glory; oh! how must they bless God, who hath again visited his people,—how take part in our joys, as they see the lamp of the temple again rekindled and rebrightening, as they behold the silver links of that chain, which has connected their country with the see of Peter in its vicarial government, changed into burnished gold; not stronger nor more closely knit, but more beautifully wrought and more brightly arrayed.

And in nothing will it be fairer or brighter than in this, that the glow of more fervent love will be upon it. Whatever our sincere attachment and unflinching devotion to the Holy See till now, there is a new ingredient cast into these feelings; a warmer gratitude, a tenderer affection, a profounder admiration, a boundless and endless sense of obligation, for so new, so great, so sublime a gift, will be added to past sentiments of loyalty and fidelity to the supreme see of Peter. Our venerable Pontiff has shown himself a true shepherd, a true father; and we cannot but express our gratitude to him in our most fervent language, in the language of prayer. For when we raise our voices, as is meet, in loud and fervent thanksgiving to the Almighty, for the precious gifts bestowed upon our portion of Christ's vineyard, we will also implore every choice blessing on him who has been so signally the divine instrument in procuring it. We will pray that his rule over the Church may be prolonged to many years, for its welfare; that health and strength may be preserved to him for the discharge of his arduous duties; that light and grace may be granted to him proportioned to the sublimity of his office; and that consolations, temporal and spiritual, may be poured out upon him abundantly, in compensation for past sorrows and past ingratitude. And of these consolations may one of the most sweet to his paternal heart be the propagation of holy religion in our country, the advancement of his spiritual children there in true piety and devotion, and our ever-increasing affection and attachment to the see of St. Peter.

In order, therefore, that our thanksgiving be made with all becoming solemnity, we hereby enjoin as follows:—

1. This our Pastoral Letter shall be publicly read in all the churches and chapels of the archdiocese of Westminster and the diocese of Southwark on the Sunday after its being received.

2. On the following Sunday there shall be in every such Church or chapel a solemn Benediction of the blessed Sacrament, at which shall be sung the *Te Deum*, with the usual versicles and prayers, with the prayer also *Deus omnium Fidelium Pastor et Rector* for the Pope.

3. The collect, *Pro Gratiarum Actione*, or thanksgiving, and that for the Pope, shall be recited in the Mass of that day, and for two days following.

4. Where Benediction is never given, the *Te Deum*, with its prayers, shall be recited or sung after Mass, and the collects above-named shall be added as enjoined.

And at the same time, earnestly entreating for ourselves also a place in your fervent prayers, we lovingly implore for you, and bestow on you, the blessing of Almighty God, Father, Son, and Holy Ghost.   Amen.

Given out of the Flaminian Gate of Rome, this seventh day of October, in the year of our Lord MDCCCL.

NICHOLAS,
Cardinal Archbishop of Westminster.
By command of his Eminence,
FRANCIS SEARLE, Secretary.

BIBLIOGRAPHY

Beck, Rt. Rev., G. A. (Editor), *The English Catholics 1850–1950*
London, 1950.
Butler, Dom Cuthbert, *Life and Times of Bishop Ullathorne*. London,
1926.
Chapman, Ronald, *Father Faber*. London, 1960.
Cumming, J., *Cardinal Wiseman, A Lecture*. London, 1850.
Cardinal Wiseman, His Oath and its Obligation. London, 1850.
Notes on the Cardinal's Manifesto in a Letter to Lord John Russell.
London, 1850.
Fitzsimons, John, (Editor), *Manning: Anglican and Catholic*.
London, 1951.
Gavazzi, Alessandro, *My Recollections of the Last Four Popes, an
Answer to Dr. Wiseman*. London, 1858.
Gwynn, Denis, *Cardinal Wiseman*. Dublin, 1950.
The Second Spring, 1818–1852. London, 1944.
Lord Shrewsbury, Pugin and the Catholic Revival. London, 1949.
A Hundred Years of Catholic Emancipation. London, 1929.
Hales, E. E. Y., *Pio Nono*. London, 1954.
Revolution and the Papacy, 1769–1846. London, 1960.
Leslie, Sir Shane, *Cardinal Manning, His Life and Labours*. Dublin,
1953.
Mathew, David, *Catholicism in England*, 1535–1935. London, 1936.
May, J. Lewis, *Cardinal Newman, A Study*. London, 1929.
Middleton, R. D., *Newman at Oxford*. London, 1850.
Mozley, Anne, *Letters and Correspondence of J. H. Newman*. London,
1891.
Nielsen, Frederik, *The History of the Papacy in the XIX Century*.
London, 1906.
Newman, Cardinal, *Apologia Pro Vita Sua*. London, 1864.
Autobiographical Writings (Edited by H. Tristram), London, 1956.

The Letters and Diaries, Vol. XI, (Edited by C. S. Dessain). London, 1961.

Pius, Rev. Father, *Life of Father Ignatius of St. Paul, Passionist, (The Hon. and Rev. George Spencer).* Dublin, 1866.

Purcell, E. S., *The Life of Cardinal Manning.* London, 1896.

Life and Letters of Ambrose Phillipps de Lisle. London, 1900.

Reynolds, E. E., *Three Cardinals.* London, 1958.

Sencourt, Robert, *The Life of Newman.* London, 1948.

Spencer, Philip, *Politics of Belief in Nineteenth Century France.* London, 1954.

Trappes-Lomax, Michael, *Pugin, A Mediaeval Victorian.* London, 1932.

Ullathorne, W. B., *Autobiography (From Cabin Boy to Archbishop).* London, 1941.

Ward, Bernard, *The Sequel to Catholic Emancipation.* London, 1915.

Ward, Maisie, *Young Mr. Newman.* London, 1948.

Ward, Wilfrid, *Life and Times of Cardinal Wiseman.* London, 1897.

W. G. Ward and the Oxford Movement. London, 1889.

W. G. Ward and the Catholic Revival. London, 1912.

Life and Letters of John Henry Cardinal Newman. London, 1912.

Warren, Samuel, *The Queen or the Pope.* London, 1850.

Watkin, E. I., *Roman Catholicism in England from the Reformation to 1950.* London, 1951.

INDEX